Complete Works of Lokuang Vol. 41

Metaphysical Philosophy of Life

Translated from the Chinese by
Carlos Tee, Ernest Li Chang-yi and Nancy Du

Student Book Co. LTD.

Contents

Preface

Traditional Chinese philosophy is centered on life. Confucianism, Buddhism and Taoism explain the meaning of life in a variety of ways. However, they all take "meaning of life" as the unifying idea behind each of their philosophical systems. Philosophy of Life is not equivalent to philosophy of living or ethics but is rather a body of knowledge based on metaphysical ontology. Philosophy of Life takes life as the myriad realities in the world and as the foundation of ethics and philosopy of living.

The Confucian philosophy of life traces its origins to the *I Ching*, or the Book of Changes. Confucianists take the cosmos as a changing body formed through the fusion of *yin* and *yang*. Following the Mandate of Heaven, these two elements continue in their changes, generating myriad things in the process. Within the generated things, *yin* and *yang* also continue their movements. For this reason, generated things show immanent movement. This immanent movement is nothing else but life.

Propagating ideas in the *I Ching*, Sung and Ming Dynasty Idealists focused their studies on the meaning of life and proposed that it is attained when man achieves union with Heaven.

However both the *I Ching* and Sung and Ming Idealists neither explained changes that occur in life; nor did they identify the source of these changes. For this reasons, I have adopted ideas of Scholastic Philosophy in explaining the creation of the universe by God. With his creative power, God made the universe, which is itself a generative power. In creating the universe, God also created generative power, which is itself a reality (substance). The "form" of this reality is God's idea of creating the universe while its matter is created by God *ex nihilo*, out of nothing. The universe is creative power constantly in motion, through which it generates the myriad things. The matter of the myriad things is derived from that of the universe while their forms are God's ideas of creating them. Generative power serves as the dynamic cause that unifies matter and form to create each thing. In the case of man, his matter is derived from parents while his form (the soul) directly originates from God.

The existence of each thing is itself life, which is also motion. To explain the movement of life, I have adopted the Scholastic concepts of potency and act. The change from potency to act is one that proceeds from reality to reality. Human life starts from parents. As soon as a fetus is conceived, it already is a reality. It grows and becomes a baby and later undergoes childhood, adolescence, adulthood and old age. All these stages proceed from potency to act. It goes on until the potency for life is exhausted, upon which changes stop to occur and the person dies.

Such a change is a substantial change. It does not immediately lead to death. Instead, as long as there is potency for life, it will always lead to acts of life. It is only when the potency for life is exhausted when death occurs.

In my discussions, Philosophy of Life crisscrosses Chinese and Western philosophies. In the process of linking these two philosohical traditions, I have met not a few challenges and difficulties. Although I have tried to come up with solutions and explanations, they may not necessarily be acceptable to all.

Articles in this collection were compiled from my three books on Philosophy of Life. The chapters do not always link with one another smoothly, for which I would like to offer my apologies.

Let me express my sincere gratitude to the Council for Cultural Planning and Development for assistance in the publication of this book. I also would like to express my thanks to the translators of the articles: Mr. Carlos Tee, Mr. Ernest Lee Chang-yi and Ms. Nancy Du of Fu Jen University's Graduate Institute of Translation and Interpretation Studies. This book would not have been made possible without their contributions.

Chapter I

The Development of Chinese Philosophy of Life

I. Primordial Philosophy of Life

Primordial philosophical ideas have developed out of philosophers' probes into life itself and its environment. The *I Ch'uan*, for instance, describes the origins of the *pa-kua* [1] created by Fu Hsi. It says:

> When in early antiquity Pao Hsi [Fu Hsi] ruled the world, he looked upward and contemplated the images in the heavens; he looked downward and contemplated the patterns on earth. He contemplated the markings of birds and beasts and the adaptations to the regions. He proceeded directly from himself and indirectly from objects. Thus he invented the eight trigrams in order to enter into connection with the virtues of the light of the gods and to regulate the conditions of all being. (*Hsi-tz'u* [Appended Remarks], Part II, Chapter 2, Baynes 328-329)

The way of human life that had been studied by ancient philosophers later served as the basis for kings and nobles in governing their people. Primitive philosophical ideas of the Chinese nation are enshrined in the pages of the *Shu-ching* (Book of History).

The *Yao-tien* (Classic of the Yao) describes how the reigning emperor commanded Hsi-ho, Hsi-chung and Hsi-shu to administer his subjects in accordance with celestial phenomena and the four seasons. At that time, people's lives were centered on agriculture. The changing of the seasons and the four directions all had close relationships with

---

(1) [Translator's Note] The *pa-kua* or the Eight Trigrams are the eight combinations of three whole or broken lines used in divination.

their agricultural activities. In fact, climate and soil conditions exert a tremendous influence on human life, livestock and farm produce.

The chapter entitled *Hung-fan* includes the following texts:

> . . . Fourth, the five arrangements: The first is the year, the second is the month, the third, day, the fourth, the stars and planets and the fifth, the calendrical calculations. . . Eighth, the verifications. . . The sovereign is to examine the character of the year; the ministers and scholars, that of the month; and the lower level officials, that of the day. If there are no aberrance in the year, month or day, all kinds of grain shall grow to maturity, government operations are wise, heroic men become eminent and peace and prosperity reign in people's houses...The commoners examine the stars. Some stars love wind and others love rain. The movements of the sun and the moon brings about winter and summer. The movements of the moon together with the stars regulate wind and rain.

This chapter deals with people's daily life, specifically the important factors necessary to achieve "growth of all kinds of grain" and "the reign of peace and prosperity in people's homes" --that is, the ability of the year, month and day to remain in smooth order and harmony.

These ideas were also clearly expressed in another work, the *Chou-li* (Rites of the Chou). The *Chou-li* records a bureaucracy that included officials governing heaven, earth, spring, summer, autumn and winter. Each official position was not identified using the customary title but rather through the different affairs of the state. These official titles clearly suggest the close interrelationship between national affairs and the weather. In the *Li-chi* (Book of Rites), a lengthy chapter entitled *Yueh-ling* (Monthly Decrees) records political activities held every month, all of them taking the weather as basis. The *Yueh-ling* of the Book of Rites is similar to the *Shih-erh yueh-chi* (Twelve-Month Records) of the *Lü-shih ch'un-ch'iu*. The latter was written by Lü Pu-wei during the reign of Emperor Shih Huang-ti, founder of the Ch'in Dynasty. The reign of Emperor Shih Huang-ti, however, failed to administer the land based on the *Yueh-ling*, whose ideas can be traced far back into antiquity. The *Yueh-ling* propounds that the reign of kings and emperors must all follow the weather which is manifested by the sun, the moon and the stars. Weather influences the life of the myriad things in the universe which are related to human life. In the first month of Spring, the book prescribes that the Son of Heaven must welcome the advent of Spring in the east. He must pray for abundant harvest from God and personally plow the field using a hoe. It is said that in this month, heavenly *ch'i* descends on the earth while earthly *ch'i* ascends to the skies. The union of heaven and earth leads to the germination of plants and trees. The ideas in the *Yueh-ling* and the *Yueh-chi* originated from ancient times. However, detailed practices and ceremonial rites were conceived only in the later dynasties of Ch'in and Han. These ideas were centered on the changes in the myriad things of the universe, which were continuously manifested in the four seasons. Changes in the four seasons are the processes of generation and transformation in the myriad things.

II. The Maturation of Philosophy of Life

By the time of the writing of the *I Ching*[2], the ancient Chinese thoughts on philosophy of life had already reached maturity. Chinese philosophers have by then formed a system of ideas.

All things in the universe are changing. This process is called *I* (change). The purpose of change is *sheng-sheng* (perpetual renewal of life). The *I Ching* says: "Change is the perpetual renewal of life" (*Hsi-tz'u* [Appended Remarks], Part I, Ch. 5). Changes come about

---

(2) [Translator's Note] The *I Ching* is one of the basic Confucian classics. It is also much cherished by the Taoists. It is divided into the texts and commentaries. The texts consists of sixty-four hexagrams and judgments on them. These hexagrams are based on the Eight Trigrams, each of which consists of three lines, divided or undivided, the divided representing the weak, or yin, and the undivided representing the strong, or yang. Each of these eight corresponds to a direction, a natural element, a moral quality, etc. (Chan, 262n). For example, *ch'ien* (Heaven) is represented as ☰.

because of *yin* and *yang*, two elements which continuously interact, resulting in the formation of things. The Appended Remarks further says: "That which lets now the dark [*yin*], now the light [*yang*] appear is Tao. As continuer, it is good. As completer, it is the essence" (Part 2, Ch. 5, Baynes 297-298).

Yin and *yang* possess different characteristics. *Yang* is strength while *yin* is gentleness. Strength leads forward while gentleness causes a retreat. Going forward represents action while a retreat means quiescence. Action leads to progress while quiescence causes accommodation. These two elements engage in mutual coordination, through which they form the myriad things. Changes of *Yin* and *yang* continue unabated. They operate in cycles the same way as night and day alternate and as the four seasons take their turn. These changes make the universe resemble a torrent of life, constantly brimming with activities which cause the endless generation and transformation of things. As Chapter II of the Appended Remarks says: "As the firm and the yielding lines displace one another, change and transformation arise... Change and transformation are images of progress and retrogression" (Part I, Ch. 2, Baynes 287-288).

In the *I Ching*, divinatory symbols [trigrams, *kua*] represent physical form while lines [judgment, *yao*] represents change. Meanings of change are explained in verbal terms. For example, Chapter VIII of the Appended Remarks says:

> The holy sages were able to survey all the confused diversitites under Heaven. They observed forms and phenomena, and made representations of things and their attributes. These were called Images [*hsiang*]. The holy sages were able to survey all the movements under Heaven. They contemplated the way in which these movements met and became interrelated, to take their course according to eternal laws. Then they appended judgments, to distinguish between the good fortune and misfortune indicated. These were called the judgments [*yao*].
> (Section I, Ch. 8, Baynes 312)

Elsewhere, the *I Ching* also says:

> The eight trigrams are arranged according to completeness: thus the images are contained in them. Thereupon they are doubled: thus the lines are contained in them. The firm and the yielding displace each other, and change is contained therein. The judgments, together with their counsel, are appended, and movement is contained therein. Good fortune and misfortune, remorse and humiliation, come about through movement. The firm and the yielding stand firm when they are in their original places. Their changes and continuities should correspond with the time. Good fortune and misfortune take effect through perseverance. The tao of heaven and earth becomes visible through perseverance. The tao of sun and moon becomes bright through perseverance. All movements under heaven become uniform through perseverance. (*Hsi-tz'u hsia* [Appended Remarks], Part II. Ch. 1, Baynes 326-326)

> Thus the Book of Changes consists of images [*hsiang*]. The images are reproductions. The decisions [*t'uan*] provide the material. The lines [*yao*] are imitations of movements on earth. Thus do good fortune and misfortune arise, and remorse and humiliation appear. (Part II, Ch. 3, Baynes 356-357)

Changes in the divinatory symbols of the *I Ching* symbolize the changes going on in heaven and earth, which lead to the generation and transformation of the myriad things. The *I Ch'uan* says: "Generation [*sheng*] is the great virtue of Heaven and Earth" (Appended Remarks, Part II, Ch. 1). Changes in heaven and earth have as their elements the *ch'ien* and the *k'un*. The former is the origin of generation and transformation. In the *I Ching*, the divinatory symbol *ch'ien* is described in the following words:

> Great indeed is the sublimity of the Creative [*ch'ien*], to which all beings owe their beginning and which permeates all heaven. The clouds pass and the rain does its work, and all individual

beings flow into their forms. . . The way of the Creative works through change and transformation, so that each thing receives its true nature and destiny and comes into permanent accord with the Great harmony: This is what furthers and perseveres. He towers high above the multitude of beings, and all lands are united in peace. (Baynes 370-372)

In turn, *k'un* is explained as:

In a state of rest the Creative [*ch'ien*] is one, and in a state of motion it is straight; therefore it creates that which is great. The Receptive [*k'un*] is closed in a state of rest, and in a state of motion it opens; therefore it creates that which is vast. (Baynes 301)

These two symbolize heaven and earth. The generation and transformation of the myriad things in the universe depend on the cooperation between heaven and earth. *Ch'ien* activates while *k'un* synthesizes. The *t'ai* divinatory symbol represents spring, a season of germination and growth among the myriad things. In the *I Ching*, the *t'ai* divinatory symbol is described as follows:

Peace [*t'ai*]: The small departs, the great approaches. Good fortune. Success. In this way heaven and earth unite, and all beings come into the union. Upper and lower unite, and they are of one will. (Baynes 301)

The union of heaven and earth leads to good weather, something advantageous to the growth of crops. This is important for farming, a task which is closely related to proper timing and the right location. The divinatory symbols of the *I Ching* explain what is "central and right" [*chung-cheng*], a condition wherein the elements *yin* and *yang* are in their proper positions. As the *I Ching* always says: "Time has a great significance." The generation of agricultural crops, the four seasons and geographical location must be integrated with time and space for them to be coordinated with the generation process.

The significance of time and space in the *I Ching* is determined by *sheng-sheng* (perpetual renewal of life), not by changes occurring in matter. The change studied in the *I Ching* is not material change. This is because change is taken as *sheng-sheng* or is life itself. The *I Ching* describes change as *shen* (spirit), something deeply mysterious in nature. Thus, the Appended Remarks says:

> As begetter of all begetting, it is called Change. As that which complete the primal images, it is called the Creative [*ch'ien*]; as that which imitates them, it is called the Receptive [*k'un*]. In that it serves for exploring the laws of number and thus for knowing the future, it is called Revelation [*chan*]. In that it serves to infuse an organic coherence into the changes, it is called Work [*shih*]. That aspect of it which cannot be fathomed in terms of the light [*yang*] and the dark [*yin*] is called Spirit [*shen*]. (Part I, Ch. 5, Baynes 299-301)

> In it are included the forms and the scope of everything in the heavens and on earth, so that nothing escapes it. In it all things everywhere are completed, so that none is missing. Therefore by means of it we can penetrate the tao of day and night, and so understand it. Therefore the spirit is bound to no one place, not the Book of Changes to any one form. (Part I, Ch. 4, Baynes 296)

> The Changes have no consciousness, no action; they are quiescent and do not move. But if they are stimulated, they penetrate all situations under heaven. If they were not the most divine thing on earth, how could they do this? (Part I, Ch. 10, Baynes 315)

Confucius had studied the *I Ching* and later lectured on it to his disciples. The *I Ching* was originally designed for divination and served as basis for predicting good and evil fortune. Good and evil fortunes are calculated using the concepts of *yin* and *yang*. Harmony augurs good fortune and the reverse means ill fate. Divination predicts the good or evil effects of things. Something is not done if evil fortune is predicted. Similarly, predicted good fortune is a signal to go ahead. For Confucius, good and evil fortunes do not depend upon things' good or bad luck. Instead, they have something to do with the goodness or wickedness of things. Good things lead to good fortune and evil things invite disaster. For him, good fortune and disaster are rewards or punishments for things done. Reward and punishment are determined by heaven and carried out by spirits.

Having associated good and bad fortune with the goodness or wickedness of things, Confucius then extended the way in which heaven and earth change as described in the *I Ching* to the way of moral behavior. Man forms part of the wholeness made up of heaven and earth and the myriad things. Thus, man's way of life also forms part of the way in which heaven and earth change. The I *Ch'uan* says:

> The Changes is a book vast and great, in which everything is completely contained. The tao of heaven is in it, the tao of the earth is in it, and the tao of man is in it. It combines these three primal powers and doubles them; that is why there are six lines. The six lines are nothing other than the ways (tao) of the three primal powers. (Baynes 351)

The way of man and those of heaven and earth are linked to form the tao of the three primal powers. The way of heaven and earth is generation while the way of man is benevolence (*jen*). On this, the *I Ching* further says:

> It is the great virtue of heaven and earth to generate life. It is the great treasure of the holy sage to stand in the right place. How does one safeguard this place? Through benevolence (*jen*). (Appended Remarks, Part II, Ch. 1)

Benevolence and generation are interrelated. In the *I Ching*, a commentary on the words of the text for the *ch'ien* divinatory symbol says: "The great man shares virtues with Heaven and Earth". Here, great man refers to the great sage or the holy king. The virtues of the sage are derived from his sharing with the virtue of heaven and earth to perpetually renew life [*sheng-sheng*].

Since the virtues of the sage overlap with those of heaven and earth, then the principles of the sages virtues and those of heaven and earth also overlap. The virtue of heaven and earth to perpetually renew life [*sheng-sheng*] arises from the coordination between *yin* and *yang* elements to cause a harmonization in time and space, and thus, to position things in what is "central and right" [*chung-cheng*]. Similarly, the virtue of the sage also comes about through the union of *yin* and *yang* elements, by which he constantly achieves the golden mean [*chung-yung*]. Thus, the actions of a sage are patterned after heaven and earth. In the *I Ching*, the commentaries on the Decision [*t'uan*]. Images [Symbolism or *hsiang*], and the word of the text [*wen-yen*] often associate human action with the way heaven and earth change. For instance, all the Decisions [*t'uan*] deal with the way of the gentleman. The *I Ching* links human life with the life of the myriad things in the universe. The life of the universe is one. Although this life is divided into different levels, they are actually linked with one another. This idea is a unique feature of Chinese philosophical thought. It is also a feature universal to all philosophical schools in China.

III. Ideas on Life in the *Chung-yung* and the Book of Rites

In the Analects, only once did Confucius mention heaven's propensity to generate. It says:

> Confucius said: ' I do not wish to say anything. ' Tzu-kung said, ' If you do not say anything, what can we little disciples ever learn to pass one to others?' Confucius said, ' Does Heaven (*T'ien*, nature) say anything? The four seasons run their course and all things are produced. Does Heaven say anything?' (*Yang Huo*, Chan 47)

Confucius taught about the concept of following heaven. For him, heaven brings good by governing the orderly turn of the four seasons, which allows the generation and transformation of the myriad things.

This idea totally overlaps with those of the *I Ch'uan*. In his teachings, Mencius[3] also did not clearly deal with a philosophy of life. However, there were two instances in his teachings that resemble ideas in the *I Ching*. In the chapter entitled *Chin-hsin shang*, he writes: "The superior man (sage) is affectionate to his parents and humane to all people. He is human to all people and feels love for all creatures" (Chan 81). Elsewhere, he says: "The myriad things are in me in every possible way."

More of this kind can be found in the *Chung-yung* than in the Analects. Chapter XXVI of the *Chung-yung* says: "The Way of Heaven and earth may be completely described in one sentence: They are without any doubtness and so they produce things in an unfathomable way" (Chan 109). The way of heaven and earth boils down to one word — generation. Heaven and Earth generate perpetually in an orderly manner based on the nature of things. They function in a mysterious unfathomable way. Such a generation process continues without end. This way of heaven and earth is followed by the sage. In the *I Ch'uan*, it says that the sage matches generation by heaven and earth with the virtue of benevolence. Thus, the sage is united in virtue with heaven and earth. The *Chung-yung* says: "Great it the Way of the sage! Overflowing; it produces and nourishes all things and rises up to the height of heaven" (Chan 110). The *Chung-yung* teaches the idea of following one's nature in one's action. This following of one's nature is called sincerity. It says:

> Only those who are absolutely sincere can fully develop their nature. . . If they can fully develop the nature of things, they can then assist in the transforming and nourishing process of Heaven and Earth, they can thus form a trinity with Heaven and Earth. (Ch. 22, Chan 107)

---

(3) [Translator's Note] Mencius (c. 370-c290 B.C.) was a follower of Confucius. He believed that man is naturally good and that the principles of moral conduct are inborn.

> Only those who are absolutely sincere can. . . know the trans-
> forming and nourishing operations of Heaven and Earth. Does
> he depend on anything else? How earnest and sincere--he is
> humanity (benevolence, *jen*)! How deep and unfathomable --
> he is abyss! How vast and great -- he is heaven. (Ch. XXXII,
> Chan 112)

Participation in the work of heaven and earth is what the *I Ch'uan*
refers to as *san-ts'ai* (three primal powers), which consist of heaven,
earth and man. The fusion of the three primal powers causes the generation and transformation of the myriad things.

Confucius is praised in the *Chung-yung* for imitating heaven and
earth, and for uniting his virtues with those of heaven and earth. He is
extolled as possessing the greatness of heaven and earth . Chapter XXX
says:

> Chung-ni (*Confucius*) transmitted the ancient traditions of Yao
> and Shun, and he modeled after and made brilliant systems of
> King Wen and King Wu. He conformed with the natural order
> governing the revolution of the seasons in heaven above, and
> followed the principles governing land and water below. He
> may be compared to earth in its supporting and containing all
> things, and to heaven in its overshadowing and embracing all
> things. He may be compared to the four seasons in their succe-
> ssion, and to the sun and moon in their alternate shining. All
> things are produced and developed without injuring one
> another. The courses of the seasons, the sun, and moon are
> pursued without conflict. The lesser forces flow continuously
> like river currents, while the great forces go silently and
> deeply in their mighty transformations. It is this that makes
> heaven and earth so great. (Chan 111-112)

This passage bears a striking resemblance to the commentary on the
words of the text of the *ch'ien* trigram as follows: "The Great Man
(Sage) unites his virtues with those of Heaven and Earth. He shares his
brightness with the sun and the moon. He matches the order of the four

seasons." Mencius once called Confucius as "the most timely of all sages." In the *Chung-yung*, Confucius is identified in spirit to the "great man" mentioned in the *I Ch'uan*. Both sages were said to have praised the generation process achieved by Heaven and Earth, which leads to the endless generation and transformation of the myriad things.

In the *Chung-yung*, philosophy of living has its fundamental roots in the concept of "following one's own nature." One's nature is the basis of human life. If man acts following his nature, then he can fulfill his nature as he develops himself. This, in turn, will allow him to develop his human nature and materiality, both of which are needed to praise heaven and earth's work of generation and transformation. The nature of the myriad things are linked together because life is interlinked. If one has developed his life, he must further develop the life of the myriad things in the universe. As the Chinese saying goes: One must fulfill himself and others.

The *Li-chi* (Book of Rites) is a collection of Confucian ideas on "rites" compiled by Tai Sheng. The chapter entitled *Yueh-ling* (Monthly Decrees) is not a work that is representative of the period of Confucius and Mencius; neither was the *Yueh-chi* (Record of Music), a collection made during the reign of Emperor Han Wu-ti by Prince Hsien of Ho-chien (in present-day Hopei Province). However, the ideas propounded in these two works are closely realted to Chou Dynasty ideas on ritual music. Let us first discuss the ideas proposed by the *Yueh-chi*. It says:

> Heaven is high and earth is low. All things are scattered in them in their own ways. The Rites were instituted in accordance with all these. These things flow ceaselessly and the union of their actions leads to transformation. Music arose according to this pattern. Planting in Spring and growth in summer: this resembles the virtue of benevolence (*jen*). Harvesting in fall and storing in winter: this resembles righteousness. Benevolence is akin to music and righteousness to the Rites.

The matching of the virtues of benevolence and righteousness with music and ritual symbolizes the generation of the myriad things in the universe. It further says:

> Animals are grouped together according to their kind and plants are divided according to their genus. That is because their natures and mandates differ. They take their forms in Heaven and acquire their physical shapes on earth. Therefore, the Rites manifest the distinctions between Heaven and Earth. The ether of earth ascends and that of Heaven descends. *Yin* and *yang* act upon each other while Heaven and Earth agitate one another. They are drummed by thunder and excited by wind and rain, moved by the four seasons, warmed by the sun and the moon, and all transformations proceed unimpeded. Therefore, music manifests the harmony between Heaven and Earth.

The union of heaven and earth, which leads to the generation of the myriad things, is the idea proposed by the *I Ch'uan*. The *Yueh-chi* also echoes the same idea. Music represents the life of the myriad things, their integration and the harmony existing among them.

The *Yueh-chi* says:

> Therefore, the previous sage kings composed music according to human nature and emotions, regulated by musical temperament and formulated with propriety and righteousness. They allowed music harmonized with the vital spirits and followed the movement of the Five Elements. This is done to keep the music from drifting away when its momentum arises freely toward loudness and to keep it from being pent up when its drive is restrained by condensed quietness. In this way, music will express great vitality without violence, and show soft feeling without weakness. These four functions coincide in the inner mind and are explicitly made manifest. They abide in their locations and never oppose one another.

Since music represents unity, then it requires harmonization. Music follows a rhythm and a melody. Everything must be just right. Only then can music effectively harmonize man emotions.

The *Yueh-chi* also says:

> If the king does practice music and rituals, Heaven and Earth, as a response to man, will show their bright influences. Heaven and Earth will work in happy union, and *yin* and *yang* will interact in harmony. The pleasant air form above and the corresponding action below will nourish the myriad things. Plants and trees will grow with luxuriant foliage, their sprouts and buds curling in lush abundance. The feathered and the winged will be vibrant. Horns and antlers will grow. Insects will come to the light and start their activities. Birds will breed and sit in their nests. The hairy creatures will mate and reproduce. Mammals will not have still births and no eggs will be broken. All these are attributed to the power of music.

Music manifests heaven and earth. All that grow are made to germinate. All that have wings are made to soar. All that have hollow horns are made to grow. Even embryos and eggs can avoid being still born. The significance and function of music are then all related to life. This explains why music received much emphasis in Ancient China. Many chapters dealing with music in the *Shih-ching* (Book of Songs) attest to the popularity of music in ancient times. These ancient music, however, were lost in the succeeding generations. What were left to us are only these philosophical writings.

However, the most direct effect of music occurs in the human heart. Music arises from the inner emotions of man and is expressed externally as sound. As Hsūn-tzu[4] writes:

---

(4) [Translator's Note] Hsūe-tzu (298-238 B. C.) was a Confucian and a contemporary of Mencius. He was more influential in the Han Dynasty than Mencius. His thought was naturalistic in temper, contrasting with Mencius' idealistic philosophy. He is known for the work *The Hsūs Tzu*.

Music is an expression of joy. This is something which human nature cannot be without. When there is joy, it must find expression in sound and takes its shape in the movement and tranquillity of the person.

Thus, music is extremely important to man.

The gentleman said: ' Man cannot be without music and rituals. For if man's heart is regulated by music, then harmony, justice, love and sincerity naturally fill the wholeness of man. And where there is harmony, justice, love and sincerity, there is also joy. Joy, in turn, makes peace; peace leads to permanence; permanence makes Heaven; Heaven makes God. Without the use of words, Heaven is still trustworthy. Though not angry, God appears awe-inspiring. All these come about when man uses music to correct introspection. '

The commentary on the above lines says:

I means harmony; *chih,* justice; *tzu,* love; *liang,* sincerity. All of these show that music can draw out the goodness inherent to human nature.

IV. Lao-tzu and Chuang Tzu: Emphasis on the Propagation of Life

Lao-tzu[5] was an absolute naturalist. He said: "Heaven and earth are ruthless, and treat the myriad creatures as straw dogs" (Ch. V, Lau 9). However, his naturalism was not an inflexible form of materialism. Rather, it is a passion for generation. In his writing, he says:

I do my utmost to attain emptiness; I hold firmly to stillness. The myriad creatures all rise together, and I watch their return. The teeming creatures all return to their separate roots. Return-

---

(5) [Translator's Note] Lao-tzu (6th C. B.C.) was the founder of Taoism, and author of the *Lao Tzu* or *Tao-Te Ching.*

ing to one's roots is known as stillness. This is what is meant by returning to destiny. (Ch. XVI, Lau 23)

The way is broad, reaching left as well as right. The myriad creatures depend on it for life yet it claims no authority. It accomplished its task yet lays claim to no merit. It clothes and feeds the myriad creatures yet lays no claim to being their master. Forever free of desire, it can be called small; yet, as it lays no claim to being master when the myriad creatures turn to it, it can be called great. It is because it never attempts itself to be great that it succeeds in becoming great. (Ch. XXXIV, Lau 51)

Lao-tzu considered Tao as the root of all the myriad things. Tao is neither the creator nor a type of dull element. Instead, it is a living subject that generates and sustains all things. Tao does not take pride in its success or laments the lack of it; neither does it act as the master. The principle of change of Tao lies in advancing as it retreats, in being strong in weakness, in proceeding as it returns. It has no actions or will and leaves everything to their natural course. For him, man's Tao of living lies in following this principle. He says:

Therefore the sage takes his place over the people yet is no burden; takes his place ahead of the people yet causes no obstruction. That is why the empire supports him joyfully and never tires of doing so. It is because he does not contend that no one on the empires is in a position to content with him. (Ch. XLVI, Lau 99)

I have three treasures which I hold and cherish. The first is known as compassion, the second is known as frugality, the third is known as not daring to take the lead in the empire. Being compassionate one could afford to be courageous. Being frugal one could afford to extend one's territory. Not daring to take the lead in the empire one could afford to be lord over the vessels. (Ch. XLVII, Lau 99)

Lao-tzu's philosophy appears very passive. But actually, it actively pursues the propagation of life. For instance, he said that man has three treasures — compassion, frugality and lack of daring to take the lead. Although these appear as passive virtues, he explained compassion as bravery, frugality as generosity and lack of daring to take the lead as the path to becoming a useful person. All these effects are very active in nature. Failure to observe these three, and to "forsake compassion for courage, to forsake frugality for expansion, to forsake the rear for the lead, is sure to end in death" (Lau 99). It can be seen from this that Lao-tzu did not seek for death by lack of activity and will. Instead, he emphasized lack of activity and will to propagate life to the highest level. Thus, he sought not for small wisdom but instead great wisdom that appeared like foolishness. He aspired not for small virtues but instead great virtues that lacked benevolence and righteousness. He sought not for little life but instead hoped for the propagation of life to the highest, even to an extent as great as Tao itself.

Chuang Tzu[6] was a philosopher who sought for the transcendental level of life. His philosophical ideas brim with life. Although Chuang-tzu had continued Lao-tzu's idea of a limitless Tao, he focused more on the reality of *ch'i*. He writes:

> In the midst of the jumble of wonder and mystery a change took place and she had a spirit [*ch'i*]. Another change and she had a body. Another change and she was born. ([Perfect Happiness], Watson 192-193)

> You have only to comprehend the one breath that is the world. The sage never ceases to value oneness. ([Knowledge Wandered North], Watson 236)

> No thing is either complete or impaired, but all are made into

---

(6) [Translator's Note] Chuang Tzu (399-295 B. C.) was a Taoist philosopher who was a minor state official. Ignored by Confucian thinkers, he has had a great influence on the development of Taoism and Zen Buddhism. His principal writing is the *Chuang Tzu*.

one again. Only the man of far-reaching vision knows how to make them into one. ([Discussion on Making All Things Equal], Waston 41)

Heaven and Earth share the same *ch'i* that permeates all the myriad things. Even human life is derived from *ch'i*. If man were able to extricate himself from all forms and colors around him and live in *ch'i*, then his life would fuse with the life of the myriad things. He could then circulate unimpeded in the universe and feel at ease in it. Chuang-tzu further writes:

> If he had only mounted on the truth of Heaven and Earth, ridden the changes of the six breaths, and thus wandered through the boundless, then what would he have had to depend on? ([Free and Easy Wandering], Watson 32)

For him, the development of life lies in leaving everything to its own nature and in maintaining their natural simplicity. Thus he writes:

> What do you mean by the Heavenly and the human? Jo of the North Sea said, "Horses and oxen have four feet--this is what I mean by the Heavenly". Putting a halter on the horse's head, piercing the ox's nose-this is what I mean by the human. So I say: do not let what is human wipe out what is Heavenly; do not let what is purposeful wipe out what is fated; do not let (the desire for) gain lead you after fame. Be cautious, guard it, and do not lose it--this is what I mean by returning to the True." ([Autumn Floods], Watson 193)

Heaven is natural. Man is artificial. Being naturally simple means maintaining what is natural and avoiding harm from what is man-made.

In the chapter entitled "Way of heaven," Chuang-tzu writes:

> Lao Tan said, "Hmm--close--except for the last part. ' Universal love'-that's a rather nebulous ideal, isn't it? And to be with-

out partisanship is already a kind of partisanship. Do you want to keep the world from losing its simplicity? Heaven and earth hold fast to their constant ways, the sun and the moon to their brightness, the stars and planets to their ranks, the birds and beasts to their flocks, the trees and shrubs to their stands. You have only to go along with Virtue in your actions, to follow the Way in your journey, and already you will be there. Why these flags of benevolence and righteousness so bravely upraised, as though you were beating a drum and searching for a lost child? Ah, you will bring confusion to the nature of man! (Watson 150)

These were Lao-tzu's words of advice to Confucius as conceived by Chuang-tzu. What it meant is that man is by nature benevolent and righteous. If someone were to teach about benevolence and righteousness, it would be artificial virtues, which would only work to bring chaos to human nature.

The *ch'i* of the universe operates without ceasing. It goes forever in cycles. Chuang-tzu writes:

Then the four seasons will rise one after the other, the ten thousand things will take their turn at living. Now flourishing, now decaying, the civil and military strains will keep them in step, now with clear notes, and now with dull ones, the *yin* and the *yang* will blend all in harmony. ([The Turning of Heaven], Watson 156)

Embrace the ten thousand things universally--how could there be one you should give special support to? This is called being without bent. When the ten thousand things are unified and equal, the which is short and which is long? "The Way is without beginning or end, but things have their life and death--you cannot rely upon their fulfillment. One moment empty, the next moment full--you cannot depend upon their form. The years cannot be held off; time cannot be stopped. Decay, growth, fullness, and emptiness end and then begin again. It is thus that we might describe the plan of the Great Meaning and discuss the principles of the ten thousand things. The life of things is a gallop, a headlong dash--with every movement they alter, with every moment they shift. What should you do and what should you not do? Everything will change of itself, that is certain! ([Autumn Floods], Watson 182)

The *I Ching* also says that changes in the myriad things are mysteriously unfathomable. In dealing with changes in the universe, Chuang-tzu said that they are inexplicable. They move and yet do not move, change and yet do not change, act and yet do not act. It is thus called self-generation [*tzu-hua*]. On this, Chuang-tzu writes:

Inborn nature cannot be changed, fate cannot be obstructed. Get hold of the Way and there's nothing that can't be done; lose it and there's nothing that can be done. Confucius stayed home for three months and then came to see Lao Tan once again. ' I've got it,' he said. ' The magpie hatches its young, the dish spit out their milt, the slim-waisted wasp has its stages of transformation, and when baby brother is born, big brother howls. For a long time now I have not been taking my place as a man along with the process of change. And if I do not take my own place as a man along with the process of change, how can I hope to change other men?' Lau Tzu said, ' Good, Ch'iu (Confucius)--now you've got it!' ([The Turning of Heaven], Watson 166)

The generation and transformation of the myriad things are as simple as nature. The birds are hatched from eggs and the fish given birth in water. Bees are generated with slender waists. Man is born viviparous. When someone gets a younger brother, the older brother cries for losing everybody's attention. All these are as simple as nature. Therefore, man must understand the reason for generation and transformation. He must first transform himself before transforming others.

When man transform himself, he thus attains great penetration [*ta-t'ung*] and becomes one with heaven and earth. Chuang-tzu says:

"If he can serve as a model for men, how much more so that which the ten thousand things are tied to and all changes alike wait upon!" ([Great and Venerable Teacher], Watson 181). Unity can be achieved with Heaven and Earth, not with men, Chuang-tzu further writes:

> If nature is trained, you may return to Virtue, and Virtue at its highest peak is identical with the Beginning. Being identical, you will be empty; being empty, you will be great. You may join in the cheeping and chirping, you may join with Heaven and Earth. You joining is wild and confused, as though you were stupid, as though you were demented. This is called Dark Virtue. Rude and unwitting, you take part in the Great Submission. ([Heaven and Earth], Watson 132)

One who takes part in the Great Submission becomes a real person [*chen-jen*, True Man] or the perfect man. Chuang-tzu also writes:

> What do I mean by a True Man? The True Man of ancient times did not rebel against want, did not grow proud in plenty, and did not plan his affairs. A man like this could commit an error and not regret it, could meet with success and not make a show. A man like this could climb the highest places and not be frightened, could enter the water and not get wet, could enter the fire and not get burned. His knowledge was able to climb all the way up to the Way like this. ([Great and Venerable Master], Waston 77)

The real person (True Man) is similar to the Confucianists' sage. It is a stage when life is propagated to the highest level, one wherein man's life becomes fused with that of heaven and earth.

V. Philosophy of Life in the Ch'in and Han Dynasties

By the time of the Ch'in Dynasty, the philosophical ideas that had developed in the Spring and Autumn Period and the Warring States Period eventually saw signs of decline. This period also witnessed the inclusion into the realm of philosophy, superstitious beliefs which can be traced to the Warring States Period. It was at this time when the idea of the Five Agents (*wu-hsing*)[7] of *yin* and *yang* that were prevalent in Han times actually emerged. Legalist teachings became popular among politicians following the unification policies of Emperor Shih Huang-ti. The scholarly value of Ch'in and Han philosophies is rather low although it had strong repercussions in the life of the Chinese people. The philosophy of life of that time can be seen through ideas in *Lü-shih ch'un-ch'iu* and those proposed by Tung Chung-shu, Pan Ku and the works of Han scholars on the *I Ching*. Ch'in and Han philosophies bear strong influences from Kuan-tzu.

Kuan-tzu said:

> The earth is the origin of all things and the root of all life. The beautiful and the ugly, the sage and the unworthy, the stupid and the eminent are all generated by it. Water is the blood of earth and circulates inside its muscles and veins. It is therefore said that water possesses complete faculties. . . The waters of the State of Ch'i are rapid and changeable and hence, its people are greedy, careless and audacious. The waters of the State of Ch'u are gentle and clear, and hence, its people are superficial and deceitful. The waters of Yueh are turbid, heavy and soaking, and hence, its people are stupid, jealous and sullied. The waters of Ch'in are stagnant and confused, and hence, its people are greedy, quarrelsome, cunning and troublesome...Hence, the birth of the sage who would transform the world depends upon water. When water is pure, the people's hearts are at ease. Men's hearts being upright, their desires do not turn dissolute. Men's hearts being upright, their

---

(7) [Translator's Note] *Wu-hsing* literally means "five actions or operations." The term refers to Metal, Wood, Water, Fire and Earth. The concept of "Five Agents," like the concept of yin and yang, go far back to antiquity and to quite independent origins (Chan 244). It is also rendered as the "Five Elements."

conduct does not become evil. Thus, when the sage reigns, he does not teach men one by one or house by house. Instead, he takes water as his key.

These ideas can be considered unique in the history of Chinese philosophy. The emphasis on water is akin to the ideas of Lao-tzu. Lao-tzu taught that goodness is comparable to water, which finds strength in weakness. Because of differences in the quality of water, persons and things generated also vary. This concept also has its parallel in the *Ti-kuan*, a chapter in the Rites of the Chou [*Chou-li*]. In Chinese history, it is often said that a scenic place always begets women of beauty.

Kuan-tzu's greatest influence on Ch'in and Han philosophies lies in his ideas of the Five Agents in *yin* and *yang*. In the chapter entitled "Four Seasons" [*Ssu-shih*], Kuan-tzu writes:

"*Yin* and *yang* therefore are the greatest principles of Heaven and Earth. The four seasons are the great paths of *yin* and *yang* while punishment and reward are the factors that bring harmony to the four seasons."

This means that the administration and decrees of kings in the four seasons must conform with the times and seasons. Any incongruity attracts disaster. Kuan-tzu further writes:

In his reign, the sagacious king would examine himself upon meeting adversity, for when he reaches the end, he will start again. Thus, virtues will grow in spring and ripen in summer, moderate in autumn and bear fruit in winter.

This overlaps with the Confucianist teaching on "birth in spring, growth in summer, harvest in fall and storage in winter."

If the sagacious king governs with virtues and according to law, the four seasons will go on in their natural course. If virtues and laws are abandoned, the four seasons will go against their course. Therefore, nothing can be achieved and disaster will surely follow.

This idea is similar to that of the *ming-t'ang yueh-ling*. In his chapter on the "Five Agents", Kuan-tzu did not explain the Five Agents (metal, wood, water, fire and earth) but dealt with the offices of the Five Agents and the laws that govern thae five sounds [*wu-sheng*]. He said:

> The sun comes every six months, making the number six the standard figure in the system of mankind. The number six is the link between mankind and heaven and Earth. The number of the way of heaven is nine, while eight and six correspond to the way of Earth and the way of mankind. With Heaven as father and Earth as mother of man, the myriad things are generated and united.

Here six refers to the six bands [yao]. Six *yang* bands represent the heavens and six *yin* bands represent the earth. Heaven is numbered nine while earth is numbered eight. Man is numbered six, with six referred to in the phrase "emphasis on the three primal powers [*san-ts'ai*] and doubling them." All these are ideas derived from the *I Ching*. Kuang-tzu divided the year into five farming periods, each period consisting of 72 days. Such a division was based on the Five Agents. Kuang-tzu's chapter on the Five Elements further says:

> ...ratify the Five Elements in conformity with the cyclical changes of season, and to establish the five office (of wood, fire, earth, metal and water) for adjusting the status of man. It's only when man and nature come into full accord that cosmic beauty can be generated. (Fang 49)

Here the five seasons [*wu-shih*] are identified as wood, fire, earth, metal and water. Each season corists of 72 days for an annual total of 360 days. Later in the Han Dynasty, scholars of the *I Ching* matched the elements wood, fire, metal and water with the four seasons, with earth made to correspond with the middle of the year. With this harmony between man and Heaven, it is said that the myriad things grow in abundance.

The *Lü-shih ch'un-ch'iu* was compiled by a Ch'in Dynasty Prime Minister, Lü Pu-wei. The work includes extremely complicated ideas that showed strong Taoist tendencies. Its views on the universe takes either [*ch'i*] as the prime element of the myriad things. Ether changes naturally to generate the myriad things. Ether is divided into *yin* and *yang* which circulate between Heaven and Earth in a recurring fashion. The chapter entitled "*You Shih Lan*" says:

> Heaven and Earth have their origins: Heaven consists of the clear air that rises above, while Earth is constituted by the turbid air that blows downward. Harmony and fusion between Heaven and Earth give rise to life. When life is revealed through natural phenomenon, there appears the sun, the moon, the day and the night. In men, there emerges differences between individuals in their characters and talents. Things are integrated and formed; segregated, in order for them to develop. If man can discern how things are formed--their blending, becoming, separating and development--then Heaven and Earth will remain in harmony.

A clear *yang* causes clear air and a turbid *yin* leads to turbid air. When heaven and Earth are joined in harmony, *yin* and *yang* are paired, leading to the generation and transformation of the myriad things.

A chapter in the *Lü-shih ch'un-ch'iu* called "*Shih-erh chi*" bears strong similarities with the "Monthly Decrees" [*Yueh-ling*] in the Book of Rites [*Li-chi*]. The year was divided into four seasons, each season consisting of three months. Months are differentiated based on the ebb and flow of *yin* and *yang*. For instance:

> In the first month of spring, the ether of Heaven descends while the ether of the earth ascends. Heaven and Earth are united. Plants germinate and grow. . . .In the second month of summer. . . the days are long and *yin* and *yang* come to life. Death and life are made visible...In the second month of autumn...the *yang* decreases day-by-day...In the third month of winter, the mandate of autumn applies and white dew descends early.

In the "*Shih-erh chi*," phenomena in the natural world, human actions and political measures are all included in one large system. Its basis lies in the vicissitudes of *yin* and *yang* during the twelve-month period. These vicissitudes trigger off generation and growth, as well as the ebb and flow of the life of the myriad things, all of which are linked with one another.

The *Lū-shih ch'un-ch'iu* has a chapter called "*Ming-lei p'ien*," which is also often called "*Kan-ying p'ien*" (Interaction). Interaction refers to the correlation between the good or evil of human activities and the corresponding ether [*ch'i*] circulating around Heaven and Earth. These interactions lead to strange natural phenomena. Good phenomena mean propitious signs while bad phenomena mean signs of disaster. They act as signs of heavenly reward or punishment. These ideas on interaction were later influenced by the concept of Five Agents, which gradually rose in popularity during the Warring States Period. Tsou Yan had compiled all the superstitious beliefs prevalent during those times and devised the order of the Five Agents. He matched the order of the Five Agents with those of the five virtues and five colors to explain the rise and fall of dynasties. These later caused the evolution of the concept of "*wu-teh shih-chung*" (the perpetuation of the five virtues). Thus, the first Chinese emperor, Huang Ti was assigned the earth element and the yellow color. Emperor Yu was assigned the wood element and the color blue. The emperors T'ang and Chou were assigned the elements metal and fire and the colors white and red. The dynasty that succeeded the Chou was assigned the element water and the color black.

In Tung Chung-shu's Ch'un-ch'iu fan-lu and Pan Ku's Pai-hu t'ung-yi, the Five Agents were assigned their relative hierarchy of harmony and contradiction. Tung Chung-shu writes:

> Heaven possesses Five Agents: the first is wood, the second is fire, the third is earth, the fourth is metal and the fifth is water. Wood is the starting point of the Five Agents, water their terminus and earth their center. Such is their natural sequence. Wood generates fire, fire generates earth, earth generates metal, metal generates water and water generates wood. Such

is their father-and-son relationship. Wood occupies the left, metal the right, fire the front, water the rear and earth the central position. Such is their generational hierarchy, with all agents mutually giving and receiving from one another. (Chapter XLII: Definition of the Five Agents, Vol.XI, Ch'un-ch'iu fan-lu)

This is the sequence of the Five Agents' mutual generation and how they are located with respect to the four directions and their center.

In Pan Ku's work, it says:

Why do the Five Agents reign in succession? It is because they generate one another in succession. Hence, they all have a beginning and an end. Wood generates fire. Fire generates earth. Earth generates metal. Metal generates water and water generates wood. . . The Five Agents do harm to each other due to the nature of the universe itself. That is, what is abundant overcomes what is scarce. This explains why water overcomes fire. What is ethereal overcomes what is dense, and therefore fire overcomes metal. What is hard overcomes what is soft, and therefore metal overcomes wood. What is concentrated overcomes what is dispersed, and therefore, wood overcomes earth. What is solid overcomes what is vacuous, and this explains why earth overcomes water. (*Pai-hu t'ung-yi*, *T'ung-teh un* Vol.3: Five Agents).

This shows that the sequence of mutual generation and subjugation among the Five Agents are phenomena occurring in the natural world. These Five Agents are five types of natural things that share relationships with one another. However, Han Dynasty Confucianists had taken the Five Agents as five variations of *yin* and *yang*, and thus reckoned them as component elements of the myriad things. For them, there are no natural objects nor human affairs in this universe. Rather, all these are derived from *yin* and *yang*, and the Five Agents. Hence, the sequence of the Five Agents became the principles of relationship among all things and events. With this development, the Five Agents finallly entered the realm of Chinese philosophy and all related scholarly ideas.

The scholarship on the *I Ching*, which became popular in Han Dynasty China, explained the different divinatory symbols using the concepts of *yin* and *yang*, and the Five Agents. Changes in the divinatory symbols where attributed to ether *(ch'i)*, which permeates the cosmos and generates the myriad things in it. The changes brought about by ehter may be measured in terms of time, such as the four seasons in a year. Changes may also be related to space and direction, such as the four cardinal points. In the Han Dynasty, scholars of the *I Ching* matched the four prime trigrams [*cheng-kua*] with the four seasons and the twelve alternating trigrams [*hsiao-hsi kua*] made to correspond with the twelve months of the year. The twenty-four bands *(yao)* of the four prime trigrams were matched with the twenty-four climatic periods. In turn, the 72 bands of the twelve alternating trigrams correspond with the 72 intervals *(hou)* each year. Finally the 360 bands of the 60 divinatory symbols match the number of days in a year, each symbol corresponding to 6 , 7 days on average. The so-called prime trigrams--*k'an, chen, li and tuei*--are matched with the four cardinal points and the Five Agents. Thus, spring corresponds to the east, wood and *chen*. Summer matches with the south, fire and *li*. Autumn coincides with the west, metal and *tuei*. Winter corresponds to the north, water and *k'an*. Earth occupies central position. The four seasons symbolize time while the four cardinal points represent space. *Yin* and *yang* and the Five Agents symbolize ether, which circulates in time and space to generate changes represented by the 64 divinatory symbols. These changes are aimed at the perpetual renewal *(sheng-sheng)* characterized by birth in spring, growth in summer, harvest in fall and storage in winter. This is how the Han scholars of the *I Ching* explained the divinatory symbols and their relationship to ether. These scholars' study of the *hsiang* and the *shu* were limited to their divinatory use. Although the divinatory *hsiang* also relates with the sequence of the 64 divinatory symbols, their explanations were merely mechanical in nature and bore no philosophical significance at all. By the closing years of the Han Dynasty and during the period of the Six Dynasties, Taoism also adopted the concepts relating divinatory symbols with ether. Thus, Taoist teachings and practices evolved, including methods for producing the *nei-tan* and the *wai-tan*, absorption of the vital *ch'i* of Heaven and Earth based on the waning and waxing of the moon, and the concoction of the so-called *chin-tan*, an elixir believed to bring immortality.

VI. Philosophy of Life in Buddhism

Buddhism takes the ten thousand dharmas as the harmony between the principal and subsidiary causes. What is actual is but emptiness and in fact possesses no real life. However, it is a popular belief that the ten thousand dharmas are all reality. How is it explained? Different Buddhist sects propose different explanations, which have a few points in common.

The universe and the myriad things constitute one reality. They all are products of man's phantasm. This phantasm comes as a result of man's erroneous belief that he is a reality.

When a person is conceived in his mother's womb, it is his strong consciousness of his prior belief in his former life that he is a being, or what is called "grasping of oneself" (*wo-chih*). This *wo-chih* remains intact after death in the previous life and reincarnates in the mother's womb. This belief possesses one's life and all the consequences of one's actions in his former life. In turn, these consequences become the seeds of action in one's present life. Because of these seeds, one continues to have feelings and knowledge. However, matters of feelings and knowledge are all derived from these seeds. Precisely because of these matters, the ego still experiences love, hate, greed and desire, and does evil actions. The latter leave seeds of evil that will develop in the life to come.

Since all the myriad things were created by the seeds in one's heart, or what is called "consciousness-only of the ten thousand dharmas," and "heart-only of the ten thousand dharmas," then they all are joined into one body. After death, man reincarnates to become man again or in the form of an animal, insect, stone or other things. Hence, not only are the myriad things fused together, they also possess life.

To exempt himself from the reincarnative cycle, man must uproot his belief that his own ego is a reality. Once this "grasping of oneself" (*wo-chih*) is abolished, the belief that the myriad things are a reality (*wu-chih*) also disappears. This results in man's attainment of nirvana, the state of Buddhahood and immortality. There are a myriad ways to abolish these beliefs in the reality of the ego and things. A common point among the different Buddhist sects consists of the need for meditation to eradicate oneself of worries. It is aimed at seeing oneself as the *chen-ju* in the silence and tranquility of one's heart. The *chen-ju* is itself Buddhahood, the absolute reality or the reality of the ego. The ego usually only sees his own body and things around him. He does not see the real *chen-ju* hidden in his own self nor in the myriad things. Once the ego sees the *chen-ju* in the depths of his heart, he then becomes aware that his own self and things are but the outward manifestations of the *chen-ju* in the same way as waves in the great ocean. Waves are caused by the activity of the ocean. Similarly, the myriad things are also activities of the *chen-ju*. They are an expression of the life of the *chen-ju*. Once he is enlightened about this truth, man attains Buddhahood and is reverted back to the substance of the *chen-ju*. He is united with the *chen-ju* and attains the state of nirvana to live for all eternity.

VII. The Idealists' Philosophy of Life

Confucian thought experienced a decline after the time of Mencius and Hsun-tzu. In the Han, Yuan, Sui and T'ang Dynasties, Confucian philosophy received much stimuli from Taoist and Buddhist ideas. By the Sung Dynasty, a new form of Confucianism started to emerge--the Idealist School. The Idealists focused their study on the nature and principles of the myriad things. Their study covered the *I Ching* and the *Chung-yung* and absorbed concepts inherent to Taoism and Buddhism. This development paved the way for the formation of metaphysical studies in Confucian humanistic philosophy.

The first to formally delve into Idealist scholarship was Chou

Tun-i[8]. His ideas are summarized in his *T'ai-chi t'u-shuo* (Explanation of the Diagram of the Great Ultimate) and *T'ung-shu*. The former expounded on the concept of *sheng-sheng* (perpetual renewal of life) which originated from the *I Ching* while the latter dipped into the ideas of sincerity and spirituality (*shen*) in the *Chung-yung*. Chou Tun-i writes:

> The Ultimateless and the Supreme Ultimate. The Supreme Ultimate produces *yang* through movements. Having reached its limit, this movement is followed by quiescence, which produces *yin*. Once quiescence reaches its limits, there is a return to movement. Thus, movement and quiescence alternate to become the source of each other. *Yin* and *yang* are distinct and their forms stand revealed. The transformation of the *yang* and its union with *yin* generate water, fire, wood, metal and earth. These five ethers become diffused in an orderly manner and the four seasons proceed in their cause. The Five Agents are derived from the one *yin* and *yang*. *Yin* and *yang* make up the one Supreme Ultimate, which is the Ultimateless fundamentally. The Five Agents are generated, each with its own nature. The true substance of the Ultimateless, and the essences of *Yin* and *yang* the Five Agents, are joined in a mysterious union and later consolidated. The *ch'ien* becomes the male element and the *k'un* becomes the female element. The two ethers interact to generate the myriad things. The myriad things engage in perpetual generation in such a way that transformation continue without ceasing. Of them, only man is blessed with excellence and is therefore the most intelligent...Great indeed are the changes. Herein are expressed their fullest.

---

(8) [Translator's Note] Chou Tun-i (1017-1073) was the pioneer of neo-Confucianism and the teacher of the famous Ch'eng brothers. He is known for his *An Explanation of the Diagram of the Great Ultimate* and *Penetrating the Book of Changes*.

Here, let us not deal with the issue of Ultimateless and Great Ultimate. Instead, let us focus on Chou Tun-i's ideas of the sequence of the generation of the myriad things. His sequence follows a combination of ideas in the *I Ching* and those of Han Dynasty scholars of the classic. He started with the origination of the *yin* and *yang* from the Great Ultimate. *Yin* and *yang* generates the Five Agents, which in turn gives birth to male and female. Male and female generates the myriad things. This process of transformation follows changes in one ether. This one ether is transformed into two ethers, *yin* and *yang*. In turn, *yin* and *yang* change into five ethers, which again is transformed into two ethers, male and female. Male and female ethers interact to generate the myriad things. This process of transformation was later accepted by the Idealists, although they expressed reservations on the issue of the origins of the Ultimateless and the Great Ultimate.

Chou Tun-i's *T'ung-shu* deals with the Five Agents. It says:

> The passive material force of water has its roots in *yang* and the passive material force of fire has its roots in *yin*. The Five Elements are nothing but *yin* and *yang*, which in turn form the Great Ultimate. The Four Seasons continue in their course and the myriad things have their end and beginning.

This idea overlaps with the *T'ai-chi t'u-shuo* (Explanation of the Diagram of the Great Ultimate). It would thus be wrong to assume that since the *T'ung-shu* made no mention of the Diagram of the Great Ultimate, then the *T'ai-chi t'u-shuo* was not authored by Chou Tun-i. The *T'ung-shu* mainly deals with the Tao of human life. It talks about the mean and sincerity. For instance, the *T'ai-chi t'u-shuo* says:

> The sage regulates himself according to the mean, correctness, benevolence and righteousness. He takes quiescence as essential, and in so doing, establishes the supreme standard for mankind.

In the *T'ung-shu*, there is the following passage:

The way of the sage consists of benevolence, righteousness, the mean and correctness. Observing them is estimable. Exercising them is beneficial and cultivating oneself to acquire them brings one close to Heaven and Earth. (*T'ung-shu*, Chapter 6)

These ideas totally overlap with one another. *T'ung-shu* also deals with the virtue of sincerity. It says:

Sincerity is the nature of the sage. For great indeed is the origination of the *ch'ien*. It is the origin of the myriad things, the very source of sincerity. (*T'ung-shu, Ch'eng-shang*, Chapter 1)

Here, sincerity is the same virtue mentioned in the *Chung-yung*. It is the fulfillment of one's nature, or what is called perpetual renewal of life (*sheng-sheng*) in the *I Ch'uan*.

In comparison, Chang Tsai's[9] philosophy is founded on the concept of ether (*ch'i*). He writes:

The Great Void which bears no shape, such is the ether in its substance. But it condenses and diffuses in its transformations through which it acquires temporary shapes. (*Cheng-meng*, Great Harmony)

The Great Void condenses to generate *yin* and *yang*, which in turn condense to produce the Five Agents. The Five Agents condense to generate the myriad things. All these transpire with the condensation and dispersion of the one ether. He further writes:

The Great Void cannot but consist of ether. This ether cannot

---

(9) [Translator's Note] Chang Tsai (Chang Heng-ch'ü, 1020-1077) was a neo-Confucian philosopher. A native of Chang-An, Chang's principal writings include the *Hsi-ming* (The Western Inscription) and the *Cheng-meng* (Correcting Youthful Ignorance).

but condense to become the myriad things. The myriad things cannot but disperse to be transformed into the Great Void. The cyclical procession of these movements is therefore inevitable. (*Cheng-meng*, Great Harmony)

This ether undergoes transformation naturally but it is not material in nature. He explains:

"All that possess shape are being. All being consist of appearances and all appearances consist of ether. Ether by nature is vacuous and spiritual (*Cheng-meng, Ch'ien-ch'eng*).

> The Ether (*ch'i*) consists of *yin* and *yang*. Their gradual production and reproduction is called transformation. That which is unfathomable in the fusion of *yin* and *yang* is called divination (*shen*).

In the *I Ch'uan*, emphasis is made on the perpetual generation by Heaven and Earth in a mysterious, unfathomable way, or more properly, described as spiritual. Chang Tsai described the transformations of the ether as mysterious and unfathomable, hence overlapping with what the *I Ch'uan* says. Chang Tsai writes:

> Sensation is the spirit of nature (*hsing*), and nature the object of sensation. Only when man acts in moderation can he attain the standard of life and conduct. Thus, to harmonize the myriad things is the divine law. To understand them is the way. To fell them is nature. (*Chang-meng, Ch'ien-cheng*)

Materiality results from the condensation of ether. This materiality has a power of interaction that is deeply mysterious. Although it involves such transformations as extension and withdrawl, motion and quiescence, start and end, these are but transformations of the one ether. For this reason, it is described as divination (*shen*) or Tao.

Since the myriad things consist of the one ehter, then all life must be mutually linked through a hierarchical order. Thus, Chang Tsai writes:

> In the process of generation, some come first and others later. This is the sequence dictated by Heaven. In terms of size and shape, some are small and some large, some tall and some short. This is the order prescribed by Heanven. Similarly, the generation of things also follow a sequence dictated by Heaven. The shapes and sizes of things likewise follow an order prescribed by Heaven. (*Cheng-meng, Tung-wu*)

Yet, the sequence and order dictated by Heaven do not separate things but rather unite them into one reality. Elsewhere he writes:

> *Ch'ien* is called the father and *k'un* the mother. We who are insignificant are found in their midst. I am thus the substance that lies within the confines of Heaven and Earth. My nature is that of Heaven and Earth, the commanders. People are my brothers. I find company in the midst of things. (*Cheng-meng*, Western Inscription, The *Ch'ien*).

This singleness of the myriad things is experienced with the human mind. In the same work, Chang Tsai writes:

> By the expansion of one's mind, one is able to embody all things in this world. . . By fulfilling his own nature, the sage prevents his mind from being limited to what is heard and seen. He views the world and sees that there is no one thing that is not his own self. This is what is meant by Mencius when he said that by fulfilling one's nature, one comes to know nature and Heaven. So vast is Heaven that there is nothing external to it. Hence, a mind that keeps things outside of it is not capable of uniting with the mind of Heaven. (Enlarging One's Heart)

In fact, this is what Mencius meant when he said: "The myriad things are in me in every possible way."

The philosophies of life of Ch'eng I[10], Ch'eng Hao and Chu Hsi[11] can be associated with one another. Chu Hsi's ideas can be taken as representative of these three because he had adopted the ideas of the first two and elaborated on them.

For Chu Hsi, the myriad things are formed from two elements: *li* (material principle) and *ch'i* (material force). Material principle is universal for all that lie between Heaven and Earth while material force is differentiated into clear and turbid. The one same material principle is the principle of life. The degree of turbidity or clarity of the material force varies. The turbid material force refers to corporeality while the clear material force corresponds to spirituality. When material principle and material force unite, the latter limits the former and thus, it is said that there is "unity and diversity in material principle" [*li yi erh shu*]. An object that has a turbid material force cannot manifest the material principle of its life. Thus, inanimate things are called "non-living" things. An object that has a relatively clearer material force may show a portion of the material principle of its life, as in the case of simple forms of biological life. Thus, based on the degree of clarity or turbidity of the material force, the material principle of life is manifested as various forms of life. Man has the clearest material force. He therefore has the most intelligent mind and the material principle of his life is manifested in its totality. Hence, it is said: "Man possesses the fullness of the material principle while things only possess some part of it."

Life's material principle is totally made manifest through man's spiritual life. Chu Hsi writes:

---

(10) [Translator's Note] Cheng I (1033-1107), a neo-Confucianist, was the younger of the Ch'eng brothers. His principal writings include: Surviving Works; Additional Works; Collection of Literary Works by Ch'eng I; and Commentary on the Book of Changes. Ch'eng Hao, the older brother, is also known as Ch'eng Ming-tao (1032-1085). They are often referred to as the Two Ch'eng's.

(11) [Translator's Note] Chu Hsi (1130-1200) was a Confucian philosopher whose writings dominated Chinese, Korean, and Japanese thought for centuries. His writings include: *The Collection of Literary Works by Chu Hsi; Complete Works of Chu Hsi; Classified Conversations of Chu Hsi; Supplement to the Reflections on Things at Hand.*

Heaven and Earth take the creation of things as their mind. Heaven embraces the earth for no other purpose than the creation of things. Since ancient times, the generation of life proceeds without end. Man and things have also attained as their mind the creation of things. (*Chu-tzu yū-lei*, Bk. LIII)

In man, this mind to create things is called benevolence. Thus, Chu Hsi further writes: "Benevolence is the mind of Heaven and Earth to create things." Chu Hsi differentiated between benevolence and love. For him, benevolence is the principle of love. A benevolent heart (mind) is one that generates life without end. Thus, he writes:

To clarify the meaning of the word ' mind ' , Chu Hsi said: ' One word suffices to cover it all--sheng (generation). The great virtue of Heaven and Earth is generation. Man receives the material force of Heaven and Earth and is generated. There- fore, this mind must be benevolent. Benevolence is then genera- tion. ' (*Chu-tzu yū-lei*, Bk. V)

Elsewhere he writes: "The mind is itself benevolence. It is not that benevolence exists outside the mind (*Chu-tzu yū-lei*, Bk. LX)."

Speaking ontologically, the whole universe possesses only one material principle of life and one circulating material force which may be either clear or turbid. Material principle and material force fuse to form corporeal nature. This "nature" is made up of matter[12] and form. It is individual nature, which includes the concepts of classifica- tion and individuality at the same time. In Chinese philosophical tradi- tion, the clarity and turbidity of material force are not exact opposites but are relative concepts. It follows a line proceeding from pure clarity to total turbidity. The fusion of material force and material principle is

---

(12) [Translator's Note] "By being united to matter, the form is ' contracted', that is narrowed from its universal and specific being to existence in a parti- cular" (Allers, "Prime Matter" 191). "In St. Thomas Aquinas' Ontology, he takes *forma* and *materia* to form the nature of things. Nature and *existentia* fuse to form ' reality' which is a concrete thing" (Lokuang, *Chu Hsi* 26).

one that leads to corporeality. They unite to form the corporeality of a substance[13], not the accidents of the substance. In contrast, accidents are the functions (*yung*) of the substance. They are formed after the substance had started to exist. Thus, the clarity or turbidity of material force does not refer to a classification of accidents but rather one of substance. A substance, with either a clear material force or a turbid one, does not differ from others in terms of its accidents. It differs in terms of its substance. When the principle and material force of life fuse, they are made manifest in varying degrees owing to the degree of clarity or turbidity of the material force. It is not that the degree of accidents differ, but rather, a difference in the substance of life. As a consequence, objects formed also differ. In actual circumstances, the fusion of life's material principle and a clear or turbid material force thus results in different things. This is a manifestation of the "unity and diversity in material principle" [*li yi erh shu*].

Man received the fullness of life's material principle owing to a material force that is the clearest of all. A clear material force means spirituality. Thus, man's life is spiritual or intellectual in nature. Man's mind is also benevolent. Since benevolence encompasses all good virtues, a spiritual life is a life of charity, righteousness, decorum, wisdom and trustworthiness. All these virtues emanate from the human heart and is manifested in his emotions. Emotion is a movement of the heart. When this movement is "central and regulated" [*chung-chieh*], it leads to virtues. The cultivation of virtues is thus a task of controlling one's passion by observing respect. Respect can be internal or external. Internal observance of respect is aimed at rectifying onself while being righteous in one's actions constitute an external obser-

----

(13) [Translator's Note] In Scholastic philosophy, "the nature of a substance is that it exists in itself, independently from another being. While accidents are in another, substance is in itself. It is what underlies the accidents, persists even if these are changing" (Allers 305). The *Dictionary of Philosophy and Religion* explains these two terms in the following way: "If by ' accident' one means that which inheres in something else, whose reason or essence is in something else, then by substance one should mean the subject of accidents which contains its own reason or essence" (556).

vance of respect. Both internal and external observance of respect depend upon single-heartedness. It consists of keeping undivided attention on the task of the moment so that it becomes consistent with the Heavenly principles. When the latter is achieved, sincerity is also attained. Sincerity is the virtue of the sage who, in turn, praises the generation of things by Heaven and Earth. Chu Hsi writes:

> Praising the generation of things by Heaven and Earth, man finds himself between them. Although all things share the same material principle, what Heaven and man do are distinguished from one another. There are tasks that man can do thoroughly that Heaven cannot. Heaven can generate things, yet farming must be done by man. Water can nourish living things, yet irrigation depends upon human effort. Fire can cook, but only man can use it to cook. Assistance in preparing materials is a task needing the help of man. How could this help not be necessary? (*Chu-tzu yu-lei*, Bk. LXIV)

In Chu Hsi's philosophical system, metaphysics is fused with philosophy of living. It is representative of the Chinese Confucianist philosophical thinking. The concepts of material principle and material force pervade the whole system. Since material principle is the principle of life, then life forms the core of his philosophy.

The central idea of Wang Yang-ming's[14] philosophy is the fulfillment of one's conscience. Conscience refers to one heart (mind). The heart (mind) is not only the seat of Heavenly principles, it is also the center of all knowledge and life. For Wang Yang-ming, the things of this universe exist because of man's heart. If man's heart (mind) is

---

(14) [Translator's Note]   Wang Yang-ming (1472-1529) was a neo-Confucian whose influence became dominant in China during his lifetime and for the 150 years thereafter. He occupied many administrative posts commendably. Posthumously, he was awarded the title of Marquis, and *Wen-ch'eng* [Completion of Culture]. His principal writings include the *Inquiry on the Great Learning* and *Instructions for Practical Living*.

unknowing, then all things would not exist at all. Something that is not known by the heart (mind) of man is not existent. Not that it is inexistent substantially, but only in man's consciousness. In this case, it would be tantamount to inexisting for man. Since all things exist because of man's heart (mind), then the heart of man unites everything into one integral reality. However, this integral reality is not only so intellectually but also in terms of their substance and life. In his work entitled "Great Learning," Wang Yang-ming explains the phrase "unity of behevolence" [yi t'i chih jen]. By it, he meant that there is a unity of life, that is, all the myriad things are interlinked in their lives. They are mutually dependent and assisting. Man's life is maintained with help of animals, plants and minerals. To live, man needs to eat and drink. He needs remedies for his illness. Thus, he depends upon animals, plants and minerals. If the substances of animals, plants and minerals are not linked with man's life, not only would they be of no use to man's life, they would also bring harm to it.

Wang Ch'uan-shan[15], a philosopher of the early Ch'ing Dynasty, adopted the concept of ether [ch'i] from Chang Tsai. For him, ether was the origin of the myriad things. However, he dropped the idea that the ether of the Great Vacuity was undifferentiated into yin and yang. Wang proposed that the substance of ether was originally divided into yin and yang. In the Great vacuity, the ether divided into yin and yang was in a state of Great Harmony (T'ai-ho) and did not manifest in the two forms. Once changes had occurred in the Great Harmony, yin and yang became manifest. Hence, Wang Ch'uan-shan proposed the idea of a "parallel structure of the ch'ien and the k'un." Changes in yin and yang follow a principle of change, which is corporeality or humanity, both of which are mandated by Heaven. Changes in

---

(15)[Translator's Note] Wang Ch'uan-shan (Wang Fu-chih, 1619-1692), a materialistic philosopher who lived at the time the Manchus were breaking up the Ming Dynasty, which he helped defend by raising his own army. His philosophy is similar to Chang Tsai. His principal writing is the *Surviving Works of Wang Fu-chih.*

yin and *yang* continue without end. Once they form an object, they continue triggering off changes within it. However, since the nature of that object was mandated by Heaven, it remains unchanged. Although the object experiences internal changes, it remains the same object. Corporeality does not remain constant after the formation of things; neither does it remain unchanged. The phrase "nature (*hsing*) grows day by day while life decreases" explains the significance of life.

Tsai Chen's philosophy focuses on the transformation of the ether and the perpetual renewal of life. He writes:

> Anything that has life cannot be dissociated from the ethereal transformation of Heaven and Earth. *Yin* and *yang* and the Five Agents operate without end because of the ethereal transformation of Heaven and Earth. This is the origin of the generation of man and all things. (*Meng-tzu tzu-yi shu-cheng*, Bk. II)

Scholars of the Han Dynasty took man's life as possessing the primeval ether of Heaven and Earth, while also possessing ether derived from parents. Tsai Chen thus proposed that man possesses an "endowed ether" and a "nurturing ether." Tsai Chen further explained:

> Endowed ether and nurturing ether are not identical. Although nurturing ether comes from an external source, it nonetheless is drawn in by endowed ether. The Five Agents have a mutually generating and subjugating relationships. When an element encounters a mutually subjugating element, it leads to harm, or even death. From this, one can see differences in their nature. Endowed ether goes well with nurturing ether because they are matching, not mutually negating. Therefore, internal and external ethers are one. They contribute to the ethereal transformation of Heaven and Earth to eventually generate things precisely because they are mutually complementing, not subjugating. (*Meng-tzu tzu-yi shu-cheng*, Bk. II)

In this process of generation and transformation, order is followed and things fall into a hierarchy. Things belonging to a lower level nurture things on a higher level. Thus, all myriad things in Heaven and Earth are destined for sustaining human life. Elsewhere he writes:

> In the *I Ching*, it says: ' The movement of *yin* and *yang* constitutes the Way (*Tao*). What issues from the Way is good, and that which fulfills it is individual nature. ' The successive motion of *yin* and *yang*, which causes the ceaseless ethereal transformation of Heaven and Earth that leads to generation, is the Way (*Tao*). Does the movement of *yin* and *yang* lead to perpetual renewal of life? Is this generation following a certain order? It is because of the smoothness in Heaven and Earth that it was said: ' The movement of yin and yang constitutes the Way (*Tao*).' Perpetual generation of life is itself benevolence (*jen*). There is no generation without first following a certain order. (*Yuan-shan*, BK. I)

In the early years of the Republican Era, Hsiung Shih-li [16] combined ideas he borrowed from Buddhism with Confucian Idealist philosophy. Although he called it a return from Buddhism to Confucianism, his idea of *sheng-sheng* (perpetual renewal of life) only preserved a small part of the outside features of the *I Ching*. The bulk of the contents of his ideas are still Buddhist in nature. He explained substance as having four meanings:

> 1.) Reality (substance) is the origin of all principles, the source of all virtues and the start of all transformations. 2.) Reality is

---

(16) [Translator's Note] Hsiung Shih-li (1885-1968) was educated at the Nanking Institute of Buddhism. He studied the *I Ching* and produced a reconstruction of the rationalistic or idealistic side of neo-Confucianism using elements from Western philosophy. His principal writings include: *New Doctrine of Consciousness-Only* and *An Inquiry on Confucianism*.

being and existing, that is, existence and non-existence. 3.)
Reality has no beginning nor end. 4.) Reality is manifest as infinite and endless function (*yung*), or better, something changing. The operation of functions, or better, something changing.
The operation of functions (*yung*) does not in any way change
the reality's perpetual renewal of life (*sheng-sheng*) and its
movements. Reality generates different virtues and natures.
Thus, it should be called something unchanging...We must
know that a reality is, in its totality, a changing, all encompassing function. That is, outside the operation of functions, there
is no reality (substance) as for example, all the ocean water
turning into waves in such a way that the ocean disappears.
That is why reality and function are not distinguished. (Reality
and Function, p.9)

In fact, this reality (substance) as explained by Hsiung, is nothing else
but the Buddhist *chen-ju*. Changes in the reality is described as
"opening and closing" [*hsi and pi*], each being a type of movement, but
not in the same way *I Ching* explains as "when *yang* moves, *yin*
follows." These "opening and closing" are not chronologically differentiated, both being terminated immediately as soon as they start. They
are constantly ending and starting. Opening acts to draw things. These
so-called "things" are not things of forms and shapes but are instead a
sphere of movement, which may be real or vacuous, or even both. This
sphere of movement becomes one when it is vacuous. When real or
condensed, it becomes a multitude. This oneness or multitudinousness
is formed and annihilated instantaneously, its reality being a reflection
of the mysterious nature of the *chen-ju*. In his writings, Hsiung Shih-li
described this phenomenon as follows: "Great indeed is the changes.
Herein is expressed its fullest (*T'i-yung*, p.238)."

In recent decades, Prof. Thomé Fang did much to promote Chinese
philosophy. He said: "Chinese philosophy is centered on life. Any
philosophical system is an expression of the essence of life ([Collec-
tion of Speeches by Thomé Fang] 79). Confucian philosophy is
founded on the *I Ching*. This classic focuses on explaining *sheng-*

sheng (perpetual renewal of life) carried out through changes *(I)*, the creative power of life. The whole cosmos is one torrent of life that flows without end, in a way that is right and central, and harmonious. The way of human life is patterned after the way of *sheng-sheng* (perpetual renewal of life) in the universe. It tends towards transcendence to the life of the cosmos and the attainment of spiritual heights, an internal transcendence occurring in the human heart. Then the human heart can appreciate the beauty of the universe. Prof. Thomé Fang writes: "...to reach the principles of the myriad things through the beauty of Heaven and Earth and to use artistic sentiments to develop the philosophical wisdom necessary for establishing a system of philosophical thoughts ("The Original Confucian and Taoist Philosophies" 14). Elsewhere, he writes:

> Life embraces within itself all beings and creatures interwoven with, and enlinked, to the great path of Tao. In its fulfillment through change and transmutation it roots itself in Primary Nature which, as the Primordial of Being, is the spring of inexhaustible energy, and passes through the steps of creative advance into Consequent Nature which, as the ultimate destiny, is the achievement of the Supreme Good. As a universal active substance, Life manifests itself in Space and, withal, conquers its limitations by the great momentum of infinite creative urge. (Chinese Philosophy: Its Spirit and Its Development, 106)

Man received the fullness of life. Hence, man's creative potentials are comparable to Heaven's.

In his work "Nineteen Essays on Chinese Philosophy," Prof. Mou Tsung-san writes in the first chapter entitled "Peculiar Issues in Chinese Philosophy":

> The principal issue developed in Chinese philosophy is life, or what we call the knowledge of life. Chinese philosophy takes life as its object, mainly by focusing on the mind [*hsin*]. It studies how we should adjust, operate and deal with our life. (15)

VIII. Conclusions

In summary, the development of Chinese philosophy started with the *Shang-shu* and reached its maturity with the writing of the *I Ching*. The philosophical thinking of Confucianism can be summarized in the sentence--"The benevolent generates life"--which pervades the whole school as one system.

At present, using Confucian philosophy of life to deal with Confucianism or even the modernization of Chinese philosophy can help accommodate both the rapid changes in contemporary society and the growing significance of new technology. This is the direction that the author follows in seeking ways to modernize Confucian philosophy. This chapter only represents a philosophical outline and is lacking in in-depth analysis. Life by itself is moving and cannot be subjected to analysis. It can only be experienced. Yet, after experiencing it, it must be explained. To achieve this, the concepts and analytical methods used by Western philosphy in explaining cosmic changes can be instrumental as we direct our efforts to explaining the significance of Chinese philosophy of life.

Works Cited

Allers, Rudolf. "Potency." *Dictionary of Philosophy*. Ed. Dagobert Runes. Lanham, Maryland: Rowman, 1964.

Baynes, Cary F. *The I Ching*. Princeton: Princeton UP, 1967.

Chan, Wing-tsit. *A Source Book in Chinese Philosophy*. Princeton: Princeton UP, 1963.

Fang, Thomé. *Chinese Philosophy: Its Spirit and Its Development*. Taipei: Linking, 1968.

Lau, D.C. *Tao Te Ching*. Hong Kong: Chinese UP, 1982.

Lokuang, Stanislaus. *Chu Hsi's Theory of Metaphysical Structure.* Taipei: n.p., 1982.

Mou, Tsung-san. *Chung-kuo che-hsueh shih-chiu chiang* [Nineteen Essays on Chinese Philosophy]. Taipei: Hsueh-sheng, 1983.

Watson, Burton. *The Complete Works of Chuang Tzu.* New York: Columbia UP, 1968.

Translated by Carlos Tee

Chapter II

Creation

I. The Constant Mobility of the Myriad Things in the Universe

In the previous chapter, we witnessed how Chinese philosophy regards every being in the universe from the perspective of existence in motion. Every being is in motion internally and is alive. However, we did not delve deeply into the substance of what constitutes life. In this chapter, we will examine the essential meaning of life from the theory of change as advocated by philosophers. Max Born writes:

> We often acknowledge something as being ' static. ' Strictly speaking, the term ' static ' does not exist. Readers must find this strange, right? When we talk about material things, we often make the distinction of dead or alive and mobile or static. This, however, is a juvenile distinction. Rocks that appear lifeless or doors, window, tables and chairs that appear immovable are actually in motion every second of the day. Why do we fail to notice their movements? It is because we are conditioned to pass judgment based solely on the external appearance of things, we resort to the impression provided to us via our senses, but these impressions are deceiving.

These are the words of a Noble Prize physicist. From the point of view of physics, everything is constantly moving in the universe. The universe is said to be infinitely big and composed of many galaxies. Light waves and electric waves connect the galaxies. These two types of waves are manifestations of power. Power has infinite energy. Power is constantly moving within and about the galaxies.

The Cosmic Theory advocated by Newton and post-Newtonian scientists believe the entire universe static. There is cosmic attraction and cosmic repulsion that counter balance each other, gravity screening covers up the ambiguity that exists between the two forces. "In other words, if the system of the universe is stable, then overall expansion and contraction could not have occurred, although slight partial changes are possible. As to the belief that our universe is static, there is obviously one difficulty in explaining the phenomena of red shifts" (Schatzman 2).

The Theory of Relativity by Einstein adopts the cosmic repulsion belief. It believes that cosmic repulsion created the ball-shaped static universe that contains dense matter. The universe itself is enclosed. However, this type of theory "still belonged to the theory of relativity and was not logical. It was only after cosmic repulsion was introduced that the objective was reached. The rationality of the argument was proven with reasons outside the realm of physics" (Schatzman 283).

Certain astrologers believe the universe was self-generated. It has always existed with no beginning and end. Schatzman further writes:

> The past like the present has the same average density. The past has no beginning, the future will never come to an end. All in all, we can say the density of the universe has never altered. New matter continue to appear to compensate for the decrease in density as a result of overall expansion. Under these circumstances, cases of self-generated matter are very rare, approximately one hydrogen atom per square meter every billion year. However, this has proven to be more than adequate.(285)

Philosophers have always studied the universe. Since ancient Greece, some philosophers have advocated the universe is in motion, Thales (624-545 B.C.) believed flowing water was the origin of everything. Anaximenes (585-528 B.C.) believed ether was the origin. Heraclitus (545-484 B.C.) felt fire, the fastest agent of change, was the basic element of the universe. The Eleatic School, however, was opposed to the concept of the earth being in motion, instead they viewed the universe as an unchanging entity. Plato and Aristotle combined the two viewpoints together. believing the universe to be costantly changing but the study of the universe should stem from the static dimension. Heraclitus once remarked that there was one fixed element in this ever-evolving universe. It was the foundation of Logos which constituted the unchanging, principal part of thought. Aristotle traced the phenomenon of change right back to its roots. The highest and foremost seed of change in the universe should life in an absolutely self-generated entity or a deity that created the universe. Philo of Alexandria (25 B.C.-40 A.D.) of the Neo-Platonic School believed it was Logos under the deity that was the Creator of the universe.

Although the Catholic theologian St. Augustine (354-430 A.D.) inherited Plato's line of thinking, he did not advocate the existence of a world of concepts. The way of the universe already existed in the logos of the Creator. The Creator created everything in accordance with his logos. The medieval theologian Saint Thomas Aquinas [1] (1224-1274 A.D.) believed everything in the universe was finite. Relatively, the entity could not be self-generated nor was it an automatic phenomenon, it had to be a pure and necessary being. This pure and necessary being is the omnipotent deity.

Immanuel Kant (1724-1804) advocated the existence of the pure reality, the Creator of all, could not be proven through pure rationale. We could not know of its existence, we had to suppose its existence based on the essential needs of our rational everyday life. George Hegel (1717-1831) placed all his attention on the spirit. He saw the spirit of everything as the spirit of the world, which is an absolute spirit. According to logical dialectics, this absolute spirit was the antithesis of non-ego, in other words, the world. Through spiritual activities such as art, religion and philosophy, antithesis is reverted back to thesis for a return to the absolute spirit.

Henri Bergson (1859-1941) envisioned the universe as *durée*. This *durée* was active and alive, it could not be separated and had no begin-

---

(1) [Translator's Note] St. Thomas Aquinas (c.1225-1274 A.D.) is known as the "angelic doctor." He is a major Catholic theologian and philosopher who attempted to reconcile faith and reason. His philosophy and theology, Thomism, have been very influential in Roman Catholicism. His most famous work is the Summa Theologica.

ning or end, it was a prosperous, ongoing life force. Alfred North Whitehead (1864-1947) believed the universe was a uniform whole composed of separate units. The entity as a whole was active and could be perceived not through rationale but rather through human perception. This belief resembled that of Chinese philosophy.

The foundation of Chinese philosophy originated with the *I Ching* which advocates the continuous change and transformation underlying all existence. The commentary on the Decision (*t'uan*) of the *ch'ien* hexagram says:

> Great is *ch'ien* the originator. All things are derived from it. It unites and commands all the myriad things. The clouds move and the rain is distributed, and all things evolve in their respective forms. . . Change is the way of *ch'ien*. It transforms everything to make them obtain correct nature and destiny.

The commentary on the Images (*hsiang*) says: The heaven moves with full power. Similarly, the great man engages in ceaseless activities." The Appended Remarks says:

> What makes the *I Ching* a great book is that it is the principle of human life and is therefore not far from us. It is also called the way for its being in a state of flux: changing ceaselessly, operating universally, alternating up and down, fusing weakness and strength. We cannot take one form of existence as standard but as a form of change. (Part II, Ch. 8)

Again, in Part I of the Appended Remarks, it reads:

> Therefore in change there is the Great Ultimate. It generates the two modes (Therefore in change there is the Great Ultimate. It generates the two modes (*yin* and *yang*) which in turn give rise to the Four Forms. The Four Forms generate the Eight Trigrams. The Eight Trigrams determine good and evil fortune. (Ch. 11)

Elsewhere, the *I Ching* says:

> The successive movement of *yin* and *yang* constitutes the Way
> (Tao). What arises from this movement is good and that which
> realizes it is individual nature. (Appended Remarks, Part I,
> Ch. 5)

From the above sentences, the *I Ching* explains the principle and
process of change in the universe. The Great Ultimate is one, it serves
as the origin of change in the univese. From the Great Ultimate, the
yin and *yang* are born, the *yin* and the *yang* then continue to evolve to
become matter. The objective and meaning of change is to create life.

The *Tao Te Ching* was created before *I Ching*, but the philosophy
of change as explained by the *I Ching* was not developed after Lao-tzu.
Lao-tzu says in the *Tao Te Ching*:

> Tao generates the one, the one generates the two, the two gene-
> rates the three. The three generates all things. All things have
> darkness at their back and strive towards the light, and the flow-
> ing power gives them harmony. (Chapter 42)

Chuang Tzu meditates on the changes of Tao as being infinite and all
encompassing. In the chapter entitled "Heaven and Earth," he writes:

> In the great beginning, there was non-being, possessing neither
> being nor name. The One was derived from it. It was one but
> possessed no physical form. When things come to possess it
> and start to exist, that is called virtue. That which has no form
> is divided and from its very start going on without ceasing is
> called destiny. Through movement and quiescence it generates
> all things. When things are generated following the principle
> of life, physical form results. When this physical form embo-
> dies and retains the spirit in such a way that all activities
> follow their own principles, that is nature. By the cultivation
> of one's nature, one will return to virtue. When this virtue is
> perfect, one will be vacuous and because of it, one becomes

great. One will then be joined with the sound and breath of things. When one is united with Heaven and Earth, this unity is intimate...

Elsewhere, he writes:

At the great beginning there was non-being. It had neither being nor name and was that from which came the one. When the one started existing, there was the one although still without form...It was found among the wilderness. It transformed into ether (*ch'i*), which changed to take a form. The form changed and thereby led to life. Life changed and it gave rise to death. It moves in a way similar to the four seasons: Spring, Summer, Fall and Winter.

Chuang Tzu believed that Tao generated the ch'i of one, and *ch'i* further gave rise to all beings.

The belief that *ch'i* gave rise to all beings was popularized in the Warring States Period. In the Han Dynasty it became the central focus of Chinese philosophy. *Ch'i* was separated into *yin* and *yang, yin* and *yang* changed into the Five Elements. The Five Elements dissolved into everything in the universe, the beings in nature and the affairs of the human world as well as the time and space that encompasses all affairs and beings. Confucian scholars in the Han Dynasty said the *I Ching* specially spoke about and, involving the changes of sixty-four hexagrams that coincided with the four seasons and the flows in the universe to form a mobile entity in the universe.

The Sung Idealist philosopher Chou Tun-i explained the "Diagram of the Great Ultimate" following the Han Dynasty scholars of the *I Ching* and the Taoists:

The Ultimate and yet also the Supreme Ultimate. The Ultimate produces the *yin* and *yang*, and the *yin* and *yang* produce the Five Elements. The Five Elements produce man and woman, man and woman produce all things.

This process of generation is a typical explanation of the generation of all beings in Chinese philosophy.

However, in the Sung Dynasty there was also the belief that the nature of all beings was quiescence. Chou Dun-yi said that "When quiescence reaches its peak, movement comes about. Similarly, when movement attains its maximum, it leads to quiescence. They each act as one another's root (Diagram of the Great Ultimate)." Quiescence precedes movement. In the *Yue-chi* of the Book of Rites (*Li-chi*), there is the belief that "man's nature is quiescent." The nature of man is quiescent, fluctuations are caused by the external world. Lu Ta-lin of the Sung Dynasty explained the meaning of the sentence "Our emotion before they are aroused is called equilibrium" in the *Chung-yung* as quiescence. This kind of thinking can be traced back to Lao-tzu's saying that "returning to the roots means stillness." In addition, in the Northern and Southern Dynasties at the end of the Han Dynasty, esoterics tended towards tracing the origin. Buddhism in the Sui and Tang Dynasties emphasized calm and peace. Confucians in the Sung Dynasty advocated that the nature of man was peaceful. Chu Hsi, however, was greatly opposed to this viewpoint. Lao-tzu's calm was a natural calm, it asked for naught but had everything, it was not still. The calm in esoterics and Buddhism was more a method of ethical cultivation rather than a calmness in essence. Chinese philosophy often advocated that the universe was constantly in motion. If we hope to study the universe, we have to rely on experience and not on analytical methods.

II. The Creative Power

Our common experiences, the experiments of natural scientists, the perception of philosophers all point to the objective reality that beings in the universe are constantly in motion. The fact that they are in motion and evolving frequently implies they are finite and relative substances. The frequent evolving signifies that there is a start and end to the evolution of the substance. The phenomena of life and death are commonly found in our universe. An evolving being cannot generate change by itself, there must be a pure act that serves as first dynamic cause in order to trigger off change. Therefore, beings in the universe are not self-generated but created.

Some philosophers and scientists advocate that the universe is a self-generated entity. Materialists and Panthesists also advocate this belief. How does a substance with beginning and end come to make itself exist before its actual existence? If this was the case, it cannot be the agent responsible for creating its existence. Furthermore according to logic, material goods cannot be their own propelling force. If we regard the universe as a deity, we have to remember that the universe itself is still a finite, evolving being. This implies that the universal deity is also a finite, evolving being. This does not correlate with the absolute aspect of the deity designed as Creator of the universe.

The Creator created all beings in the universe, the Creator is a pure and absolute spiritual substance.

The Creator is a form of pure act, this entity is a pure act wholly without any potency[2]. The Creator is also an absolute substance, it substance is absolute wholly without change. The nature of the Creator is also absolute.

The pure and absolute entity that created all beings in the universe is not self-generative. Unlike Lao-tzu who believes Tao gave birth to all beings in the universe, the essence of Tao is vague and unstable, it is self-generative and all beings are a result thereof. Tao is embodied in all beings. The essence of all beings is Tao. Chuang-tzu believes in the essential equality and value of man and matter. Confucianists believe the Great Ultimate (the chaotic mass at the start of time) gave birth to the *yin* and the *yang* which in turn gave birth to all

---

(2) [Translator's Note] Potency, as opposed to act, "is the capacity of being or of being thus" (Allers, "Potency" 244). Motion is the passing of a subject from potency to act. In the *Summa Theologiae*, St. Thomas Aquinas explains motion in this way: "Anything which moves is moved by something. Nothing indeed is moved save according as it is in potency with regard to that towards which it is moved. Nothing moves, on the contrary, save according as it is in act, For to move a thing is to make it pass from potency to act" (Gilson 59).

beings in the universe. Confucians however did not mention whether the Great Ultimate was self-generative. Although Chang Tsai spoke about the *ch'i* of the Great Void in the same manner as Lao-tzu spoke of Tao, he did not mention whether it was self-generative.

The pure and absolute entity that created all beings in the universe has to transcend the universe, not have the same nature and essence as other beings in the universe. To create all beings in the universe, the Creator does not have to use its own nature and essence but rather use a power unique to the Creator, creative power.

Creative power is the external power of the absolute entity in the same manner as the beings that are created are outside of the Creator's absolute substance. Therefore, creative power is not the intrinsic essence of the Creator but rather the external manifestation of his essence. This force is the first dynamic cause. It can also be seen as the ultimate dynamic cause.

Regardless of whether it be the first or ultimate dynamic cause, creative power is an omnipotent power. The principle of all beings in the universe is the result of the wisdom of the Creator. The Creator creates each being according to His wisdom just like human beings act according to their own ideals or principles. Catholic teachings tells us that everything in the universe enjoys the beauty and benevolence of the Creator.

The Creator created the universe because of a desire to share His beauty and benevolence with the people and things of this world. Creative power stems from the will of the Creator. The Creator possesses an omnipotent will which creates out of nothing and brings forth existence out of nothing. The first chapter of Genesis in the Bible describes the creation. The word "said" is used throughout, ' God said let there be light, and there was light '; ' God said let there be fishes in the sea, and there were fishes in the sea, let there be living creatures on land and there were living creatures on land.' This form of narration is symbolic. The word "said" symbolizes the will of the Creator. With a simple command, the will of the Creator was immediately manifested out of nothing. All creation is beautiful and benevolent as it bears the beauty and benevolence of the Creator. Chapter I of Genesis says, "God saw everything He had made, it was very good" (1:31)

The Creator is a pure act, above change. However, He is not rigid and lifeless. Instead the Creator is a most lively and flexible reality. Neither is creative power emitted from the Creator lifeless and static. It is a strong, sustaining force. Therefore, the act of creation was not completed all at once but is rather an ongoing process of progression and formation. However, the Creator is an absolute substance that transcends time and space, thus the Creator does not relate to time and space in his process of creation. He is only present in the now while to all beings in the universe, the process of creation takes place within the framework of space and time. In Genesis, the symbolic six days is used to depict the process of creation. Scientists used the theory of evolution to describe the process of creation. Genesis also mentions the process of creation occurred in the symbolic six days while on the seventh day God rested. This signifies creation is not self-generated, but a form of hard work. Jesus also says in the Bible: "My Father goes on working, and so do I" (Jn, 5:17). This signifies the process of creation is an ongoing one, continuing right into the present.

III. Generative Power

By way of creative power, the Creator created generative power. Generative power generates all beings in the universe.

By way of creative power, the Creator created generative power. Generative power and creative power and interlinked and inseparable. Once they are separated, generative power as well as the universe would vanish into nothingness. The two parts are interwoven, not only in terms of work dynamics, but also in terms of their existence. Generative power is derived entirely from creative power.

Generative power is a form of power with its own properties, principle and potentiality. As the term power denotes, generative power is constantly in motion, in fact, its essence is motion. The essence of motion connotes that its properties are not fixed. The properties of generative power are on the whole constant. Generative power is not an absolute substance therefore it is a finite relative substance. No matter how large a finite substance becomes, it still has certain confines. The confines remain constant in change.

The essence of generative power is in the entire universe. The essence of the universe is finite and constant. However, the properties of the essence and not fixed. In the initial stage, it is very unstable. Lao-tzu described "Tao" as:

> The substance of the great Life completely follows Tao. Tao brings about all things so chaotically, so darkly. Chaotic and dark are its images. Unfathomable and obscure in it is the seed. This seed is wholly true. In it dwells reliability. (*Tao Te Ching*, Chapter 21)

Chang Tsai describes the Great Harmony and the Great Void as "the Great Void is formless and ethereal, it gathers and dissipates in numerable changes." He writes:

> The Great Harmony is known as the Tao. Because in it there are interacting qualities of floating and sinking, rising and falling, movement and quiescence, therefore there are engendered in it the beginnings of the emanating forces which agitate one another, overcome or are overcome by one another, and contract or expand, one with relation to the other.

> Vast and unseeable is the Ether as the Great Void. Yet it rises and falls and spreads about, never stopping for a moment. Is not this what the changes speak of emanation? Or what Chuang-tzu describes as the ' wonderful air ' which living creatures blow against one another? Herein lies the pivots of vacuity and solidity, movement and quiescence, and the beginnings of *yin* and *yang*, and hardness and softness.

The property of generative power can be determined through change. In terms of concept, being is the most simple concept. Initially, they had no content. Later, once content was determined, there were organic and inorganic beings. Organic beings were further divided into plants and animals, after animals there were human beings. This is a conceptual change from simplicity to complexity, from void to substance. In terms of astrology, at the beginning of the universe, there were the stars and the clouds. They evolved to become galaxies, the galaxies evolved to become individual planets, earth being one of the planets. With earth's evolution, there were minerals, plants and animals. Lastly, there were human beings. This is the astrological and biological evolution from chaos to order, from lowly to advanced beings. The property of generative power is simplest yet richest. Simplest in terms of its essence and richest in terms of its changes as it holds the properties of all beings in the universe.

Within the essence of generative power lies its principle, the principle of all beings in the universe. The principle of generative power is derived from creative power. The principle of creataive power belongs to the principle of the Creator's wisdom. The Creator created all beings in the universe. He created his own blueprint and decided on the objectives of creation as well as the principles and process of change motivated by generative power. This is what we term the natural law of the universe. The Tao of the heavens and the Tao of the earth mentioned in the *I Ching* and the creation of all beings in the universe by the Creator did not take place at one specific moment, but was rather the result of continuous change. Rational exists in their evolution and principle exists behind each being. In the *I Ching*, it is aid: " *Yin* and *yang* constitute the Tao, it is benevolent to pass the Tao on, and its success lies in its nature." The nature of beings originate in the changes of *yin* and *yang*. But in the *Chung-yung*, it is also said: "What heaven has conferred is called nature" (Chapter 1). The changes of *yin* and *yang* are destined in heaven, therefore the principle of beings are regulated by the Creator. The Creator selects a principle from his wealth of wisdom which serves as the nature of every being the Creator also regulates the substantive nature of each individual being.

For instance, Chu Hsi says human beings are composed of principle and *ch'i*, the *ch'i* of human beings is confined by the principle of human beings. The substantive nature of each human being refers to the nature of his *ch'i*, the principle of a human being is confined by the clarity and turbidity of his *ch'i*. Chu Hsi's students asked him what determined the clarity or turbidity of *ch'i*? Why did one person's *ch'i* differ from another person's *ch'i*? The reason is not principle as the common principle of all human beings is humanity. Neither is the reason *ch'i* because ch'i cannot determine its own turbidity and clarity. The Chinese attribute it to "fate." One is born into fate. You are born clever, I am born stupid. Your ch'i is clear, mine is turbid. We share different fates. Practically speaking, we can call this the will of the Creator, or the will of heaven. The principle of every individual being or individual human being is also the principle bestowed to generative power by creative power. The principle of generative power is manifested as different forms of "potency."

The principle of generative power is not the highest form of principle. The highest principle is the wisdom of the Creator, all beings share the Creator's wisdom. Neither is the principle of generative power an amalgamation of the principle of all beings in the universe. The reason being the principle of all beings in the universe did not actually exist at the start of the universe when creative power gave rise to generative power. This is rather like the debate in Chinese philosophy about whether the principle of *yin* and *yang* existed in the Great Ultimate or in the Great Void. In the Great Ultimate, there is no distinction between *yin* and *yang*, therefore the principle of *yin* and *yang* did not actually exist. Principle and ch'i go hand in hand, if there is the principle of *yin* and *yang*, there must be the ch'i of *yin* and *yang*. If we assume the principle of all being in he universe already existed when creative power gave rise to generative power, that would imply all beings in the universe were created and generated at once, at the same time.

The principle of generative power is "potency." In Western philosophy, they talk about potency. Potency is energy that has not become reality, but has the potential to become reality. Potency is not a passive void, nor is it passive illusion, instead it is active possibility. This possibility is hidden within actual existence. Under the right conditions, when activated by certain forces, it can become reality. The principle of all beings is hidden in the essence of generative power. Generative power continues to move, thus causing the essence of generative power to change. With these changes other beings are generated. Every change contains its own principle, when principle is combined with essence, a being is realized. This potential principle is much like the "beginnings of goodness and natural powers" mentioned by Mencius. The beginnings of goodness and natural powers Mencius referred to is the potency of man. The principle of generative power is the nature of all beings. Prior to the actual realization of each being, the principle of each being constitutes the potential of generative power.

Chu Hsi once proposed the "unity and diversity of principle." From the viewpoint of life, there is only one kind of life. The reason why the lives of beings in the universe differ is because their *ch'i* differ, *ch'i* limits principle. The principle of generative power including the principle of different types of beings and the principle of individual beings all differ. Only when principle matches up with essence can a being be realized. This is because principle confined essence, and not the other way around. The principle of generative power originates from the wisdom of the Creator. The wisdom of the Creator is an absolute wisdom that grants generative power its boundless principle.

The most important aspect of generative power is its "power." The "power" of generative power is the activating power of all changes in the universe. It is also the power to generate life. Generative power derived its power from creative power. Creative power is the source of power not only at the moment of creation but also during the continuing process of change, from the beginning of time to the present and onto eternity. Generative power cannot be separated from creative power just like electric current cannot be cut off from the power supply.

From the beginning, generative power promoted change. The order and process of change proceeded in accordance with natural law established by the wisdom of the Creator. The process of change is gradual and onward. It proceeds from the lowly to the more advanced beings. Through change, "beings" are generated. The essence of generative power and the principle of the being combine to become reality. The generation of a being is only that, it must not be equated with creation of a being as it is not sprung from nothingness. The principle of a being is the potential found in the essence of generative power, the essence of generative power is composed of the elements found in the essence. The elements merge together because of their nature, generative power bonds them together. Generative power bonds the elements together and ensures their continued bonding. Only then can a "being" exist. Generative power is found and exists in every being. This kind of existence is one that is in motion as it is attributed to generative power. The *I Ching* advocates that *yin* and *yang* continue to change in beings. Wang Fu-tzu belongs to the school of thought that says "life diminishes day by day while nature is born day by day." Physicists also explain that the elements found in substances are often in motion. This kind of movement occurs within the body of the being, it is what we term life. The *I Ching* also says: "life brings about change." A human being has different parts to his body that holds together because of life. If life is lost, the body will break down and disintegrate. A tree or a flower holds together because of life. If life is lost, the tree and the flower will disintegrate. A stone or a plank remains one whole because a central cohesive force holds all the molecules together. Once the central cohesive force is lost, the stone or the plank will disintegrate. This central cohesive force is generative power. The cohesive force for trees, flowers and human beings is life, which is generative power.

In the entire universe, generative power serves as the power of existence and change, in other words, it is existence and change of the universe. Within each being, generative power serves as the power of existence and change. In other words, it is the existence and change of each being.

Generative power enables each being to become an individual existence. The basis of individual existence is the principle, which confines the changes of generative power so an individual existence can be realized.

The entire universe is alive due to the changes of generative power. The changes of generative power allow the elements in the essence to form an individual existence in accordance with the principle. A being is not the result of changes in another being but rather the result of generative power. Change is progressive. It progresses in accordance with the natural law, but this is not the Theory of Evolution. The principle of another being is not born out of another being but rather comes from the potential of the essence of generative power, with the changes that occur in generative power, the potential becomes a reality.

The entire universe is one generative power. The changes that occur in the universe are part of one change. It is a single change that embodies or is dividied into innumerable portions of changes. The portions of changes are interconnected and interrelated. Therefore all beings in the universe are interconnected. Wang Yang-ming once proposed "the unity of *jen* (benevolence)." Chinese philosophers, whether they be Taoists or Confucians, believed all lives in the universe were unified and interconnected. The natural world and the human world could not be separated. Generative power is the life-giving force of the universe, it is also the existing life-giving force in every being.

To explain what generative power is, we can look to the concept of *ch'i* in Chinese philosophy. At the beginning, generative power was rather like the Ether of the Great Void, its essence is the Great Harmony. The Ether of the Great Void contains the power and principle to change, it gradually changes, first to *yin* and *yang* then to the Five Elements. It then changes to beings thus we say all beings are formed from *ch'i*. However, the two are still different in many ways. Generative power is not an essence like *ch'i* that embodies all beings. It is rather the power to generate that is not divided into *yin* and *yang* and the Five Elements. However, the similarities lie in the changes of *ch'i* that generate all beings and also reside within every being. We can also use Bergson's "elan vital." This life force (*elan vital*) is constantly active so the universe becomes an inseparable continuity, or *durée*. However, Bergson's life force (*elan vital*) lacked content. Generative power is the life force with essence, with principle, it is generator of the living universe.

All forms of "power" within the universe have essence, principle and force. We can take the example of electric power, it has its own principle, own essence and own force. The essence of electric power is made up of the bonding of material molecules. The bonding of the molecules occur in accordance with the principle of electric power, therefore the bonding is the result of motion.

The substance of generative power is essence as well as power. The principle is within the essence and within the power. The principle, essence and power are all in one and cannot be separated.

Generative power has substance, power and principle. Its substance is the entire universe. Therefore the universe is generative power. The essence of the substance of generative power can change and the change is activated by the power in generative power. The activation of change by generative power is in line with the principle given to generative power by creative power. Generative power is the universe, which appears to resemble the Great Harmony advocated by Lao-tzu and Chang Tsai. However, generative power does not resemble Tao or the Great Harmony as it is not only present at the beginning of the universe but is present in time and space, in the past, in the now and in the future. Generative power continues to evolve. This is unlike saying Tao is in all beings or *ch'i* is in all beings. All beings belong to generative power and all beings belong to the universe. All beings are constituent parts of the universe, therefore all beings are also constituents of generative power.

Works Cited

Gilson, Etienne. *The Christian Philosophy of St. Thomas Aquinas.* New York: Random House, 1956.

Schatzman, E.L. *The Structure of the Universe.* Vol.2, trans. Shih Yeh-chang. Taipei: Kuang-wen.

Translated by Nancy Du

Chapter III

The Cosmos

I. The Cosmos Is Infinite Power (Energy)

In *The Structure of the Universe*, Schatzman writes:

> The universe consists of stars, which cluster together into galaxies of myriad shapes. Observable cosmic matter shows an extremely low average density, something in the vicinity of three hydrogen atoms in every ten square meters. Nevertheless, these matter form exceedingly complex heavenly bodies. Galaxies, consisting of stars, are found in every direction as far as our human eyes can see. Stars are constantly being born and constantly in the process of evolution. Galaxies too are being born, developing and dying. Our knowledge of the evolution of stars may be substantial, yet our understanding of the evolution of galaxies is remarkably dismal. (33)

As galaxies evolved, mighty explosions led to emissions of electric waves. A number of these galaxies show telltale signs of having experienced a series of explosions. Stellar systems made up of galaxies are also in the process of evolution. Some are star clusters several billions of years old. Quasars, hundreds of times more uminous than the brightest of the spheroid galaxies, are unchallenged in magnitude as energy sources. The energy they can emit is trillions of times higher than what the sun can radiate... The pathway of light is obstructed by the presence of matter, a phenomenon which led to the idea of curved space... The human race is still engaged in the continuous process of ascertaining whether the universe is an open hyperboloid or a closed flat circle. The Hubble-Humason Relation and electric wave disturbance coming from the farthest corner of space seem to suggest a closed, spheroid model... The universe is approximately ten billion years old. According to calculations, extraordinary cataclysmic events (the so-called Big Bang) occurred during this period. (342-343)

In his book *Cosmos,* Carl Sagan writes:

> The Big Bang resulted in matter and energy. For an undetermined period of time, the universe assumed no definite shape or form. . . Impenetrable darkness enveloped the universe. In this emptiness were found atoms of hydrogen. Everywhere, dense gaseous mixtures were accumulating and growing while globular bodies consisting of matter gradually collapsed. Two drops of hydrogen were larger than the sun. In these globular bodies, nuclear energy, hidden in potency within matter, was first manifested. Thus, the first generation of stars was born. The universe was filled with immense light. (20)

In the beginning, the cosmos was a cloud of gas, perhaps an enormous and closed ellipse or, perhaps a gigantic expanding body. Trapped inside the gaseous matter was unimaginable power which triggered the cataclysmic "Big Bang." Later, it gradually formed into the stars and the galaxies. The mighty explosion of the universe was triggered by the power within the cosmos or the cosmic power itself. Regarding the relationship between energy and matter, Heisenberg says in his work *Physics and Philosophy*: "Matter and energy per se are similar concepts. Therefore, we say that all basic particles are made up of energy" (37). Heisenberg further writes: "Energy transforms into matter, allowing fragments of the basic particles to remain the same basic particles" (37).

Thus, we can derive several notions from natural science.

1. The cosmos is moving. It is constantly in motion and undergoing change.

2. Changes in the cosmos reflect its possession of a moving force.

3. In the very beginning, the cosmos was made up of a ball of gas or nebula; formless, shapeless, and utterly dark.

4. Stars were created by an explosion. Stars emit light.

5. Power exists between stars, such as light, electric wave and so on.

6. Light advances following a curved pathway and is obstructed by objects on its way.

7. All matter in the universe are created by energy. They are all considered as "power." In physics, energy is used to represent matter.

8. The cosmos is in motion because of power. From its movement, all things are created.

Armed with these fundamental concepts, let us study the cosmos from the philosophical angle. The cosmos is a unity and not a multiple, although its volume is infinitely immense and intergalactic distances are extremely far. The galaxies are joined to one another by energy, as are all things in the universe.

This moving cosmos was a product of the creative power of the Creator. This creative power is transformative, possesses infinite power and is known as generative power.

II. The Matter and Principle of the Cosmos

Generative power possesses its own "matter," which constitutes its body. In the beginning, the matter of the generative power assumed no certain form because it was moving. It resembled the Tao of Lao-tzu, which he described as having a hazy, indeterminate nature, "elusive and vague, whose essence is very real; in it are evidences" (*Tao Te Ching,* Chapter 21). It was also analogous to Chang Tsai's *ch'i* (ether) of the Great Vacuity (*T'ai-hsu*) or the Great Harmony (*T'ai-he*) which "ascends and descends and moves in all ways without ever ceasing" as galloping wild horses do (*Cheng-meng, T'ai-ho* [Great Harmony]). Both Lao-tzu's Tao and Chang Tsai's *T'ai-ho* refer to the origin of the cosmos. In the beginning, the cosmos assumed no definite shape, yet cannot be taken as formless. "No definite shape" refers only the exterior form. Since the whole of the cosmos is matter, then it must have a form of its own. However, in so far as the exterior form is concerned, the shape of the cosmos is indefinite. That is because once its essence and form are made definite, it can no longer change within itself to generate things.

The generative power possesses its own principle (*li*) which is its own nature. The principle of generative power is a principle in action. And because of its principle and action, there exists an ordering of parts.

The universe consists of galaxies made of stars. In between these stars and galaxies is matter. Substances making up this matter and these stars are the same substances that make up the universe. However, it is also possible that some primeval gas or nebula of the universe did not explode to form the galaxies. Naturally, his primeval gas also forms part of the matter of the universe. Cosmic matter is the matter of the generative power, and is, therefore, the matter of all things in this universe.

The principle (*li*) of the cosmos is also the principle of the generative power. Does it embody the principle of all things in the universe? This issue reminds us of the problem of *li yi erh shu* [unity and diversity of principle] expounded by Ch'eng I and Chu Hsi. Both Ch'eng and Chu propose that the whole universe possesses only one principle which is shared by all things in different degrees. In this way, different things possess different principles. The degree of sharing is determined by the clarity or turbidity (*ch'ing chuo*) of the *ch'i* [material force]. The "unity of principle" refers to the principle of life or the "principle of existence" in each thing. Different things possess life in different degrees. To explain this, Chu Hsi pointed out that the principles (*li*) of things vary in their degree of completeness.

Since the universe is an integral substance, then it must have a principle (*li*) of its own. The universe became the "universe" owing to its own principle. It also changes because of this very principle. The cosmos was created by the Creator. Its matter and principle owe their existence to the creative power of the Creator. The matter out of which the cosmos was created came from nothing. This creation out of nothing is the real meaning of the word "creation." This is possible since the Creator is all powerful. The principle (*li*) out of which the cosmos was created did not come from nothing but was bestowed on the cosmos as conceived in the mind of God. This is similar to the construction of a building. The engineer uses external materials to construct the building according to a blueprint based on his idea. The construction materials make up the matter of the building while the blueprint is its principle. The latter was conceived in his mind. Outside God, there is nothing. He created the matter of the universe using his divine power. With his infinite intelligence, God determined the principle of the cosmos. Thus, God created the universe with his creative power following the principle he himself set. He created the matter of the universe *ex nihilo*. Matter and principle together formed the universe. This principle of the universe is the principle of the universe *per se* and is not the principle shared by all things. All things generate through changes caused by the generative power of the universe. The principles of things are not encompassed in the cosmic principle. Matter cannot be generated while principle cannot be divided. These are two important principles. Matter and principle fuse to form something. Matter cannot generate principle. Principle (*li*) is non-material. It is abstract, made up of no parts and indivisible. The principle of one thing cannot be derived from the principle of another thing. Thus, where principle comes from is a question asked in philosophy. Matter comes from previously existing material. Viewed in an abstract manner, origin is not a question for both matter and principle. Abstractly speaking, we only talk about what matter and principle are. We never deal with their origins. Concretely, however, must ask where they come from. The matter of all things in the universe is derived from the matter of the cosmos. In Chinese philosophy, the matter of all things is called *ch'i* (material force). Concretely speaking, this *ch'i* is cosmic *ch'i*. The *ch'i* of the cosmos is one. Regarding the principle (*li*) of all things, Sung and Ming philosophers all thought that principle (*li*) is embodied in the *ch'i*, with the exception of Chu Hsi who proposes that li and ch'i stand on an equal footing and exist at the same time without precedence over each other. However, Chu Hsi did not explain the origin of *ch'i*. Instead, he denied the existence of a primeval principle *(li)*. Neither did Western philosophy pay attention to this issue, because Western philosophy explains the substance of things in an abstract, metaphysical way. Only when dealing with the origins of life is this issue brought up. Western philosophy takes the soul as a living creature's principle and the center of life. Where does the soul come from? Ordinarily speaking, the soul is derived from other souls of the same species of living thing. The vital principle of a flowering plant comes from its seeds whose life is derived from seed-bearing flowers. However, difficulties arise in explaining the origin of a human soul. A human soul cannot come from the souls of the parents since the soul is a spiritual being.[1] The parents' souls are indivisible and therefore the soul of their offspring cannot come from them. Catholic Scholastic philosophy proposes that the human soul is created by God. This process can be explained in two ways. One proposes the creation of the soul at the moment of conception after which the human fetus starts having life. The other proposes a soul-creating capability which God endowed on the universe in the beginning of time. This soul-creating capability acts at an opportune moment when the ovum is fertilized after the parents' union. At the moment of fertilization, the soul is endowed. This capability was created by God in the beginning of the universe. This latter explanation is also applied to the evolution of other things. The principle of superior beings cannot be derived from inferior beings in the process of evolution because inferior beings cannot encompass superior beings. The evolution of inferior beings to superior ones is also an endowment from the Creator in the beginning of time. However, the difficulty lies in whether the Creator concretly bestowed inconspicu-

---

(1) [Translator's Note] Being "translates three Latin terms, which, in Scholasticism, have different significations. *Ens* as a noun is the most general and most simple predicate; as a participle it is an essential predicate only in regard to God in Whom existence and essence are one, or Whose essence implies existence. *Esse*, though used sometimes in a wider sense, usually means existence which is defined as the *actus essendi*, or the reality of some essence. *Esse* quid or essentia designates the specific nature of some being or thing, the ' being thus' or the quiddity" (Weedon 36).

ous matter on these things when he endowed them with principle in the beginning of creation. Is this only a type of abstract theory? If inconspicuous matter was bestowed, how can it be that superior forms of principle--even the principles of purely spiritual souls--are included, since the principles of matter *per se* are of a lower level? This is difficult to explain theoretically. St. Thomas Aquinas believed that the process of creation is continuous as a consequence of he cosmos' inability to subsist by itself and its necessity to be sustained by the Creator. The cosmos also cannot exist by itself and must need the continuous support of the Creator because its very existence is derived from the Creator. Emptiness *per se*, the cosmos cannot by itself maintain the existence it derived from the Creator. It constantly needs the support of the Creator. This support is continual creation in itself. The word continuation appears meaningless when applied to God because God is beyond time. Continuation is only applicable to the universe. The theory of continual creation is adopted in order to explain the origin of the human soul, that is, the soul is created by God.

I used to accept both of these explanations. But after a long period of consideration, I came to believe that only the process of continual creation can be used to shed light on the origin of the principle (*li*) of things. Thus, we say that using his creative power, the Creator created the matter of the universe. All later changes in the universe are derived from the changes done on its existing matter. In the process of change, it is the generative power that changes. The generative power often fuses with the creative power, receiving from he latter the "power" to change the generation process. It also receives the principles (*li*) of different types of changes. Wang Ch'uan-shan said: "Nature (*hsing*) becomes more constant as time goes by while the Mandate of Heaven decreases with time." *Yin* and *yang* continue to undergo change, each change following the Mandate of Heaven. While nature continues to grow, the Mandate of Heaven goes on decreasing. The generative power constantly changes following principles set by the Creator. These principles are in turn derived from the creative power of the Creator. The principles of all things are all derived from the creative power and each of these principles is unique. Chu Hsi said that the nature of things comes from the clarity or turbidity of the *ch'i*. Where does the turbidity of things come from? Chu Hsi failed to offer an explanation. Ordinarily he said: "It's life!." That is, it is destined by God.

The cosmos possesses its own matter, principle and power. Its power is the generative power. In its process of generation, the generative power is infinite, constantly changing like a galloping wild horse. All things in the universe have matter, principles and powers of their own. The matter of all things is all derived from cosmic matter. The principles of all things are all derived from the principle received by the generative power from the creative power. The powers residing in all things are all derived from the generative power.

III. Power

In dealing with the universe and all things, both Chinese philosophy and Western philosophy discuss in a formal way such topics as nature, matter, principle and, even, existence, all of which are abstract concepts. Yet, they miss one concrete and important issue. Western philosophy proposes that nature and existence combine to form an actual being. However, it fails to clarify how this process of combination can be possible. It is generally accepted that existence is concrete nature; that with existence, nature actually exists. But since existence in Western philosophy is an abstract concept, how could it become existence in a concrete way. This is an important issue. In Chinese philosophy, Chu Hsi proposes that principle (*li*) and *ch'i* (material force) combine to form a concrete being. But Chu Hsi did not explain how this combination comes about. Actually, this issue, common to both Chinese philosophy and Western philosophy, is related to power.

Aristotle said that four causes are required for things in the universe to change, namely: material cause, formal cause, efficient cause and final cause. Of these, efficient cause is the most important. It starts the process of change and combines material and formal causes with the resultant formation of something with a final cause as its objective. When the efficient cause triggers change, it does so using its own power to thus join matter and form. Thus we can say that the union of matter and form, or of material force and principle, are made possible by the power of the efficient cause. Aristotle also proposes that all things in the universe can act as efficient cause to one another. They have the power to trigger off change. However, this power comes from existence. All things in the universe cannot make themselves exist by themselves, because they are all relative beings. The efficient cause can be ultimately traced to the Absolute Being (the Creator). They come into existence from the Absolute Being and ultimately receive power from the Absolute Being.

The whole cosmos is in action, a process which goes on constantly. The power of the cosmos permeates the whole universe and the myriad things. The power of the myriad things is derived from the power of the cosmos which is the generative power. The latter comes from the creative power of the Creator.

The whole cosmos is generative power which finds action in the whole universe. The matter of the whole cosmos, which is the matter of the generative power, is the domain of action of the generative power. Generative power acts within the noumenon itself. The principle (*li*) of the whole universe is the principle of the generative power which acts based on its own principle. When the generative power acts to generate something, it combines the principle derived from the creative power with some cosmic matter to form the thing. The formed thing thus acquires both matter and form and exists because of the generative power. As this thing exists, it continues to maintain power from the generative power and constantly acts within itself. Thus, we can say that the existence of something is the existence of action.

The power of the generative power in the thing itself makes possible the joining of all elements of the thing based on the latter's own principle. The thing also acts based on its principle. For instance, the existence of man is an existence *in actus*, and ordinarily known as life. It is the power to generate. The generative power of man *per se* comes from the generative power of the cosmos. The soul is the seat of man's generative power and the principle of man. Man's principle is derived from the creative power of the Creator and endowed through the generative power of the universe. Man's own generative power, obtained through its own principle, is life, which is the union of mind and spirit. Man's life unites body and soul and joins together all parts of the body. Scholastic philosophy proposes that the whole human soul resides in the entire body and all its parts. This idea means that man's abstract principle resides not only in the entire person but also in each of his bodily parts. For instance, when one limb becomes crippled, it no longer has life and thus, ceases to be a human limb. It becomes something else. When one's soul and body separate, that person loses his life. He no longer is a person but only a corpse. A person's being depends upon his existence, which is life and also generative power. Similarly, a flower's being depends upon existence. A flower's existence is also life and generative power. Once a flower loses life, it is no longer a flower; all its parts then separate from one another.

Within the universe, power joins together all the parts to form the universe and keep it existing and changing. In any object, power makes possible the joining of the parts to form that object. It also maintains its existence and keeps the parts from falling apart. Power also keeps actual beings constantly in action and changing.

Any object has its own power which keeps its existence. A rock keeps its parts together by virtue of its own power. Also by virtue of this power, a rock has internal movements. A rock will not by itself separate its parts but instead wears down owing to actions outside itself. In physics, rocks are often described as constantly undergoing movements and changes in their internal elements.

Things that have internal movements by virtue of their own power are said to be living. Life is nothing but one's internal movements. This internal movement proceeds based on each object's own principle and thus, differs from object to object. Some of these objects share common internal attributes thereby forming species. Ordinarily, these objects are classified into systems of "life" based on their degree of "immanent action." For Chu Hsi, it is the turbidity of the material force (*ch'i*) that leads to different levels of manifestation of the principle (*li*). Thus, life is manifested in different degrees. Man is endowed with the fullness of the principle of life. The principle of life is fully manifested in man. Thus, human life is classified to be the highest. Speaking in a concrete manner, man's principle (*li*) was bestowed by the Creator by virtue of his creative power and through the generative power. Human life is based on its own principle. Thus, man possesses a human principle, a human generative power and a human life.

Chinese philosophy covers changes in the cosmos and stresses the concept of power. It sees the cosmos as a torrent of life. Chuang-tzu proposes that heaven and earth's one and original creative force roams in the universe, pervading the myriad things. Man, nourished by this force, unites and interlinks with the myriad things in the universe.

It is not that Western philosophy pays no attention to cosmic power. Because this issue enters the realm of creation, it must be dealt with in theology. Western theology devotes one whole chapter in its discussion of creation. Roman Catholic faith proclaims: "Father, all creation rightly gives you praise. All life, all holiness comes from you through your Son, Jesus Christ our Lord, by the working of the Holy Spirit" ("Eucharistic Prayer III," *Roman Missal* 673). The "working of the Holy Spirit" is the crative power of the Creator. After the creation of the universe, the Creator continues to "generate life and make the world holy."

The science of physics focuses on the study of "energy." It takes the whole universe from the viewpoint of dynamics. Matter is energy and the relationship between matter is energy. The whole universe is one network of power. Galaxies are held together by power. The same is true with stars. Things on earth are also generated by changes triggered by generative power. With power, they are substained and interlinked.

As we philosophize, we cannot neglect this scholarly issue of the cosmos by simply relegating it to the realm of the abstract. The universe is a moving, changing universe. Similarly, each thing is also in motion and undergoing change. Therefore, every time we discuss the Philosophy of Life, we always take the universe and all things in it as living.

Works Cited

Allers, Ruddolf. "Matter, prime." *Dictionary of Philosophy*. Ed. Dagobert Runes. Lanham, Maryland: Rowman, 1964.

-----. "Substance." *Dictionary of Philosophy*. Ed. Dagobert Runes. Lanham, Maryland: Rowman, 1964.

Belmonte, Charles, Cecilio Magsino, and James Socias, eds. *Daily Roman Missal*. Manila: Studium Theologiae, 1989.

Heisenberg, Ernest. *Physics and philosophy*.

Sagan, Carl. *Cosmos*. trans. Su Yi-ning. Taipei: Kui-kuan.

Schatzman, E.L. *The Structure of the Univers*. Vol.2. trans. Shih Yenchang. Taipei: Kuang-wen.

Weedon, William S. "Being." *The Dictionary of Philosophy*. Ed. Dagobert Runes. Lanham, Maryland: Rowman, 1964.

Translated by Carlos Tee

Chapter IV

Life

I. The Meaning of Life

In Thomistic philosophy, life is an attribute of physical bodies. With life, physical bodies can achieve self-activation and self-actualization. Self-activation refers to the phenomenon wherein a physical body, which is already in existence, can initiate its own activities and therefore serves as its own driving force. Self-actualization, on the other hand, describes the fact that the purpose of a physical body's activities is usually to develop itself. Here, development is done following one's own nature. Such development does not always have to be in the direction of reinforcing or increasing one's energy level of life. Rather, it is also possible that the energy level of life will be diminished or decreased as a result of development. Using this line of thinking, Western philosophy and the natural sciences divide all matters in the universe into two groups: living and non-living things. Non-living things are those physical bodies that do not possess the ability of self-activation and self-actualization. Minerals, for example, are non-living things; so are machines. All the computers and robots that we employ in modern times are considered to have no life.

On the contrary, Chinese philosohy regards the universe as a whole body that is constantly changing. Furthermore, the changing of the universe is in the form of the changing of *ch'i*, a process which is both automatic and self-realized. Therefore, in Chinese philosophy, the whole universe is a living body. What gives life to this body are the two changing forces of *yin* and *yang*. From the transformations of *yin* and *yang* emerge a new entity within which *yin* and *yang* continue to change and metamorphose. These are internal changes intended to develop the body as a new life. Thus, the Book of Changes says: "Change is the generation of life" (Chapter 5, Part I, *Hsi-tz'u*).

In traditional Chinese philosophy, no distinction is made as to which are living things and which are non-living things. Every physical body is considered a living thing with *yin* and *yang* continuously changing inside. Of all things, minerals are a special case. The manifestation of life in minerals is suppressed because their *ch'i* is too turbid. Therefore, in actual reality, minerals can be catgorized as nothing.

I once wrote an article for the Journal of Chinese Philosophy (*Chung-hua che-hsueh hui nian-kan* Issue Number V) entitled "Philosophy of Life." In it, I described the views about life as espoused in traditional Chinese philosophy and explained what it means by saying that life is the generator of life itself. I would like to summarize my main points in the following lines.

Customarily, the meaning of life is taken to be derived from the fact that life is the product of activities that are both initiated and completed by itself. Under this criterion, the two major groups of living and non-living things can be defined. Minerals are non-living things in the sense that they are static and without the ability to act and realize themselves. Animals and plants, on the other hand, are living things since both have self-activated lives and are capable of developing and eventually realizing themselves. The differentiation is made based on how the "potency" of a physical body is actualized. While the potency of living things is mobilized from within for self-development, non-living things have to rely on external forces to activate their potency and they themselves remain inactive and have no prospect of development.

As opposed to a clear-cut dichotomy. Chinese philosophy advocates a system of continuum that contains many intermediate states. Furthermore, substance is used in place of driving force as the determining factor of life. Both Ch'eng Yi and Chu Hsi made the same proposition that there is but one common life principle in the universe. By articulating the concept of "unity and diversity of principle." Chu Hsi contends that everything in the universe shares the same life principle. Although there is only one common principle, its manifestations when combined with *ch'i* take on many different forms because *ch'i* has various degrees of clarity and turbidity. The existence of physical bodies in the universe is the proof of life but the actuality of each existence is determined by a specific variety of *ch'i* that makes the existence a reality. Diverse actualities of existence in turn give rise to correspondingly diverse actualities of life. Thus, the "unity and diversity of principle." Everything in the universe shares the same one and only principle of life. It is *ch'i* that makes the manifestations of the principle specific and diverse.

There is only one principle of life, but when combined with *ch'i*, principle develops into disparate forms and engenders disparate lives. Chu Hsi says: "Humans possess principle in its totality; other physical beings have only received a portion of it." He proposed that the principle of life manifests itself in its totality in humans and only partially in other physical beings. As a result, human life represents the whole principle whereas all other beings possess only a portion of life. A partial life as such is characterized by the clarity or turbidity of *ch'i* which is held up as a linear scale of different degrees rather than two polar opposites. Therefore, everything in the universe has a life. They differ only in their level of sophistication. The notion of scale can also be found in the science of biology as well as philosophy where living matters are defined to cover a whole range from the lowest to the highest forms. The only exception is minerals which are treated as non-living things.

However, in traditional Chinese philosophy, even minerals have lives of their own. The basis for this school of thought is that *yin* and *yang* elements within minerals and mountains go through constant changes just as they do in animals and plants. In ancient times. Chinese people always believed that things like mountains and hills all possess their own spirit. Therefore, massive rocks were considered to be deities that had accumulated enough spirits and power, and so were trees that had lived a thousand years and flowers that were especially rare and hard to find. Moreover, traditional Chinese thinking has it that mountains and rocks contain something called "vital vein" that forms the essence of life. These vital veins of mountains not only make up the hill structures but also serve as the joints within the mountains that bind rocks together. If these vital veins are damaged or severed, rocks will then come tumbling off the mountains. An example of this is when mountains are opened up for the building of roads or uses, rocks will be falling down because vital veins are destroyed. From the perspective of the natural sciences, the falling of rocks is just a natural phenomenon and has nothing to do with the biological world. The ancient Chinese belief, however, has a different view. Under this view, everything in the universe is connected in life. Any change in one part of the network will have implications for the whole system. Wang Yang-ming proposed the "unity of benevolence (*jen*)". Every entity or physical body in the universe forms part of the wholeness of life.

An individual is an independent entity. All constituent elements of an individual combine to form a single entity and these elements are closely connected in it and inseparable. The life of an individual is in its cohesive force and at the center of each life is what we generally refer to as its spirit. Spirit is not only the core of life, but also the core of the cohesive force. Once life is terminated, the activities of the individual entity will stop and its cohesive force will also cease to exist. Therefore, after people die, the body disintegrates. Every individual, be it a mineral such as a rock or a mountain, has its own cohesive force. Without it, a rock could not stay together as a rock and a mountain could not keep its form and identity either. The cohesive force of an individual cannot be coming from the quantity aspect of the reality (substance), which is simply a description of one element on top of another. Quantity itself does not possess the cohesive force to bind every element together to form the individual. We often say that material things are divisible whereas living things are not. However, material things are only divisible theoretically but not down to the level of individuals. Once divided, individuals will cease to be. Western philosophy contends that cohesive force exists because of substance. Therefore, substance is indivisible. As a matter of fact, substance is indivisible only because it is possessive of a cohesive force. Cohesive force is not quantity, but quality. Furthermore, it is an internal force, not external. From the point of view of Chinese philosophy, cohesive force is no other than the life-giving force and it is due to this life-giving force that the formation of substance from individuals is accomplished. To me, this life-giving force is nothing but generative power.

The concept of life we are discussing here is derived from the concept of internal changes espoused in Chinese philosophy. Since changes are the "becoming" processes that lead from "potency to act," the "becoming" process is life itself. Finally, the driving force of "becoming" lies in generative power.

What is the meaning of life? Life is "existence." "Existence" is the action of constant changes. The action of constant changes is life, which is generative power. The existence of a substance is made possible by the formation of individuals from all the prime matter and principles both embodied in and acted upon by generative power. The existence of individuals is not only driven by generative power but is also maintained by it. I exist because I am given life by generative power. Life changes and its maintenance again has to rely on generative power. Therefore, my existence is life. Life is the action of changes. The action of changes is generative power.

II. The Formation of Life

Life is formed by changes. Changing in turn has a starting point, an end point and a dynamic process. The starting point is "potency"; the end point is "act"; the dynamic process is "becoming." "Becoming" and "act" are inseparable. Everything in the universe acquires its existence through continuous "becoming" from "potency" to "act." For every entity, existence is never a static phenomenon. It is never the case that just one movement from "potency" to "act" will stop the process and the achieved "act" will settle into a fixed state. On the contrary, existence will continue to happen and is composed of recurring cycles of "potency to act," or a non-stop process of "becoming." Therefore, the "act" here is not a finished state; rather, it is constantly evolving, which is the reason for the term "becoming."

"Becoming" is the process of turning "potency" into "act" and in fact is just "act" or reality (actual being) itself. The process continuously leads from potency to act and therefore we have non-stop actualization and creation. In theory, as the process by which "potency" is turned into "act," "becoming" is often known by another term: "actualization," to be distinguished from "realization." Nevertheless, practically, "act" will result whenever "potency" is actualized. For instance, I am in the state of reading whenever my potency of reading is actualized regardless of how much I actually read. This is true with every being in the universe. Within this scheme of life, there are the following elements at work: body, potency, driving force, self-becoming and act. Body is a reality, also known as "being" or "existence." Next, potency is derived from the principle contained in generative power. What happens then is that the body, which originally did not exist, becomes reality under the action of the "potency to exist" sparked by another body. Once a reality, the body will be continuously driven by generative power using the internal potency to exist, leading to act which guarantees the continuous existence of the reality.

The changing process we just presented is the changing process of "existence," which is the same as saying the changing of the substance. What it really describes is the continuous "becoming" process of the "being" or the "existence," a process which develops from potency to act. In addition to that, there is also the changing of accident, which accounts for the changes in the quantity or quality of "being" or "existence." For instance, I know I exist. Since I am only born once, for me to go on living requires my "potency to exist" to continuously and automatically lead to act. Likewise, when I read, my potency for reading has to be actualized and kept on for as long as I read. Without it, I could not be reading. Furthermore, this potency of mine to read has to continuously lead to act; otherwise, I am not getting results, that is to say I am not actually reading.

"Act" is "potency" becoming a reality. For "potency" to become a reality, generative power is needed to actualize it, and after that, the process to "act" is itself-sustained. Naturally, we may imagine that there is a series of actions linking the states of "potency" and "act." From the point of view of metaphysics, however, "act" is no other than "potency" actualized and "becoming" and "act" are actually one and the same. The actualization of "potency" is not an action and it does not require a process. It in itself is the actualization of "potency." For instance, as soon as I stand in front of a mirror, my reflection will immediately appear in the mirror. A mirror has the potency of showing people's images. By standing in front of the mirror, I then satisfy the precondition for the actualization of the mirror's potency and serve as its driving force. The point is, the minute I position myself in front of the mirror, my image is immediately reflected and that means the mirror has actualized its potency of showing reflections without having to go through any process. Therefore, "becoming" is the result of a potency actualized; "becoming" is "act" and "act" is "becoming."

Although "act" and "becoming" are one and the same, they do have different meanings. The term "act" implies accomplished, finished and "potency" realized. What is conveyed is the existence of a terminus as well as a static quality. On the other hand, "becoming" gives the feeling of being progressive and dynamic. It is true that "act" in itself can also represent the state of existence or being, but in view of the fact that the existence of a substance is a dynamic evolution from potency to act rather than just a static state, "becoming" is the better and more suitable term for describing the existence of a substance.

There are two aspects to the relationship between "act" and "potency": one is the essence involved, the other is the sequential order of the two. In terms of their essence, "potency" and "act" are two of the same kind. As for the sequence, "potency" happens before "act" and is originally independent from "act"; once "act" is latter achieved, "potency" and "act" will then become one and inseparable. There are two kinds of "potency": the potency of the substance and the potency of the accident. The potency of the substance can be described as the "potency to exist," meaning that the substance has the capability of existing and existence is a property of the substance. On the other hand, although the potency of the accident also belongs to the substance, it is nonetheless of a different nature. Its characteristics are such that the potency of the accident can either be spiritual or corporeal. It can either be capable of changing or currently undergoing change. Finally, the changing can either be in terms of quality or quantity. As "act" is achieved, it does not become a fixed state but goes on as it is. To explain this, we can use the analogy of the existence of a child. People often say a child exists because it is born. Actually, there is more to it than just birth. When a child is born, its existence is a result of the actualization of the potency to exist within its substance. Indeed, the child is now existing. However, this existence is only as long as the continuous "actualization" of the potency to exist within the child's substance through the process of "becoming." Once the dynamic process stops, the child will cease to exist. To say a child exists is to say it lives. To live not only requires the "potency" of living but this potency of living or existence has to be constantly transformed to the state of actualization. Otherwise, existence will no longer be possible and death will occur. In other words, a child's existence relies on the potency to exist within its subsance continuously being actualized through the process of becoming. Therefore, "act" cannot be separated from "potency" and "act" cannot survive on its own. Once a state of act is achieved and the resulting substance is in possession of the potency to exist, the state of act can only be maintained as long as the potency of existence is always in the process of being actualized.

The *I Ching* says: "The movement of *yin* and *yang* constitutes the Way (*Tao*). What issues from the Way is good, and that which fulfills it is individual nature" (Chapter 5, Part I, *Hsi-tz'u*). It takes one *yin* and one *yang* to drive the transformation from potency to act. As the two elements come together, physical bodies are formed and their existence results. As long as the combining of *yin* and *yang* continues, the existence will also continue. Echoing this ivew, Wang Ch'uan-shan says: "Essences converge everyday; life forms everyday." The existence of everything in the universe is made possible by what Aristotle referred to as the ultimate or the highest cause that incessantly creates *ex nihilo*. This ultimate cause is a pure substance containing only forms of act and no element of potency. It creates the universe from nothing by using its own force. Its force of creation reaches everything in the universe and ensures the continuation of existence by bringing every entity into a connection where mutual activation is at work. Roman Catholicism teaches that God is creative power. The Roman Missal says:

> "Father all creation rightly gives you praise. All life, all holiness comes from you through your Son, Jesus Christ our Lord, by the working of the Holy Spirit." ("Eucharistic Prayer III," 673).

For every "potency" there is, a driving force has to be provided before actualization can be achieved. Originally, the "potency to exist" of a substance is realized upon activation by an achieved. Children only start to exist because their parents give birth to them. Once a substance is already in existence, however, the recurrent process of potency becoming act is driven by the substance itself. With oneself as the driving force, the process of changing as life thus acquires its meaning. As for the potency of an accident, it can either be actualized by the host substance or by an external force. For instance, I can either move on my own or be made to move by others. Changes of this kind are the manifestations of life rather than the reason of life. Both the starting and the continuation of the existence of a substance are the result of the "potency to exist" becoming "act." The difference is in the source of activation. While the driving force for the starting of existence comes from outside, the continuation of existence is driven from within. Although both driving forces are derived from the same one force of creation, they are released from different places. For he start of existence, the driving force is produced in a different substance, as opposed to the production of driving force in the substance itself for the continuation of existence. Every power in the universe comes from the same force of creation. As generative power passes through a substance, it becomes available to be used by the substance to either activate itself or another substance.

Becoming is a self-driven process with the self-evolution of potency into act. Self-evolution means that once "potency" is actualized, "potency" will be realized.

The meaning of life is the same as the meaning of "existence." What is "being"? "Being" is the reason for "entities" to be "entities." "Being" implies "existence," which in turn indicates the continuous changing of potency into act. Life is the phenomenon of potency incessantly changing into act. Therefore, "existence" is life.

Life is a dynamic concept. Nothing in the universe is the result of "one act of a simplistic becoming." Rather, a dynamic process of potency developing into act is always involved and life itself is the continuous becoming of potency to act.

III. Characteristics of Life

Chinese philosophy holds the view that life is formed by *ch'i* through the changes of *yin* and *yang*. As such, life is not purely material in nature. In both the *I Ching* and the rationalist doctrine prevalent during the Ming and Ch'ing dynasties, the changes of *yin* and *yang* in the universe are considered to be the perpetual renewal of life. Perpetual renewal of life is divine and unpredictable. It is called *shen* (mysterious) or spiritual.

The *I Ching* says:

> Change (*I*) was made on a principle of accordance with heaven and earth, and shows us therefore, without rent or confusion, the course (of things) in heaven and earth. . . (The sage) comprehends as in a mold or enclosure the transformations of heaven and earth without any error; by an ever-varying adaptation he completes (the nature of) all things without exception; he penetrates to a knowledge of the course of day and night (and all other connected phenomena); it is thus that his operation is spirit-like, unconditioned by place, while the changes which he produces are not restricted to any form. (Chapter 4, Part I, *Hsi-tz'u*)

The successive movement of the inactive (*yin*) and active (*yang*) operations constitutes what is called the course (of things). . . That which is unfathomable in (the movement) of inactive and active operations is (the presence of a) spiritual (power). (Chapter 5, Part I, *Hsi-tz'u*)

Change (operations forming the change) are the method by which the sages searched out exhaustively what was deep, and investigated the minutest springs (of things). ' Those operations searched out what was deep:' --therefore they could penetrate to the views of all under the sky. "They made apparent the minutest springs of (things):" --therefore they could bring to a completion all undertakings under the sky. ' Their action was spirit-like:' --therefore they could make speed without hurry, and reached their destination without traveling. (Chapter 10, Part I, *Hsi-tz'u*)

Chang Tsai, in his work "*Cheng-meng*," frequently mentions how *ch'i* is transformed into spirit. It says:

The Ether (*ch'i*) is clear, and for this reason, it cannot be obstructed. Not being obstructed, it is spirit. Turbidity, the opposite of clarity, leads to obstruction, which in turn, causes physical form. (Great Harmony)

When the Ether (*ch'i*) is clear, it penetrates; when turbid, it obstructs. When clarity reaches its maximum, there is spirit. (Great Harmony)

The Ether (*ch'i*) embodies two elements (*yin* and *yang*). Their fusion is called divination. When they separate, there is change. (*Ts'an-liang*)

That which is unfathomable is divination. Divination that proceeds with order is the law of Heaven. (Way of Heaven)

Divination is a virtue of Heaven; change, the way of Heaven. Virtue is the substance of Heaven and the way its function. Substance and function together make the Ether (*ch'i*). (Divination)

Everything will be brought to light when the divine law is made manifest. Spirit prevails regardless of time and space. (Divination)

The Ether (*ch'i*) consists of *yin* and *yang*. Their actions lead to change. The fusion of *yin* and *yang* is unfathomable and is called divination. (Divination)

Divination and change in the universe result from the power of Heaven, not man. Only when man reaches the highest goodness can he understand the divination and change in the universe. (Divination)

Change (*I*) indicates a penetrating intelligence and extensive knowledge of the course of the universe, which only the one who is rich in virtues can understand. (Divination)

The *I Ching* says:

The great attribute of heaven and earth is the giving and maintaining of life. What is most precious for the sage is to get the (highest) place--(in which he can be the human representative of heaven and earth). What will guard this position for him? Benevolence." (Chapter 1, Part II, *Hsi-tz'u*)

The giving of life is a demonstration of great virtue on the part of the heavenly universe, with the sage joining in the virtue of heaven and earth, and in which virtue and benevolence thus abound. According to Chang Tsai, this is a picture of "bountiful virtue and lavish benevolence." Therefore, life is not material. It is not of a purely material nature. Instead, life is spiritual, which resides in a physical body. It is inseparable from the physical body and is by no means material-like. Compared with materialist dialectics, which regards the universe as derived from a single matter, this Chinese view is fundamentally different. Since life is generative power, it is anything but material.

Another characteristic of life is that it is interlinked. In Chinese philosophy, *ch'i* is constantly circulating in the universe and never ceases to undergo transformation through changes in *yin* and *yang*. Everything owes its being to *ch'i* whereas *yin* and *yang*, existent and incessantly changing inside every entity, are what gives life to these entities. As a result, everything is connected in life. Wang Yang-ming mentioned "unity of benevolence" in his work entitled the "Great Learning." Here, benevolence refers to life. Thus, he actually meant to say "unity of life." The *I Ching* says:

> In (all these operations forming) change, there is no thought and no action. It is still and without movement. But, when acted on, it penetrates forthwith to all phenomena and events under the sky. If it were not the most spirit-like thing under the sky, how could it be found doing this? (Chapter 10, Part I, *Hsi-tz'u*)

> Thus, a door shut may be pronounced (analogous to) Khwan (or the inactive condition), and the operation of the door (analogous to) Khien (or the active condition). The opening succeeding the being shut may be pronounced (analogous to what we call) a change; and the passing from one of these states to the other may be called the constant course (of things)." (Chapter 11, Part II, *Hsi-tz'u*)

Generative power extends to every being and serves as their driving force. The internal manifestation of each being is life itself while the external manifestations are the phenomena of life. For both, the driving force is the same, namely generative power. The same generative power resides in all beings of the universe but its manifestations vary from one to another. In the general treatment of philosophy, the manifestations of beings are considered to correspond to their unique properties and nature. Since the properties and nature of all beings are both principles derived from the essence of generative power, then the manifestations are according to these principles.

As explained earlier, life is not material and life links with one another. Relative to any being or entity, the life inside permeates throughout the whole system and reaches every element. The universe as a whole also has a life and the life extends to everything in it. Looked at another way, the life of the universe is also an accumulation of all the lives of everything in the universe. In that sense, each individual life is independent but not isolated. All things are interconnected through generative power. When any one constituent is hurt, the whole system suffers. Things in the universe exist in different scales, some large, some small. While the effects of minor destruction are not readily appreciable, the negative impacts of major and sustained destruction will immediately show. Presently, the natural environment is under various threats and many natural objects are being destroyed. As a result, both things of nature and the human race all suffer since their lives are all being affected.

It is not surprising then that Confuciansm advocates the great harmony of the whole universe. While Mencius said that "The myriad things are in me in every possible way," Chang Tsai also painted a very similar picture: "*Ch'ien* is referred to as the father and *k'un* the mother...People are my blood brothers" (*Cheng-meng, Ch'ien* and *K'un*). The underlying thought here is actually much akin to the concept of charity in Roman Catholicism. Catholicism teaches that God is the Creator of all things and we love all things because we love God. Furthermore, the purpose of God's creation is to sustain the lives of humans.

The third characteristic of life is its principles. Chinese philosophy views life as the changes of *yin* and *yang*, and these changes all follow certain paths. The rationalists called these paths of changes "principles." For Chu Hsi, they are the principles of life. Life activities are dictated by these principles and whose full representation is nothing other than human life. The principles of human life are described as "nature" in the *Chung-yung*. It says: "What Heaven has conferred is called nature; an accordance with nature is called the way; the regulation of the way is called instruction" (Chapter 1). Humans lead their lives by exercising what is in their nature, a phenomenon embodied in the concept of "truthfulness" as mentioned in the same book: "Sincerity is Heaven's way; to be sincere is Man's way" (Chapter 22). The *Ta-hsueh says*: "The Way of learning to be great (or adult ducation) consists in manifesting the clear character..." Clear character refers to good human nature. Therefore human life is about demonstrating good nature, the same thing as "fulfilling one's nature" in the *Chung-yung*.

Mencius believed that human nature is all benign and benevolent. All the good aspects of human nature are validated and exemplified through the heart and human life is therefore spiritual. The purpose of spiritual life is to fulfill the goodness of human nature, which includes the four constituents: humanity, righteousness, propriety and wisdom. To live human life is to cultivate these four constituents of goodness and develop them into corresponding virtues. That is what Mencius meant when he said "cultivating the nature and *ch'i*," especially cultivation of the "flood-like *ch'i*."

For rationalists, the words principle, heaven, nature, life and mind all describe the same thing. To follow the principles is to exercise what is in one's nature. In turn, this is equivalent to rectification of one's mind or observing heaven's orders. Wang Yang-ming even took this one step further. He believed that no principles are to be found outside the mind and the heart is nothing else but the conscience. A moral life is a life that fulfills what the conscience demands.

Generative power acts according to the principles. In other words, the characteristics of life are determined by the principles and not by the content. The principles that dictate the generative power are bestowed on all entities by creative power and serve as the element of "potency" within the generative power. When conditions are right for the "potency" to develop into the state of "act," generative power will activate the process and a reality will come into existence through the process of "becoming."

Spiritual life is not only the full extent of life and the highest point of life; it is also a moral and ethical life.

A moral and ethical life is the kind of life that a most sincere person, as can be found in the *Chung-yung*, will have when all potentials within the person's nature are realized. To realize the potentials in one's nature is to praise the work of generation and transformation by Heaven and Earth (the Universe). By doing so, one participates in the virtues of Heaven and Earth. In the *I Ching,* the *Commentary on the Text of the Ch'ien* says: The sage unites his virtues with Heaven and Earth." Elsewhere in the book, it says:

> It is the great virtue of heaven and earth to generate life. It is the great treasure of the holy sage to stand in the right place. How does one safeguard this place? Through benevolence (jen). (Appended Remarks, Part II, Ch. 1)

The sage who shares with the virtues of heaven and earth is a benevolent man.

When joined with the virtues of heaven and earth, the human spirit transcends and is above all things. This is the same as Mencius' "flood-like *ch'i*" that pervades every corner of the universe. However, the human psyche is nothing other than spiritual life. Therefore, a spirit transcending all and everything is the same as saying the human mind transcends all and everything. As Professor Thomé Fang said, the spiritual life as espoused in Confucianism is one that is transcendent. But the other aspect, spiritual transcendence is also within the human mind and therefore will manifest itself as an internal life as well. Just as Sung Dynasty's Chang Tsai pointed out:

> By expanding one's mind one is able to embody the things of the whole world. If things are not thus all embodied, there will be something that remains external to the mind. The minds of ordinary men are confined within the limits of hearing and seeing, whereas the sage, by completely developing his nature, prevents his mind from being restricted to hearing and seeing. As he views the world, there is in it no one thing that is not his own self. This is what Mencius means when he says that through the complete development of the mind one may come

to know one's nature and know Heaven. So vast is Heaven that for it there is nothing external. Therefore, a mind which externalizes things is incapable of uniting itself with the mind of Heaven. (Enlarging One's Mind, *Cheng-meng*)

Chu Hsi once said:

Heaven and Earth take the production of things as their mind. In the production of man and things, they were endowed the mind of Heaven and Earth as their mind. Therefore, with reference to the character of the mind, although it encompasses and penetrates all and leaves nothing to be desired, nevertheless, one word will cover all of it, that is *jen* (humanity). (*Jen-Shuo, Chu-tzu ta-chuan, Wen-chi* [A Treatise on Jen, Complete Literary Works of Chu Hsi, Collected Writings], Bk. LXVII)

Principle is nature. Nature is mind. Mind is itself benevolence.

What marks the highest point and the completeness of life is benevolence and benevolence is life, or generative power. Generative power is derived from creative power which in turn comes from the Creator. The Creator creates on the basis of "love," which is the same as "benevolence." The life of the universe is the continuous generation of new lives and benevolence results when the process is in full operation. Confucius used the concept of benevolence to link all his philosophical ideas. Thus, benevolence became the hinge of all virtues.

Viewed from the perspective of the Cahtolic Church, God creates everything in the universe from nothing and also sustains them. The concepts of time and space do not apply to God. It is the same divine power that both creates and preserves everything in the universe. This divine power links everything together and ensures their everlasting existence through reproduction. St. John writes: "...for God is love" (1 Jn 4:8). Human beings are created in the image of the Lord, so love also fills the human heart. Furthermore, benevolence, which is love in essence, links man with God. Benevolence brings man and God together.

IV. The Substance of Life

Existence is a result of change. The word change refers to the transition from potency to act and life itself is the successive process of potency becoming act. But, is life a reality or a function?

In Western philosophy, "nature" and "existence" combine to form "being" and "being" is the substance of "existence." But actually, "being" in here is equivalent with "the being". In other words, the principal entity. For instance, "I" is a "being," whose "existence" is "my existence." One key element of Chinese philosophy is the concept of *sheng-sheng* [perpetual renewal of life]. Each "existence" is an example of this perpetual renewal of life, which is a process of change. The principal entity of the perpetual renewal of life is the changing subject that proceeds from "potency" to "act." This subject is "the living." Therefore "the being," "the existing" and "the living" all refer to the same entity. When examined closer, "the being" is no different than "being," the existing," "existence," and "the living" life. Although we differentiate between the two terms of each pair, they are actually one and the same thing. That is why the concept of "unity between reality and function" is often dealt with in Chinese philosophy.

1. The Substance

Normally, when I say *I exist*, "I" is the principal entity and "exist" is subordinate to "I." Or, if I say I am a being, "I" of course is the subject while "a being" is the predicate. The subject and the predicate as such converge on a single identity: "I" is a being and the being is "I." This is not to deny that "I" as used in here has a richer meaning than "a being." "A being" simply refers to a reality, whereas "I" is a being with specific qualities. But still, in a statement like *I am a being*, "I" and "a being" are one and the same in the sense that this "being" is none other than "I."

"I" is the principal entity. Anything that belongs to "I" belongs to this principal entity. When we say "my body, my spirit, my intelligence, my personality, my movement, and so on," the principal entity is always "I." Unlike the concept of subject in logic and language, however, the "I" here is a principal entity as discussed in ontology. In logic and linguistics, a principal entity is the same as subject. A subject is not necessarily a noun; it can also be an adjective or verb. *The dog is white* is an example of a noun being the subject of a sentence. But *white is pure* has a subject that is an adjective and *Giving a speech is fun* chooses a verb to be the subject. From the ontological point of view, adjectives and verbs are all adjuncts, that is, that they cannot stand on their own but have to be attached to a principal entity. For instance, *white* only exists when something is *white*. Likewise, *giving a speech* needs to be associated with a person as its principal entity since it cannot exist by itself. Therefore, from the ontological perspective, a so-called principal entity has to be "a being" with an indepdent existence. Such a principal entity, then, is a *substantia*.

"I" is a principal entity, so "I" is also a substance. Furthermore, "I" is a substance because my "being" is an independent entity and I am "an independent being." A "being" has to be independent for it to be a substance. The reason is obvious. Everything that belongs to a substance is considered to be a part of it. Suppose a substance is not an independent entity but just a part of some other substance. In that case, everything that belongs to the substance will also belong to the other one and the substance is actually just an adjunct, not a substance.

What I have illustrated above is proposed by Scholastic philosophy. Personally, I have a different view. I am of the opinion that "the being" is "being"; "the existing" is "existence"; and "the living" is "life." In other words, "the being," "the existent" and "the living" are the substances while "being", "existence" and "life" are the manifestations, or the adjuncts. "The existent" is the same as "existence" and they are "life." Life is the successive processes of potency becoming act. Since this is a changing process, by inference, "the existent" is also constantly changing. But doesn't this imply that there is no static substance but only dynamic changes? Of course, this argument can not find support in ontology. But to me, this kind of changes corresponds to the process of potency becoming act and results in "the existent" or "the living." Each act that is attained initiates another cycle that starts from potency and which leads to yet another act. Therefore, act is a substance to potency. Only this substance is not static and never changed. Instead, it is dynamic and constantly changing.

In both Western philosophy of more recent times and Chinese philosophy, there have been scholars that reject the concept of substance. Although their theories are varied, generally they have one thing in common and that is they all consider *substantia* to be an empty concept without any real meaning. Each person has a life that is always evolving and changing. Other than that, is there anything else? Life is not just body or mind. But the critics of ontology do not recognize there is such thing as the human substance in addition to body and mind. By the same token, they do not accept that there is any substance to a desk besides the wood or stone it is made of. Despite the denial on their part, however, normally when we say "I," we don't just refer to the body, or just the body and the mind together. Likewise, when we say a desk, we don't just mean the wood or stone material by that. Rather, "I" refers to the principal entity of "my life" and it just happens that this principal entity also has a body and a mind. But "I" is not just my body or my mind. "I" has meanings different from just body and mind. "I" is a principal entity composed of a body and a mind. It is living and it is life. Although it changes all the time, it is also congruent throughout. Therefore, what exactly is this principal entity? As we said earlier, it is not the body or the mind. It is a living entity that is composed of a body and a mind. This living entity is constantly changing through a successive process that leads from potency to act. Therefore, there is a whole succession of "acts." To our own reasoning, this succession of "acts" is the principal entity, the "I" that we are conscious of. On the other hand, there is also the feeling part of ourselves that equates our body with our principal entity. Only our feelings cannot be relied on for that purpose. This is because feelings are aroused by and directed at fleeting forms and colors, whereas our intellect is our true vehicle for knowing the congruently changing "I," the principal entity of each and every transformation. As such, this principal entity is also the substance of our existence. Therefore, our substance is only known to our intellect. Hence, the living entity that is composed of a body and a mind is none other than our own substance, but only our intellect understands this. Furthermore, this substance is not a fictional creation of the intellect. Rather, it has a genuine existence. Our feelings take it as our body and emotions, but our intellect knows it is the substance.

Let me cite another example. When I see a desk, I may see a brown, square piece of wood in my eyes, but my intellect tells me it is actually a desk, a substance by itself. If one rejects the concept of substance, then one denies the difference between understanding through feelings and understanding through the intellect. One only accepts interpretations arrived at through feelings and does not recognize the possibility of obtaining knowledge through the intellect. But, philosophical assertions should also match our normal thinking patterns. Normally, we refer to a desk as a desk and not as a piece of wood or stone. We also describe ourselves as having a body and a soul. Never will we say we are a body or a soul. In other words, to a normal mind, "I" is a principal entity of life.

Or we can even suggest the existence of the concept of *substantia* in our mind is also reflected in the way we talk. When speaking, we first use a subject and the rest of the sentence, such as predicates, verbs, adverbs and adjectives, are all subordinated to the subject. Correspondingly, there is also a principal entity in our thinking patterns that acts as the substance while the rest are accidents, or adjuncts. Therefore, grammar reflects our way of thinking which, in turn, is a representation of the way our intellect functions. The utility of the human mind is to identify a substance that is an "independent being." An "independent being" is an independent being and cannot combine with another "independent being" to form a substance. When I am aware of an object, my eyes see the shape and the form but my intellect identifies its substance. The crux here is that a substance is not in a quiescent state. Rather, it is a repetitive succession of "acts." A substance is a reality of oneness, like one person or one desk. Our feelings detect all the different colors and forms but our intellect recognizes the oneness behind these colors and forms. As a result, I am one and I am a substance. You are also one and you are a substance. It is existence that creates this oneness. Existence constantly changes the state it is in and that is life, or generative power. A substance is a life on the premise that a substance is an independent being. Existence constantly undergoes changes and that is life; but life is also a force that gives life. My substance is a living entity. Therefore, according to logic, I must have a life. But besides that, practically, I am the life since without the life, there would not be me. Thus, I am the life, but this life is not just a purely theoretical life. This life contains essence and it also has a body that is constantly changing. As a conclusion a substance is an existence containing essence, a concrete existence, a concrete life. It is itself generative power possessing essence.

2. The Accidents (Function)

My life, a principal entity, is very complicated and contains may different components. I have a body. The body includes various organs. It has colors, a height and a weight. I also have a mind whose faculties include intellect, will, emotions, talents and dispositions. In addition, there are many relationships centered around me. All of the above are mine; they belong to me. Basically, the body and the mind are the two halves of my substance. The rest are either part of the body or the mind. These, therefore, are the accidents. In Western philosophy, accidents are grouped into nine categories: quantity, relation, quality, place, time, posture, action, passion and habit. Of the nine, posture, quantity, place and time are related to the body, while relation, quality, action, passion and habit are dependent on both body and mind. The accidents are all contingent upon the substance and they are the elements of my life that do not have an independent existence. When my life undergoes changes, these are the elements actually involved and they are often the agents of manifestation. For instance, my life has different aspects to it, such as physical, mental, intellectual and emotional, etc. These various aspects all belong to the principal entity of my life and their contents amount to the manifestation of my life. The principal entity of my life is the successive actualization of potency. Every time such actualization is achieved, the different aspects of my life are triggered off and become an integral part of my life. In the process, they constitute the outward manifestations of the many facets of my life's principal entity. Stated more clearly, the reason I am a "being" is because I exist. I exist because I live. I live because I have physical, mental, intellectual and emotional activities. These activities at once constitute and serve as the manifestations of my life and my life reflects the principal entity behind it.

Chinese philosophy views the principal entity to be Reality (substance) and the accidents to be functions. Nevertheless, the definitions for reality and substance are often varied. For instance, Chu Hsi once said:

> Substance is the principle and function its purpose. Substance exists as naturally as ears can hear and eyes can see. When eyes are opened to see and ears are turned to listen, it is their functions that are working. Therefore, inhabitants of Kiangsi refer to substance as an abstract concept and function as the purpose of things. (*Chu-tzu yü-lei*, Bk. 6)

In this particular passage, Chu Hsi takes principle (*li*) to be Reality (substance) and activity as function. He did not always stick to this classification although he did mostly treat subjects as reality and verbs as function.

Chu Hsi further writes:

> When we said that substance and function possess no certain forms, we were merely making remarks in random. What if the myriad things make up one great substance and function? Then substance and function possess their own definite forms. What is intrinsic to things is the substance, and what is derived from it is function. For instance, our body is the substance and action its function. Heaven is the substance. When heaven generates life, it is function. Earth is the substance. When its give rise to life and the myriad things, it is function. From the perspective of *yang*, it is the substance and *yin* is the function. From the perspective of *yin*, it is the substance and *yang* the function. (Chu-tzu yu-lei, Bk.6)

Between reality and function, the former serves as the foundation while the latter grows out of it and does not command a dominion of its own. For instance, in terms of the function of the eyes, eyes are the reality and seeing is the derivative function. But as far as the location of the eyes is concerned, the whole body becomes the reality and the eyes are the function. One of Chu Hsi's preferred way of explaining reality and function is as follows:

> Substance is the essence of things while function is that which can be operated by men. Take the example of a fan. The substance of a fan consists of sticks handle, and paper pasted together. When man uses it to fan, its function is performed. The same is true with the ruler and the balance. The scales and weights are their substance. Used to measure or weigh something, their function occurs.

Wang Yang-ming at once treats the reality of the mind as the heavenly principle (*Yang-ming Ch'uan-shu* [The Complete Works of Wang Yang-ming], Vol. I, 28) and as the vehicle to react to the rights and wrongs of the world (*Yang-ming Chuan-shu*, Vol. III, 14).

Li Kung of Ch'ing Dynasty did not favor differentiation between reality and function. He was of the opinion that great sages of the old times never separated these two. It was not until the Sung Dynasty that the separation was started. He considered the practice a mistake. Li said:

> Everything has been explained by the sages, from Fu Hsi to Confucius and Mencius. For this reason, scholars of later periods must observe their teachings and refrain from making innovations, which lead to mistakes. The Sung Dynasty scholars, for example, separated the Tao into substance and function. They took the former as the principal part and the latter, the subordinate.
>
> Lao Tzu took non-being as substance and being as function. In fact, the Sung scholars followed Lao Tzu in distinguishing between substance and function. In Chou Tun-i's Diagram of the Supreme Ultimate, he took the mean, benevolence and

sensation as the function of the Supreme Ultimate, and correctness, righteousness and quiescence as the substance. However, in his commentary on the *Chung-yung*, Chu Hsi referred to mean as the substance and harmony as the function. If Chu Hsi were right, how could Chou Tun-i interpret the mean, benevolence and sensation as function and correctness, righteousness and quiescence as subjstance? Both Chu Hsi and Lu Hsiang-shan[1] were influence by Lao Tzu and Buddhism. However, Lu was misled while Chu Hsi failed to develop his own theory, having wavered about the two schools. (Discourse on the Error of Sung Distinction Between Substance and Function, Bk. 13)

Lao Tzu started the discourse on reality and function but it was in Buddhism that the discourse was expanded and enriched before the Rationalists of the Sung and Ming Dynasties adopted the practice. Buddhists believe that "all the myriad dharmas are ephemeral except the eternal *chen-ju.*" In other words, each and everything in the universe other than the *chen-ju* is just a manifestation relative to the only substance there is, which is the *chen-ju.* In other words, the *chen-ju* is the pure act and everything else is but a generated phenomenon. Let me cite the example of waves and sea water. Waves are a phenomenon that exists because of sea water and waves are also none other than sea water itself. Therefore, Buddhists advocate the unity of reality and function. Chu Hsi, nevertheless, was critical of the Buddhist thinking. He argued that although reality and derived from the same source, they are two separate things. He writes:

If principle and function share one origin, then from the point of view of principle, it is the substance and phenomenon its

---

(1) [Translator's Note] Lu Hsiang-shan(1139-1193) was a Chinese philosopher who worked as a District Keeper of Records and professor at the national university. He also served as magistrate during the few years preceding his death. He continued the major emphases of Cheng Hao and developed the idealistic wing of neo-Confucianism. He opposed the views of Cheng I and Chu Hsi. His principal work is the *Complete Works of Lu Hsiang-shan.*

function. However, principle itself includes phenomenon, and thus they share one origin. Although the distinction between principle and phenomenon is slight, they can still be distinguished. From the point of view of the phenomenon, it is conspicuous while principle is obscure. This is because phenomenon forms part of principle. I have given much attention to your letter in which you made an observant analysis of principle and phenomenon. You said that ' principle comes ahead of phenomenon. Therefore, the two are not identical. For this reason, Cheng I commented that principle and phenomenon share the same origin. Nevertheless, the distinction between them cannot be neglected.' I say that we must avoid vagueness in the distinction between principal and phenomenon prevalent nowadays. (*Chu-wen kung wen-chi*, Bk. 40)

One of scholars of the contemporary period, Hsiung Shih-li, was also an ardent supporter of the unity of reality and function. Hsiung identified the *I Ching* as the basis of his theory. But actually, the classic does not touch upon the issue of reality and substance and Hsiung simply figured it out in his own interpretation of the book. Hsiung had a theory on the universe. He proposed that the universe is built from "prime forces." These fundamental building blocks first combine to form vibrating "minute divisions," which in turn conglomerate into "small assemblies" and then the entire body. Whereas minute divisions are vibrating agents, the entire body is the embodiment of proliferation. Proliferation is multiplication and with multiplication, the entire body becomes the great function that has at its core the two constituent parts of mind and matter. Therefore, mind and matter are not the reality itself but are instead the function. For Hsiung, the reality refers to the prime forces and the function is in the proliferation. As such, prime forces and proliferation become indistinguishable in the same manner as reality and function are undifferentiated.

From the perspective of life itself, life is my "existence" and life is change. Both "existence" and "life" are ontological attributes. In addition, "life" is the continuous actualization of potency with the "act" being the principal entity of "life." Consequently "life" and "existence" are practically indistinguishable. In theory, "life" is change whereas "act" is both the terminus of the previous change and the starting point of the next change. In that light, the two do not seem to be the same meaning. As a matter of fact, to me, life is the function in contrast to "act" or "the living" being the reality. So, indeed, theoretically these two are not equivalent. But still, they are one in the practical sense. Life is function and the manifestation of life is a sum of all the different constituents, including the physical, mental, intellectual and emotional aspects of Life. These different spects of life are all accidents. They are all functions. The meaning of an accident or the so-called "function" is in the fact that each accident reflects the principal entity and the principal entity is manifested by the accidents.

For example, I am the principal entity of my life and I am also "existence." My life or my "existence" therefore is presented by the various aspects of my daily life. Likewise, a desk is represented by its material, be it wood, stone or metal, and by its color and shape. The "existence" of the accidents is attached and dictated by the "existence" of the substance. Changes are the content of "existence." The changes of the accidents, as they are contingent upon the changes of the substance, are initiated by the substance and made to represent the substance's changes.

Substance exists because of generative power. Similarly, the association of substance and accidents is also due to generative power. For instance, my life leads to my existence. And it is also generative power that puts the limbs on my body together and matches their colors and shapes. Without my life, my existence will be gone and the association of my limbs, as well as the association of colors and shapes, will also disappear. In conclusion, accidents are the external forms of existence. They are the representation of life and the manifestation of generative power.

3. Life and Existence

"Life," when its meaning understood, is equivalent to an actual being. And an actual being conveys the same meaning as "existence."

"Being," of course, is the opposite of "non-being." "Non-being" means that something does not exist whereas "being" represents existence, which is another way of saying "life." If you ask me whether my parents are around and my answer to you is "they are," then that means my parents exist in the sense that they are still alive. However, if my answer has been "they are not," then you will understand that my parents have passed away and they are not around, not alive anymore. Again, if I reply by saying "my father is, but my mother is not," then it is clear that my father's life is still in existence but my mother no longer lives.

Or, I can ask you whether you have the Twenty-Four Histories in your book collection and your reply might be "there is not." This tells me that this series does not exist in your personal collection although these books may be in some bookstore or library.

Then, I ask you again if there is a moon tonight. The answer "there is" means you have seen the moon. If you have not seen it, you would have replied "there is not."

Let me cite another example. I ask, did you closed a door? If the answer is positive, that means you have taken the action to close the door, so the effect of the action exists. On the contrary, a negative answer means that the action of closing a door has not been taken and its effect does not exist.

I have presented above the different ways how "being" and "existence" are related to each other. Generally speaking, "being" implies "existence" and vice-versa. Nonetheless, there are different variations to this relationship. In the case of my parents, "being" and "existence" have an absolutely unequivocal correlation. My parents either exist or not exist, since I can only possibly have one natural father and one natural mother. In terms of the Twenty-Four Histories, however, the correlation between "being" and "existence" is a relative one. In the example given above, while the books obviously exist, they are not to be found in my personal collection. The same holds true with the moon. Here, the correlation is relative because there is visual perception involved. While the moon itself always exists, we only say it is there when we can see it. Therefore, although "being" and "existence" are closely tied together and once there is "being," there is "existence," their correlation still depends on the nature of the "being." Only when the nature is determined can we be sure about the correlation. This is because it takes "existence" for "being" to become a reality. Whether or not "existence" is life is another issue that is even more complicated.

In Western philosophy, the discourse on "being" is based on the concept of "nature." In Chinese philosophy, however, the starting point is "existence." Scholastic philosophy proposes that when "nature," consisting of *forma* and *materia*, is combined with "existence," an actual being will materialize. But the theory fails to address the "existence" part adequately. In Chinese philosophy, objects composed of two elements: material principle and material force [*ch'i*]. Material principle corresponds to nature and material force to existence. Material force may be clear or turbid. As a result, material principle is limited by material force. Furthermore, material force is ever changing, so "existence" is also constantly solving and in fact is "life" itself. Likewise, "being" is changing and is life too. Personally, I also explain philosophy of life "being" starting from "existence" as point of departure. "Existence" is the generative power within an object. It brings matter and principle togeher through which it produces a reality. Generative power always resides inside the reality which continues existing and changing. Existence and changes are all part of generative power. As a matter of fact, generative power within a reality can also be thought of as the force of life of the reality.

In terms of the relationship between "existence" and life, every "existence" of a principal entity is life. For a principal entity to exist, its potency must continuously become act and this what life is. The "existence" of an accident, on the other hand, does not necessarily involve the successive actualization of potency. Therefore, it is not life. The actual existence of a principal entity (substance) is real "existence," whereas the existence of an accident does not qualify as real existence since it is dependent on the principal entity.

The meaning of "being" is even much broader. Anything with an existence is "being," just like in the examples given earlier. In contrast, only "actual being" is "existence." It implies a principal entity that atually exists. This is not the case with "being" since it need not be associated with a principal entity, "the being," unless it is an actual entity. When "the being" is used to denote an actual entity, it is even better called "this being," as Heidegger did. What is significant about this choice of term is, "this being" is always "the existing," which is also "the living." In summary, therefore, "actual being" is "existence"; and "existence" is "life." "Life" and "existence" are one and the same thing. If it is "existence," it is "life." On the other hand, if we compare "life" and "being," only "actual being" specifically is the same as "life." We have explained that "actual being" is "existence," and thus it is also "life." For the more general "being," it has nothing to do with "life." The equivalence is between "actual being" and "life," but not "being" and "life." Life, of course, is the generative power within an actual entity.

"Existence" presupposes "nature." I am an actual being, which is "existence." And my existence is defined by my nature. Existence and nature are inseparable. As soon as I became an embryo, my existence began. Prior to that, I did not exist. When my "actual being" has not taken shape in the world, my existence is only a limited and relative one. Once I began to exist, I became my own "actual being" and "existence" is always with this "actual being." Thus, I exist. I am the "actual being" and I am I. My "nature" and my "existence" are simultaneous phenomena. Although it may seem that nature should precede existence since my "nature" defines my "existence," they actually occur at the same time. As Chu Hsi also said: "There is no separating between material principle and material force. There is no difference in their time of occurrence."

The Creator's creative power led to generative power. Generative power has both matter and principle. For instance, electricity is such a power. The Chinese think of matter as *ch'i*, so we call electricity "electrical *ch'i*" in our language. Other examples include light, heat, fire and so on. They are all generative power and they all have matter and principle. Of the two, matter is constantly changing in form and principle is equipped with all kinds of energies. There are energies of the substance and there are energies of the accident. Principle comes from generative power and therefore is determined by the Creator. Generative power, on the other hand, undergoes constant changes. As a result of these changes, matter (*essence*) and principle combined to form the object (Reality). The existence of the object is given by generative power. As a matter of fact, existence means that generative power is residing within the reality. Therefore, "existence" is itself generative power.

There are theories both in Western and Eastern philosophy proposing that "existence" creates individual qualities by restricting group characteristics. In Scholastic philosophy, for example, the concept of *materia* is used to explain this. *Materia*, which is material in nature, has the aspect of quantity. "Existence" then specifies the quantity to make it real. But in so doing, it also introduces a restriction on one of the group characteistics. Likewise, Chu Hsi uses clear *ch'i* and turbid *ch'i* to represent specific restrictions on material principle. I do not think either theory can really resolve the issue. Because the ultimate questions are: why the quantity is so and so and why *ch'i* has this degree of clarity. Once the insufficiency is recognized, it gives weight to my belief that the Creator decides what material principle to bestow and that generative power is derived from creative power. St. Augustine took issue with Plato's world of concepts and held the view that the universe is a product of the Creator's wisdom and that every object plays a role and shares the concept in that grand design. God creates human beings and our concepts are derived from God's wisdom. In other words, we all share in the wisdom of God, which is the origin of our concepts. Moreover, our personalities are also shaped by God. My personality is not just a concept. It is actually a complicated entity; it is "I." Conversely, there must be a concept representative of "I," and that is my personality. In epistemology, "I" happens before "my concept." Ontologically, however, "I" and my personality come into being simultaneously. "I" is my personality and my personality is "I." In this case, personality and "existence" converge as one. If I am to explore my roots, I will find out that "my concept" had all along been envisaged by God's wisdom. I exist because God takes "my concept" from His wisdom and enables me to exist. "My concept" is actually the principle within the matter of generative power that is derived from creative power.

What about the relationship between "nature" and "existence"? "Nature" is not "existence." Nature defines "existence." For instance, my "existence" is determined by my "nature." Nature is the principle of realities. In addition to principle, each reality also has a matter constituent, the matter that is within generative power and includes all *materia*. Generative power blends principle and matter (*materia*) to create realities. Therefore, the relationship between nature and existence also involves matter. For example, even if my "nature" and my "existence" start to merge and become one, without my matter, that is, my mind and my body, there would not be me. Furthermore, matter is determined by principle and principle and matter together limit generative power to such as extent that it becomes the force of life of the created reality. Hence, to be more exact, existence is defined by principle and matter together. Nature does not define existence and existence does not define nature.

What is "existence"? "Existence" is the "act" of "being." "Realization" implies "potency" and is none other than the successful culmination of "potency." When I talk about "being," I think of it as a concept without asking whether it is real, ideal or possible "being." Naturally, I could not be talking about "impossible being" since that would be a contradiction of terms and "being" would then just appear meaningless. "Being" is most complete when all the possible meanings of "being" are fully realized. When that happens, "being" has been transformed to "existence" from its state of "potency" and "being" becomes real and actually exists. In the meantime, "existence" and "nature" are merged and that gives rise to real being and real existence. Real existence is a succession of constant changes that lead from potency to act. "Life" then results and life is also generative power.

As explained, "existence" is "act" and "existence" is "becoming."

If is not static or stagnant but an ever-changing state. "Becoming" is a process for self-atualization and therefore is generative power since self-actualization is the meaning of "life." "Existence" can either be interpreted as "becoming" or as "life." Likewise, a real "being" is an "existing" being. An existing being is also "becoming" and therefore is "life." Here, "becoming" is the same as "sincerity" as discussed in the *Chung-yung*. One passage in this classic says: "The sincere man is one who realizes himself." For an existing being, the "becoming" never stops because if it does, there would be no more "existence." When I am in possession of myself, is due to my "existence" continuously undergoing self-actualization and that provides me my life. Once the process of self-actualization stops, my life stops and I will no longer exist. With that, "myself" will then become unattainable. This explains why continuous self-actualization is one way of describing generative power.

"Existence" is "becoming" and "existence" is "self-actualization." However, the process of self-actualization is not entirely intiaited by oneself. The beginning of my "being" is the beginning of my "existence." Therefore, it is also the inception of "becoming" and the starting of "life." In the very beginning, the driving force doesn't come from myself. Rather, it must originate from a "being" that is larger than my life. My parents gave birth to me, but in essence, their lives are not higher than mine. Although they initiated my life, the driving force doesn't come from within them. Lieh Tzu once said:

> Whatever is born cannot generate other things. Whatever came as a fruit of change cannot change other things. Only those that are not born can generate other things and those that do not come as a fruit of change can transform other things. Those that have generated other things will necessarily generate other things and those that have transformed other things will necessarily transform other things. This is the root cause of constant generation and transformation. . . That which is not born seems to be the only one while that which does not change transforms other things and returns to itself. (Lieh tzu, T'ien-jui)

Parents were born by their own parents. Since whatever is born cannot generate other things," parents do not have their own dynamic force to give birth to others. The source of life must necessarily originate not from someone born by another life. The sentence "Only those that are not born can generate other things" means that they originate from their own selves. "That which is not born seems to be the only one" is unique and originates from himself. He gives his creations generative force which propagates an endless generation process. Thus, parents' lives generate the lives of their children. Therefore, in the process wherein an "existent" generates another "existent," it originates from the "Absolute existent" and is propagated by generative power.

A "being," by definition, is already an "existent." For the "existence" to be sustained, the energy of the "existent" must also continue to be in "existence." As a matter of fact, it requires a supportive force for my life, for example, to continue to exist. Any being that is not self-sustained owes its existence to the "subsistent being." For such existence to carry on, the "subsistent being" must continue to impart life to it. Once the act of imparting is terminated, the dependent existence will cease to be. God is the Absolute Being and my life is a gift from Him. One act of giving or blessing alone does not make my life less dependent. My life is only as long as God's blessing. As Wang Yang-ming said, "Nature grows day by day and life materializes in its midst." Continuous blessing generative power which is inseparable from creative power. Creative power brings blessings from God.

4. Life and Nature

"Nature" is the reason why a being is a being. As such, it is the principle that defines "existence." What therefore is *principle*? Both Aristotle and Saint Thomas referred to principle as *forma*, but Scholasticism and Chinese Rationalists contradicted with each other in their choice of term. Chu Hsi was of the opinion that principle constitutes nature and *ch'i* (material force) makes the form. While form is obviously a visible characteristic, principle is totally without form or image. Therefore, principle is metaphysical and beyond perception and *ch'i* is subject to perception. On the other hand, Aristotle and St.

Thomas held *forma* to be principle, which is beyond perception and *materia* to be the other half that is subject to perception. The difference between the two schools of thought, actually, is just how "form" is defined and interpreted. "Form" is like a mold that gives each object it specifications. When Chu Hsi said that "*ch'i* makes the form," what he really meant to say was that "form is made of *ch'i* with *ch'i* being the material constituent of form. But how does form take shape? Why does *ch'i* make each particular form? The answer lies in "principle." That is to say, "principle" defines and specifies *ch'i*. As mentioned in the previous section, "nature defines existence." Likewise, form is determined by nature and is made of *ch'i*. Therefore, principle is actually the underlying form, the *forma* or the *forma substantialis*. But, of course, on the outside of an object is another form that is visible. Such visible form is the physical shape of the object and is distinguished as the *forma accidentalis*.

"Nature" is principle and principle is the *forma* that makes the being what it is. For Plato, nature is "concept" and can be found in the world of concepts. His theory is that objects which are considered of the same group actually share in the one "concept" representative of the group. Similarly St. Augustine believed that the "concept of form" for each group is to be found in God's wisdom. Objects belonging to this group share the same "concept of form" that is bestowed by the Creator. St. Thomas, in contrast, had a two-sided view on this topic. Epistemologically, he considered "nature" to be the common attribute observed by our intellect and that is shared among objects. In our mind, nature is a concept. On the level of realities, however, nature is indistinguishable from the objects themselves. The other side of his view follows an ontological way of thinking. That is, nature precedes the actual physical presence. Theoretically, then, "being," "nature" and "existence" are three different concepts. When "being" is discussed, both "nature" and "existence" are set aside. When "nature" is brought up, it is not to be confused with either "being" or "existence." In like manner, "existence" is also dealt with independently from "being" and "nature." But practically, these three cannot be separated from one another and "nature" and "existence" will always combine to create "being," which is also referred to as the "existing being" or "reality." In other words, "life" is what it is. To sum it up, Aristotle and St. Thomas viewed nature as having two elements, *forma* and *materia*. In contrast, Chu Hsi considered material principle to be the only constituent of nature and *ch'i* is outside the realm of nature. *Ch'i*, to be more exact, is on the level of the physical world and is concerned with the individuality of nature.

At this moment, I am a "being." My "being" is "I." There are various levels in my being. First, I am a human being. Then, I am a man, a philosopher and a priest of the Catholic Church. "I am a human being" is the foundation and the core element of the being of "I." The rest of "I" is all related to this fundamental identity of "I" and only exists because of it. Compared with other people, I am human as others are. Hence, there is nothing to compare between me and the others on that level. We are all the same. My uniqueness is only discernible when the rest "I" besides the human identity is also examined. In that case, we will all be different: you, me, him or her. The "human" attribute is our "nature." "Human nature" serves as the foundation of our respective being and it is also a foundation common to you, me, him and her.

Human nature is the common denominator for every human being. It is a concept, an understanding our intellect has of the human race. Objectively, this concept has a sound basis. The other side of the same coin, however, is that each person is also an individual and no two individuals are the same. The individualities that make us all different consist of some additional qualities that are superimposed on our human nature. Practically, these qualities can also be thought of as constraints. Plato believed in the theory that there is only one concep. that corresponds to humans in the world of concepts. Every person that lives in the physical world shares in this concept in different degrees. Our individuality, then, is a result of this difference. Chu Hsi thought otherwise. He explained that all human beings share the same material principle but people have clear or turbid *ch'i*. This clarity and turbidity of *ch'i* accounts for the disparate behaviors of different people. Disparate behaviors are the expressions of the nature of our physical matter and *ch'i*. This nature is our individual personality. Nevertheless, both Plato and Chu Hsi failed to identify the origin of the different degrees in their respective theories. Personally, I believe human nature (principle) is the concept used by the Creator to create people. Our personality is an indication as to what extent the Creator is willing to let us share the underlying concept of human nature. The Creator makes the rules and these are the practical principles. These principles, dispensed from creative power to generative power, reside in the matter of generative power. Within the same matter, there are also the matter bestowed by creative power. Matter and principle, then, through changes occurring through generative power, combine to form the being of a reality.

In Scholasticism, human nature includes *materia* which is matter of a reality (substance). For Chu Hsi, on the other hand, there is only material principle included in nature and *ch'i* is just the physical matter of a reality. For example, I am a human being. Then by definition, I should have a body and a mind. Scholasticism considers the soul as form and the body as matter and both are within the human nature. Chu Hsi took principle to be the abstract human nature and viewed both mind and body as *ch'i*, the matter of human beings that lies outside the realm of nature. When mind and body are merged, they constitute the nature of the matter of *ch'i*. It is only in this way that *ch'i* was included in Chu Hsi's discourse on nature. Personally, I am of the opinion that matter is separated from principle and thus, also from nature. Matter is specified by principle. Any given principle must have matter (prime element) corresponding to it. Here, I introduce the term of prime element, a concrete matter. For instance, the human body is composed of prime elements.

Thus, nature is principle and individuality is specified nature or specified principle. How the specification should be in each case is determined by the Creator.

The relationship between life and nature is such that life is defined by nature. For example, my life is determined by concrete nature, that is, my individuality. My life is mine and it is a life that exists because of my individuality. It is then evident that my "existence" is also limited by my "individuality." The specification of my life is that it is mine, and this comes on top of the more fundamental and general characteristics of human nature. With human nature alone, my "existence" is not yet firmly established. Only when the secondary characteristics of my individuality is superimposed on human nature will there be "I," my "existence" and my life. Once superimposed, "my identity" and "human nature" become one and inseparable. As far as my "existence" or my "life" is concerned, "human nature" and "my identity," are completely identical, both sharing in a concrete nature.

Translated by Ernest Lee Chang-yi

Chapter V

Act, Motion and Change in Existence

I. Existence

In the chapter entitled "Metaphysical Issues" of my book, *Sheng-ming che-hsüeh* [Philosophy of Life], I explained that existence is itself life. And that since life is living, then existence is constantly undergoing change. An existing reality is an integral. A change in the integral is a metaphysical issue. "Since a change occurs in my wholeness, why is it that I don't change into another me? Or immediately annihilated? The reason lies in the fact that life is one. My life has a united nature. Life acts following its nature. When I live, it is me mandated by Heaven that lives. As long as this Mandate of Heaven remains one, then I remain I. I do not die but instead continue existing."

Let me explain this issue of change in the integral that does not lead to death but instead causes continued existence.

The term "existence" has three grammatical derivatives: It can be used as a verb (*existere*), as in the sentence "He exists (*Ille existit*)." As an adjective (*existens*), it is expressed as "existing" as in the sentence "He is [an] existing [being] (*Ille est existens*)." Its noun form is "existent" (*ens*). In philosophy the term "existence" embraces all these three meanings in an undifferentiated way.

In my mind, the concept of existence is an actual, intentional being, not an empty concept. This intentional reality differs from the external form of the reality. The existence of an external reality is an integral, ever-changing existence. In contrast, the intentional being in my mind is quiescent and individual existence. It is purely existence and excludes all complexities and motion.

Philosophy of Life explains existence from the perspective of the external reality. For it, existence is integral and is motion. Thus, there arise the issues of existential motion and change. In Western Existentialism, being is explained in terms of the "ego." It deals with the actual existence of man. This existence is an integral one, and at the same time, an actual individual. In its explanation of being, Existentialism characterizes the "being-ego" as anxiety and emptiness. Anxiety describes the "being-ego's" relationship with God. Emptiness draws the line between the "ego's" worldly being and the cosmic world. All these explain "existence" from the perspective of its relationships. In Hsiung Shih-li's "New Doctrine of Consciousness-Only," being is explained as a "living actual existent being." What Hsiung called "life in the living world" does not refer to life in its usual ordinary sense. A living being is constantly in motion. A living being is an ever-flowing stream of life. . . . The term "living world" refers to that which possesses an origin, pervades everything and circulates in the four directions, and which is in act from the beginning of time until today....In other words, the reason why man is an existent living being and why man exists is because of his present life perceptions. That goes to say that these life perceptions guide man to the *Tao*. Thus, these perceptual experiences are not the usual cognitive experiences, but rather those experienced by the substance. Any "being" mentioned in the context of the "living actual existent" can be taken as a "living actual existent being" (Lin 18). Explaining life as the experience of fusing with the substance of *Tao* and reality as a being that lives this life differs to some extent from Hsiung Shih-li's ontological explanation. This is because life as the experience of fusing with the substance of *Tao* is an idea derived from combining Zen Buddhism and the Taoist concept of *chen-ju*. Being as explained by Hsiung can be considered to have three forms. "First, being as the root of being." This is in keeping with the idea of a "quiescent" being in his concept of "reversion to quiescence." It possesses unlimited possibility. Second, being as "indeterminate and unobjectified", with its substance manifested by itself freely. It is the world formed following the idea of "discernment through perception." Third, being as determinate and objectified". This is the world determined and abstracted by human mind and consciousness (Lin 20). All these explanations were derived from Buddhism.

In Philosophy of Life, "existence" refers to the external, actual existence, or each thing in itself. Each thing possesses an immanent action called life. For this reason, "existence" involves the issue of change.

To further deal with this problem, let me first explain these three terms: action, motion and change.

Action is the act of the reality based on its own nature. It is not the action arising from potency but rather *actus purus* (pure act). Motion is an action from potency to act. Change is the action of material reality. Since material realities are made up of matter, they change whenever matter moves. Material realities change when they undergo motion.

II. Act

A reality that only possesses act, and pure act at that, is an absolute reality--God himself.

God's nature is life.

St. Thomas Aquinas divided act into two types: First Act and Second Act. First Act is the substance. Second Act refers to action. God's substance is act. God's action is his substance (St. Thomas XIV.9.4).

St. Thomas also said that: "God's substance is life. Because the intellect is life, God's nature is his intellect. Therefore His nature is life (St. Thomas XVIII.a.3)."

St. Thomas affirmed that God is the greatest act, pure and perfect (*cum Deus sit maxime in actu ac simpliciter perfectus*) (XXV.a.1.c)."

Thus, God absolutely does not change. St. Thomas wrote: "Since

God is the first being, absolutely simple and with an unlimited nature, then He does not change (*Deus cum sit primus ens, omnino simplex, et per essentiam infinitus est simpliciter immutabilis.*) (IX.a.1.c)."

God has no potency whatsoever. He does not have accidents. God's actions are his very substance. Since God is life, then he necessarily has actions. God's actions are actions of the substance. They are the act of "existence" and not the actions of accidents. The act of God's existence does not result from a process leading from potency to act, but is rather pure and simple act. This type of act is beyond our imagination. It can only be inferred through the intellect.

For St. Thomas, life is immanent movement, a movement towards development of the self. He also said that the term "life" originally referred to substance and being, that is, substance and being of an immanent nature. It may also sometimes be called vital operation (*Vitae nomen substantiam et esse illus naturae cui convenit se movere, proprie significet; non nunquam vero minus proprie vitalem operationem.*) (XVIII.a.2.c). God is living. Substance is life. It cannot remain on a stand still but instead always in act. God's existence is itself his act.

III. Motion

Motion results from the passage from potency to act. In the case of angels, which are spiritual beings, motion does not lead to change. This is so because their substance is spiritual.

St. Thomas affirms that angels are spiritual beings, not composed of matter and form and are not corruptible. He said: "Those who take angels as composed of matter and form are wrong." (*Errant qui angelos ex materia et forma compositos esse affirmant.*) (L.a.2.c).

St. Thomas takes intellect as the manifestation of life. He affirmed that God possesses life because He possesses intellect. At the same time, he also affirmed that angels have intellect. Regarding angels' intellect, he posed the question whether or not it is itself angels' substance. God's intellect is God's substance. Actions of creatures cannot constitute their substance. Thus, angels' intellect too cannot be their substance. (*Cum selus Deus actus purus exis*ens, sit suum intelligere, nulla cujusve creaturae actio est idem quod substantia ejus; nec etiam ipsum intelligere angelorum idem est substntia ipsorum.*) (LVI.a.1.c).

Intellectual cognition is an action, not a substance. Angels' substance is spiritual being. They are created by God, and therefore, a relative reality. They are in act through potency. Before their creation, angels did not exist. Only after creation did they start existing. Angels' existence is a living one, not motionless. A life is the life of the integral. Therefore, existence is also the existence of the integral. An angel lives, and therefore, its existence is in motion, a motion derived from potency to act. However, angles possess no matter. They do not consist of matter and form. Therefore, the existential movement of angels does not involve change. We may then ask, do intelligence, will, feelings and actions, which all result from the intellect, also change? We humans are psychophysical [1] beings. Our intellect gives rise to ideas, feelings and impressions. These lead to change in the human mind. Ideas may increase or decrease. Similarly, feeling and impressions may grow stronger or weaker. Angels are spiritual beings. Their intellectual and emotional actions are directly carried out without going through concept or impression. Thus, these actions do not lead to any change although they remain in operation.

St. Thomas explained angels' intellectual cognition by affirming that they know themselves owing to their own nature. They know other things through the "principle" existing inside the things. This natural "principle" is a sharing of the Idea of the Creator. (*Cum angelus sit intelligibilis subsistens, seipsum per substantiam intelligit*) (LVI.a.1.c) (*Angeli cum superiores rebus materialibus et corporalibus sint, materi-*

---

(1) [Translator's Note] Here, the term "psychophysical" should not be confused with its usage by Curt J. Ducasse (1881-1969). Rather, it is borrowed to express the meaning of the original Chinese *hsin wu he-yi* , which means "the union of body and mind." The word should also be interpreted as such in other parts of this translation.

alia omnia cognoscunt per species intelligibiles existentes in eis, inquam-tum in illis sunt intelligibiliter.) (LVII.a.1.c). Angels do not have sense organs. They cannot directly get into contact with material things. They can only know through natural ideas that form part of their own nature. They cannot know human affairs in a direct manner but rather through God's idea of supremacy over created things. Angels' know-ledge and emotions are actions that lead to no change at all.

The substance of angels is life itself. Their existence is life, which is also motion. We say that angels' motion is carried out from potency to act. In its entirety, angels' existence is motion from potency to act. This substantial motion is neither creation nor annihila-tion. How is this explained?

Life always proceeds from potency to act. Every baby is born due to the ability to procreate. They did not exist before being born. The existence of babies started at the moment of their conception inside the mother's womb. The baby's potency to start existing is derived from its parents' bodies. The parents have been existing, and therefore, in act. Thus, the baby's potency to start existing rests on "act." It leads from the potency of an act, that is, the potency of parents' procreation, to another act, the baby's conception.

Of course, this is not the real start of angels' existence. Angels are created by God. After their creation by God, angels exist forever. Their existence is life and motion. The angels' creation is an "act." In this act, there is the potency to exist, from which it proceeds to act. In turn, there is in "act" the potency to exist, which leads to another act. In this way, angels continue to move, live and exist. What starts motion is generative power. Angels' generative power originates from God's creative power. These two powers are constantly joined together, with generative power continuously starting motion that leads to angels' existence. Angels are spiritual in substance. They cannot be annihilated. They constantly exist and their motions go on continuously. This eternal motion does not consist of creation and anni-hilation. Instead, it is always towards "act" or is always a process of creation or its continuation.

What if someone poses the question: How can existence be motion? In theory, the concept of existence" is itself "existence." It does not include motion. In real terms, however, existence is "motion." An actual motion is always connected to "existence" because generative power is "one."

IV. Change

All the myriad things in the universe are material objects, except man who is a psychophysical being. Motion of material things involves matter, which always leads to change.

St. Thomas once expressed his views on whether or not life exists in the myriad things of the universe. He said: "What is known in the proper sense as living thing is a reality that makes itself move through some form of movement. Movement may mean an incomplete one, such as the potency to exist, or may refer to a complete movement, such as intelligence and feeling. Thus, anything that moves by itself or acts is a living thing. Anything that does not move by itself or act cannot be called a living thing but only a semblance of it." (*Ex quo patet quod illa proprie sunt viventia, quae seipsa secundum aliquam speciem motus movent, sive accipiatur, motus proprie sicut dicitur actus imperfectus, id est existentia in potentia, sive actus accipiatur communiter; prout intelligere et sentire dicuntur moveri; ut dicitur; et sic viventia dicantur quaecumque se agunt ad motum, vel operationem aliquam. Ea vero in quorum natura non est ut se agunt ad aliquem motum, vel operationem, viventia dici nonpossunt, nisi per aliquam similititudinem.*) (XVIII.a.1.c)

St. Thomas propounds that anything that moves by itself is a living thing and possesses life. Life means possessing sentient activities. However, the sublime meaning of life lies in actions of the intelligence. According to him, anything that can move by itself, regardless of the type of movement, is called a living thing. Thus, he used "life" (living) in the ordinary sense of the word and in the sense of the natural sciences. In the latter, we used to consider minerals as non-living because they cannot move by themselves. However, modern physics now proposes that any material object experiences self-movement within itself. In fact, its degree self-movement determines its characteristics. In my explanation of Philosophy of Life, I proposed that generative power moves without ceasing within each thing. Each material object is thus a living thing, possessing life in a way that matches St. Thomas' basic ideas.

The existence of the myriad things and man is by substance, motion that is ceaseless. The moving force behind all motion is generative power. Motion of material beings are always material in nature. Man's motion, although psychophysical in nature, also possesses materiality. Material motions lead to material changes. This is so because material beings' motion is always accompanied by change. The faintest motion leads to a change in position. Thus, when man and the myriad things move, change always occurs. In fact, the existence of man, plants and animals is always undergoing change, thereby manifesting presence of life and showing actions of life. These changes are changes occurring in the whole, although theoretically, they are determined as accidental changes. Since substance and accidents together form an integral, any change in the accidents is also a change in the integral. Therefore they are also changes in the existence or of life itself.

In man and the myriad things, motion in the living substance proceeds from potency to act, as it is with angels' existence. However, angels have a spiritual substance, which experiences no change or annihilation. Therefore, angels continue moving without experiencing death. They are always living.

The life of man and the myriad things is substantially motion, which involves material changes. These changes lead to dissipation. When their material is dissipated to such an extent that they lose vitality, so much so that they are no longer fit to be triggered off by generative power, then motions stop, eventually leading to death. For instance, man's vital actions lead to bodily changes and constant dissipation of the body's material. When the body is so dissipated it can no longer move, then it becomes unfit for triggering off by generative force. When vital actions stop, man dies.

When a person is alive, his existence is always in motion. This existence and motion is a process leading from potency to act. It resembles moving pictures. During projection, a film is a moving existence, a living one. The substance of moving pictures is scene after scene of films, each of which is an "act" that has the potency to move. Electricity triggers off the film's potency. The films move, and together, form a living story. It is because of electrical power that they move to form a story, and thus, become a moving existence.

The ego's existence is a life constantly undergoing motion from potency to act. This process goes on with potency and act alternating from one to the other ceaselessly. Each act resembles one movie film. Joined together, these acts form a living story--the ego's existence. When the egos body becomes so dissipated (or because of sickness) that it can no longer move, then it loses the potency to live. Failure to proceed to "act" thus leads to death. In ancient Chinese philosophy, cosmic changes and the generation of the myriad things are attributed to a cyclic process called *Ta-hua* (Great Transformation) occurring within the cosmos. This Great Transformation is said to be the moving force behind all changes.

All organisms undergo such a motion, which always starts with generation and finally ends in annihilation. The existential motion of minerals goes on very faintly, leading to very little internal changes. However, because of the dissipation of the substance or because of destruction by an outside force, during which a reality loses the ability for motion, it disintegrates and stops existing.

The existence of each reality is motion. Since motion is differentiated into higher or lower levels, life is also classified that way. The motion of the absolute reality does not proceed from potency to act but is instead pure act. His life is perfect and represents the highest level. The existence of angels, spiritual in nature, proceeds from potency to act, but leads to no change. It consists solely of motion. Angels' life is eternal and is classified at a high level. Human existence is psychophysical, proceeds from potency to act, and is accompanied by changes in the corporeal body. When the corporeal body is dissipated, motion becomes impossible and it eventually dies. Man's soul then starts a life similar to the angels'. In the case of material things, their existence involves both motion, change and annihilation. Life is one, the life of the Creator. The life shared by creatures is differentiated into categories.

On the issue of whether or not God exists within the myriad things, St. Thomas gave an affirmative answer. He reasoned out that God's existence is itself His nature. (*Deus cum sit ipsum esse per essentiam, est intime in omnibus rebus.*) (VIII.a.1.c). He explained that God's existence in all things does not consist of having part of His nature in the collective nor in the form of accidents inhering in the substance. Rather, it is the presence of the creator in the things through triggering power. All things were created owing to God's moving force. They exist because of God's creative power, existing because of God's existence, which they share with. Since God's existence is life, then all the myriad things also share with the life of God.

Generative power, derived from God's creative power, is the moving force of things, or even, the life of things. As long as generative power resides in something, that thing possesses life and exists. Once it loses generative power, then all motions stop and life is terminated. A person possessing generative power within his whole body can move, and thus, has life and is existing. Once he loses generative power, he stops all motions and life stops. He dies and ceases existing.

There are two types of motion in man and the myriad things. One type is accidental change, such as physical and intellectual changes. Although this change occurs by the motion of substance and happens on the accidents, it belongs to the integral reality, or to the existence of things. Change in the ordinary sense are either quantitative or qualitative, both of which lead to no metaphysical difficulty. The other type of motion involves the motion of substance, or one that involves existence or life itself. This motion leads to metaphysical difficulties. Substantial changes may only be either generation or annihilation.

Change in an already existing substance may only be generation or anni-hilation. How is it possible for change to lead to *sheng-sheng* [perpe-tual generation of life]? This difficult issue has already been dealt with in my discussion on the existential motion of angels. It is explained through a process from an initial potency to "act" towards the second "act." The potency of the second "act" leads to the third "act." In turn, the third "act" leads to the fourth in an endless process from the "act" of the starting point of the motion towards the "act" of the motions terminus. This process always goes on from "act" to" act." Since "act" is existence and life, then the process goes from existence to existence or from life to life. This explains why it is *sheng-sheng* [perpetual generation of life]. The power behind motion is generative power. Moving force and the mover overlap. Therefore, generative power is also existence and life. When motion leads to the last "act," act loses the potency to live, whereby motion stops and the thing dies.

I dare not say that this explanation thoroughly solves metaphysi-cal difficulties and thus, cannot say that it is acceptable to all. These issues require further analysis and study.

Works Cited

Lin, An-wu. *T'sun-you yi-shih yü shih-chien* [Being, Consciousness and Practice]. Taipei: Ch'e-ta Books.

St. Thomas. *Summa Theologica*. I.9.VIII-LVII.

Translated by Carlos Tee

Chapter VI

On Accidents

I. Change in Life

Following Aristotle's philosophy, Scholasticism takes the nature of things as being made up of matter and form. Nature and existence together constitute the reality (substance). All realities are not quiescent. They are constantly in motion because "existence" is itself generative power. The generative power of things originate from cosmic generative power. In turn, the generative power of the cosmos is derived from the creative power of the Creator. The generative power of things possesses "form" that unites with "matter" which is material in nature and whose component parts are thus made into one. The materiality of "matter" is quiescent. In contrast, form is non-material in nature and shares in the generative power of the cosmos. Form is constantly in motion. In the case of man, his form is the soul, which is directly derived from creative power. The soul does not originate from cosmic generative power. The soul is the root of man's life. It exists in the whole of man's body as well as in all of its parts. Each of the pores of our skin must possess the soul in its entirety for it to continue living. Once they stop living, they lose the soul and turn into dead skin, after which they are dissociated from the rest of the body.

For Chu Hsi, things are composed of material force (*ch'i*) and principle (*li*). Principle corresponds to nature while material force corresponds to physical form. Principle is abstract and quiescent. In contrast, material force is concrete and dynamic. Principle must unite with material force for existence to occur. In traditional Chinese philosophy, material force is always reckoned as dynamic. It circulates without ceasing. The dynamism of the universe is derived from the material force of Heaven and Earth, known as Great *Ch'i* or Primeval *Ch'i*. Great *Ch'i* circulates around Heaven and Earth, generating the myriad things in the process. Human life is also dependent on the Primeval *Ch'i*. The Taoist teaching on "Nurturing of Life" (*Yangsheng*) gives importance to the conservation of the Primeval *Ch'i*. However, the Chinese also believe that "spirit" is the root of life. For this reason, rites for calling back the spirit of the dead form part of Chinese religious practices. The spirit also consists of material force, known as positive (*yang*) *ch'i*. In Confucianism, positive *ch'i* is taken to be dynamic while negative *ch'i* is quiescent. Both dynamism and quiescence are characteristics of material force. Principle is merely an abstract reason. Ordinarily, all of man's actions consist of material force. Each of these actions also has its own principles.

Chinese and Western philosophies do not agree on this point. Chinese philosophy differentiates between *hsing-shang* and *hsing-hsia*. Thus, actions of things are classified under *hsing-erh-hsia* which corresponds to material force. Principle (*li*) is *hsing-erh-shang,* which is an abstract realm. No discussion is ever made on dynamism or quiescence. However, in the generation of things in the universe, the dynamic force that leads to generation, although formless, is clearly discernible. In the *I Ching*, this dynamic force is called "the ingenuous" (*shen-miao*). Yet, this dynamic force that leads to the generation of the myriad things is also *ch'i*, or the cosmic material force also known as Great *Ch'i* or Primeval *Ch'i*. This is the reason why Chang Tsai and Wang Fu-chih considered *ch'i* to include both *hsing-erh-shang* and *hsing-erh-hsia*. *Ch'i* that is *hsing-erh-shang* takes no form and is called *shen* (spiritual, mysterious). This *ch'i* of the *hsing-erh-shang* type corresponds to "spiritual beings" in Western philosophy.

In Western philosophy, things are divided into spiritual and material. Spiritual things are formless. They are dynamic. In contrast, material things possess a form and are quiescent. Man's actions come from life, which in turn is derived from the soul. The soul is form while the body is matter. Actions of the body are triggered off by the soul. When the soul leaves the body, what remains of the latter is a lifeless corpse.

No distinction is made between spiritual beings and material things in Chinese philosophy. Instead, it distinguishes between the clarity and turbidity of material force. A clear material force tends to disperse itself while a turbid material force inclines towards condensation. The dispersion of material force means dynamism. A higher degree of clarity in the material force leads to "spirituality." The human mind, for instance, is formed with clear material force. Thus, its nature is vacuous and spiritual. This mind is itself the soul. This vacuous and spiritual mind in Chinese philosophy, taken as a spiritual being, overlaps with that of Western philosophy. In the latter, however, the soul is taken as form while in Chinese philosophy, the human mind is material force and prime matter. Actually, material force is prime matter or is material in nature; it cannot be spiritual.

In the case of man, his "form" is the soul, which is spiritual in nature. Among the myriad things in the universe, "form" is not material either. Non-material things, as the name implies, are not matter; neither are they spiritual. This point is difficult to explain. The "form" of the myriad things is spiritual but is not spiritual being. Only when joined with prime matter can they exist. Separated with matter, form ceases to exist. In contrast, man's form, the soul, is spiritual being. It can exist by itself.

Since form is dynamic, then each thing is also dynamic. We normally take living things as dynamic and non-living things as quiescent. Actually, the form of non-living things is also dynamic, albeit only visible in a very small degree. The motion of the form of things is immanent. It is life itself.

The motion of the form is united with the motion of matter. Matter is material in nature and made up of components. Once matter goes into action, the relationships among its internal components undergo changes. Thus, changes occur in the thing itself. Although material change occurs in matter, it is actually a change in the very thing itself. For this reason, it is a change in the substance. In Western philosophy, change in matter is accidental change. However, it is my personal belief that this change is a "change in life."

Change in life can be divided into two levels. Change in the first level is life's process of change from potency to act. This change proceeds from a reality that possesses the potency to a reality in act. In actual terms, it means a process leading from parents' potency to a fetus. In turn, the life potency of the fetus continues to lead to act, thus leading to a succession of changes--infancy, childhood, youth, maturity and old age. Once a reality in act loses its life potency, these changes stop going on and the person dies.

The second level of change consists of the changes in "matter" accompanying the change in the first level, or the change from life potency to act. Since a fetus' formation, growth continues to lead to changes in the body. This second level of change is the external manifestation of the first level of change. It is corporeal change. In philosophy, this is usually termed accidental change. We will call this change "manner of life."

II. Accidents

Again, following Aristotle, Scholasticism differentiates realities into substance (*substantia*) and accidents (*accidens*). Substance is also known as subject. Aristotle explained substance as "the subjects to which predicates belong and are not themselves predicates of anything else." This explanation puts the emphasis on the "subject." Substance is that which subsists without depending on others for its existence. In contrast, accidents depend on others in order to exist. Actually, each reality is an individual, which necessarily possesses accidents. After studying how accidents differ, Aristotle devised the following categorization:

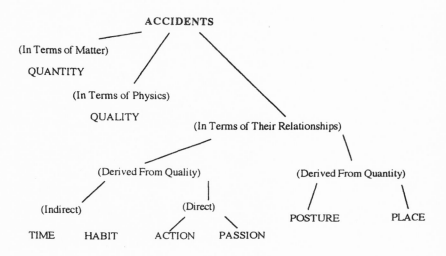

Accidents are divided into nine categories, namely: quantity, quality, relation, place, time, posture, action, passion and habit.

From these categories, we can see that the so-called accidents do not constitute substance but are instead form. When we normally refer to accidents, we usually have the idea of "subsistence" at the back of our mind. This has been the case since the days of Aristotle. This is the idea of" self-subsistence" or of "accidental subsistence." The term "accidents" is not directly associated with substance." The so-called accidents, are material in nature. As we know, matter attains a nature by the fusion of *materia* and *forma*. What are the *materia* and *forma* of these accidents? In terms of form, each of these accidents has a "form" of its own which serve as such, and is at the same time, where its significance lies. Color, height, size, speed and others are all "form." How about their matter? In fact, they have none of it. They have as their substance, the substance of the subject they adhere on. For instance, a color is the color of a certain object. Color itself is not an object. Any object has its own "existence." Because they have "existence," then they are "subsistent," or even, "self-subsistent."

When sugar crystals are dissolved in water, the "existence" of sugar and water fuse to form one existence. It is not that sugar subsists by adhering to water. Thus, the so-called accidents or adjuncts are not material objects. Rather, they are various types of "form." This form is not itself *forma* but is instead accidental form.

Accidental form traces its origins from matter, which is made up of components. When matter moves, the relationship between components experiences changes, which are manifested in an outward manner--accidental form. Changes in matter occur within time and space. Aristotle's categorization shows that accidents are derived from material and physical sources. A material source is related to space while a physical one has something to do with time. The components of matter cannot occupy the same position. This explains the concept of place. When components move, positions change. Motion in a material object extends from one component to another. It always involves a "before and after" and for this reason, it is related to time. We can thus say that accidental form is the relationship that occurs between time and space. Aristotle's categorization is also based on the relationship among the different accidents.

From the perspective of Chinese philosophy, accidental form is "function" (*yung*). Chinese philosophy explains things from the angle of substance, through which "function" is also dealt with as it emphasizes the unity between function and substance (reality).

The "existence" of things is vital power or generative power itself. Generative power endows dynamic force on form to fuse with matter. The dynamic force belonging to form is constantly in motion, through which change occurs in matter. Our body is constantly changing from the moment of birth to the time we die.

Material change can be classified into two: substantial change and change in the external form. The form of things are also of two types: substantial form and external form. Substantial form is derived from *forma*. The human body is composed of the torso and extremities, each one in its own proper position. Man's body has substantial form. It stands erect with the head sitting squarely on top of it. A dog's body has its own substantial form. This substantial form, which cannot be changed, is a limitation set by *forma* on *materia*. Each thing has its own substantial form. If this form is deficient, that person would be disabled. External form is a physical form resulting from the material exterior adhering on the substantial form. This physical form can be altered.

The "existence" of things is life, which is constantly in motion. For this reason, things change. When things undergo changes, their substantial form remain unchanged. What change are the accidental forms. Changes in the accidental form are usually related to quantitative change in space and qualitative change in time. Thus, Aristotle classified change in the universe into two types: substantial change and accidental change. Substantial change is either generation or annihilation while accidental change are either quantitative or qualitative. Changes in material life are of two levels, as we have explained above. Change in *materia* is of the second level. In turn, this second level of change is further classified into two: material substantial change and change in the accidental form. Material substantial change is a change in the matter of the substance without any change in the form of the substance. For instance, when a person's body grows, its form does not change at all. It remains the form of a human being. However, in this case, the body's substance changes. The components of the body's matter increases in quantity. Ordinarily, this change is called quantitative change. It is a type of accidental change. However, material components are not accidents but rather belong to the substance. Since the body is made up of components, if components are indeed accidents, then the body's substance would cease to exist. The addition or reduction of bodily components does not affect the body's existence. This bodily change is a change in the substance. In addition to this change in matter and substance, change in life also includes change in the external accidental form, such as height, consistency and color. These changes are myriad and are themselves changing with much frequency.

Qualitative change is also called change in the attributes of things. These attributes are capabilities or potencies, and even, talents. *Forma* possesses attributes. The same holds true with *materia*. These attributes are themselves the accidents. Changes in attributes are called accidental change because they are changes occurring in the accidents. Attributes cannot be called things precisely because of limitations set by *materia* and *forma*. All potencies are originally the substances of *materia* and *forma*, only that they face limitations in their functions. Let me cite an example. All human beings have intelligence. This intelligence differs from person to person. Some are more intelligent while some are less. This difference is a limitation. Chu Hsi believed that what limits talents or potencies is the clarity or turbidity of *ch'i*. A clear *ch'i* means great talents while a turbid *ch'i* means the opposite. A clear *ch'i* means goodness while a turbid *ch'i* means evil. We hold the view that this limitation comes from personality, which in turn, comes from the Creator. In traditional Chinese philosophy, this is called mandate, or specifically, the "Mandate of Heaven."

Therefore, the so-called qualitative change is a change in function (*yung*). When life moves, the potencies of the substance are necessarily put into action. When potency, which forms part of the substance, is activated, function results. Qualitative change is a change in potency. This change in potency is achieved in time. Since function is motion and since motion of things involves a "before and after," which is merely form, then function is not substance (reality).

However, just like quantitative change, qualitative change is also classified into substantial change and change in the external form. Qualitative change is a change in the attributes, which are limitations set on potency or talent. When attributes change, these limitations also experience changes. This latter type of change must be called substantial change. When in function, potency or talent manifests itself in the exterior. This manifestation (change) is accidental change. Thus, when a person gains more intelligence with study, it shows up in his actions. This is a change in the external form.

III. Conclusions

Accidents are neither things nor the form of things. Each substance (reality) is made up of *materia* and *forma*. Matter possesses a substantial form derived from *forma*. The components of substance share various external relationships. Each of these relationships has its own "form"--accidental form. These accidental forms, such as color, quantity and location, manifest various limitations of the subject, which thus becomes a concrete object. *Forma* possesses a power and is constantly in motion through which it enters into various relationships, which are called attributes. Ordinarily, attributes are considered as potencies. Potency is not an accident. All objects have their own substances, which consist of matter and form. In comparison, potency possesses no matter. Thus, potency or attributes are the various relationships of *forma* with the external world. To cite an example, man has a *forma* which is the soul. It shares various relationships with the outside world and performs various functions. Man is a relative being, not an absolute one, which is pure act. Before they received their existence, relative beings did not exist. Their existence resulted from a process leading from potency to act. This represents the first level of change in life. Once a relative being starts existing, it enters into various relationships with the outside world. These relationships also proceed from potency to act. What we ordinarily refer to as potency of relationships is itself *forma*. The *forma* of each reality has the principle of external actions. Thus, when a reality acts, it does so based on this principle derived from the *forma*. Thus, what we normally call potency is itself this principle. *Materia* also has its attributes, such as texture, taste, etc. These are the principles of *materia's* relationship with the outside world and which are derived from *forma*. Thus, man's ability to speak comes from man's *forma*. The hardness or brittle nature of a piece of wood is also derived from its *forma*. If attributes or potencies adhere in the substance, they do so not as a thing but as power. This power is itself generative power or the motion of life. In the Philosophy of Life, we take attributes or potencies as the outward manifestation of life. Life is action. Among relative beings in the universe, action always involves a "before and after" and uses the body or objects as tools to perform actions. Action therefore has form. Explained more concretely, the existence of a reality is motion or life. When life acts, it leads to changes. It makes all the limitations of *materia* experience change, that is, the component parts of matter increase or decrease in quantity, in which case, it is called quantitative change. When life acts, the changes that occur make all the limitations of *forma* experience change. This means that the characteristics of the reality experience change. Thus, a person becomes brighter or duller, more violent or mild-mannered. These are qualitative changes. Both qualitative and quantitative changes cannot alter *forma*; nor can they change a reality's substance. For this reason, they are called accidental forms.

Accidental forms are manifestations of life or living. A person's life is an endless series of qualitative and quantitative changes. Life is activity. The life activities of the universe and the myriad things in it constantly lead to change. Changes in the life of the universe and the myriad things can be classified as follows:

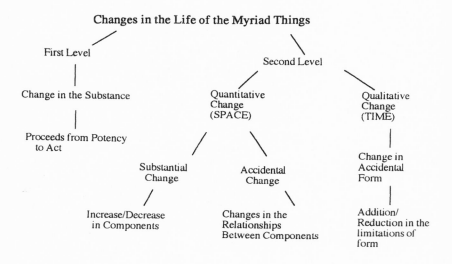

Translated by Carlos Tee

Chapter VII

Duality and Change: Yin and Yang

I. Action and Motion

In the Chinese language, *hsing* (action) and *tung* (motion) are two characters joined together to form a term that expresses movement.[1] In his exposition of the philosophy of action, the late President Chiang Kai-shek distinguished these two characters by explaining variations in their meaning:

> What makes potency converge is matter and what releases potency is power. Although potency, power and matter are three separate terms, they require each other as they perform a function leading to the formation of an integral thing. Therefore matter is power itself and vice-versa. These two are inseparable. However, potency, not matter, is the substance. (Chiang, "Sun" 2047)

> Thus, we are made to understand that action and motion are two different things. Motion is not identical to action but action may include certain types of motion. Whereas action is constant, motion is temporary. While action is necessary, motion is incidental. Action is voluntary whereas motion is most often passive. Action is obedient to the laws of nature and attuned to human feelings. . .Viewed in terms of their value and the results they bring, while motion can lead to good or evil

---

(1) [Translator's Note] In Chinese, a term may be composed of one or more characters. In this case, the Chinese term for "movement" is made up of two characters *hsing* and *tung*.

action can only lead to the good. . . . The "action" we are dealing with here is never to be confused with motion in its ordinary sense " (1244).

President Chiang Kai-shek considered action as the natural development of human nature, and thus, belonging to the substance of man. Any motion exterior to the nature of a person who moves belongs to that person's functions. Potency and characteristics belong to the substance of man. Potency brings forth power and power is action. When expressed exteriorly, action is motion.

Let me explain further the meaning of these two characters based on the late President Chiang Kai-shek's definitions of action and motion, i.e., action as the development of life and motion as the movement of matter.

The substance of life is being. Being is a concrete reality whose existence is power itself. Described in terms of substance, power has no structure of its own. It is not made up of parts but is instead a pure integrity. The existence of the Absolute Being is itself His substance. The power of the Absolute Reality is also His substance. The Absolute Reality--God--has being as His substance. His being is perfect. It cannot change but is constantly in act. Thus, he is called *actus purus*. Unchanging and unmoving while at the same time having no potency whatsoever, He is constantly living. He is the "unmoving perfection" (*wu-wei erh ch'eng*).

The act of God is not derived from potency. His is a constant and everlasting perfection. The substance of God is a pure unity and is indivisible. Therefore, the being of God is constantly in act within Himself. His act is Pure Act, unmoving, unchanging and not generating. The power of the Pure Act is its own substance. It is not a function but is life itself. The life of God is itself His own being and also his own substance. Since he is perfect being, then there is no development in him whatsoever. He is pure life.

The substance of man has a psychophysical nature. The life of man, therefore, is a psychophysical life. This psychophysical life is a "living" life. This psychophysical activity is also a psychophysical motion. With motion, there is change and generation. A psychophysical life begins and ends in time. Therefore, it involves development, thus indicating change and generation. Hence, man's life is a process of motion that leads to change. Viewed in terms of its substance, we can say that the substance of human life possesses the power to develop. This power is itself generative power. By nature, generative power causes natural development, and is, therefore, action. Since man's substance is psychophysical and since generative power develops the act of life (or the psychophysical act), then the substance of human life is also motion. Thus, we can also say that the development of human life is movement.

Generative power leads to movement which causes dual changes in man's life--both physical and spiritual. For generative power to create changes, it must not itself be pure power. Even if all pure powers were to work together, they still would not create change. For change to occur, two factors are required. Two types of powers, not one, are necessary to cause material and spiritual changes in man's life. These two forces fuse in a multiplicity of ways that lead to varied consequences. The manner in which these two powers combine lies in nothing else but the unifying principle or the form of things. When these two forces fuse, they bring forth the matter of things.

A unity [one] is pure and incapable of change. Duality is the moving force behind change. The cosmos is ever changing in its generation of the myriad things in the universe. The myriad things themselves constantly undergo change in search of their own development. The creative power of the Creator brought about the generative power which is itself the universe. Therefore, it must be that the cosmic generative power is not one and simple but instead constitutes two. Cosmic generative power encompasses two types of power which fuse together to form things. The Chinese classic "*I Ching*" says: The successive movement of *yin* and *yang* constitutes the Way (*Tao*). What issues from the Way is good, and that which realizes it is individual nature." (Chan 266) The two types of generative power can also be called *yin* and *yang*.

Life is existence. What existence is mutually involved with is corporeality. Since existence is life, then it must be constantly undergoing change with the aim of development. The principle (*li*) of change is corporeality while the power behind change is generative power. The generative power that leads to change cannot be one but instead must be two.

Chang Tsai affirms that "*Ch'i* (ether) exists in dual modes. It extends (*shen*) and transforms (*hua*), and all things in the universe are generated without end" (*Cheng-meng, Ts'an-liang*). Ch'eng Hao writes:

> All the myriad things have their opposite counterparts. When there is *yin*, there is *yang*. When there is good, there is evil. As *yang* increases, *yin* decreases, and as goodness is augmented, evil is diminished. This principle can be extended far and wide. Man only needs to know this principle." (*Erh-Ch'eng Ch'üan-shu*, Book 2, *Yi-shu*, Part 1, *Ming-tao yu-lu*, Part 1)

The Creator used his creative power to bring about generative power, which has a dual nature. Did the generative power split into two from an original one, or was it made up of two types from the very start? Once created, generative power was the universe itself. Once the universe existed, it started to move. At the moment of its creation, generative power was of two types which were distinguishable but inseparable from one another. In Chinese philosophy, there was the issue of whether *yin* and *yang* were one *ch'i* in the beginning or two. Both Chou Tun-i and Chang Tsai proposed the unity of the substance of the *ch'i,* and its later division into *yin* and *yang*. However, Wang Ch'uan-shan proposed that the *ch'i* possessed a dual substance (*yin* and *yang*) although it was still not yet manifested. Wang's idea was derived from the *I Ching* whose divinatory symbols were formed by the juxtaposition of — and --. There is no question of anteriority or posteriority between the two. Both — and -- existed at the same time. This led to Wang's conclusion on the "parallel construction of the *ch'ien* and the *k'un* (male and female principles)."

Generative power consists two types of power. Thus, the universe is likewise of two types of power, which initiate all changes in it. These two, although differing in ther attributes, are constantly joined together. Their union leads to the formation of a new combined object.

What are the attributes of these two types of power? Since power is not material, we cannot talk about its attributes. We can only describe power as either strong or weak. To explain the concepts of *ch'ien k'un* and *yin-yang*, the *I Ching* only mentions such terms as hard and soft, advance and retreat, action and station. The two powers of the generative power are two different powers that mutually regulate one another.

Mat is separated into male and female. Man exists as male or as female. This is not chance, nor an *accident*, but is something related to one's nature. Abstractly, man is a rational animal. But in terms of existence, man exists as male or female. The genders are two types of generative power which unite to procreate a new human being.

The two types of generative power initiate motion in the myriad things in the universe. With motion, there comes change and with change generation is brought about. With generation, new things are brought forth.

Ordinarily, we say that a man is the better half of a woman and vice-versa. Man and woman join to become one life. Only in this way does human life become complete. The rest of creation need *yin* and *yang* to unite and generate new things. Constant and never-ending change in the universe is due to the ceaseless operations between these two generative powers. In fact, Chinese philosophy proposes that *yin* and *yang* make up the myriad things in the universe. These myriad things are either *yin* or *yang*, thus forming the Chinese philosophy of contrasting pairs. Thus, we have: heaven and earth, sun and moon, night and day, hot and cold, long and short, big and small, fat and thin, strong and weak, hard and soft, dry and wet, indulgent and strict, justice and self-interest, wise and foolish, and other contrastive pairs. Of course, these terms have their parallels in western languages and thought. However, they are not taken as philosophical principles in the West. In Chinese philosophy, these terms were formed mainly due to differing substantial factors, that is, they are made up of *yin* and *yang* elements. In human life, one must aspire for the middle ground between these contrasting pairs, neither surpassing nor falling behind. The *I Ching* discusses principles of changes in the universe, the very same principles governing *yin* and *yang*.

II. Change

In Western philosophy, change is often seen as a motion involving one element. Using dialectics, Hegel expounded on movement. For Hegel, change involves thesis, antithesis and synthesis. Marx and Lenin adopted dialectics with emphasis on antithesis, using it as a means for their struggle. Bergson, however, proposes that life is continuous and uninterrupted unilinear motion, which he likens to an ever-flowing river. He describes it as *dureé*. In Chinese philosophy, cosmic changes, which lead to multifarious effects and the generation of myriad things, are the union of *yin* and *yang* elements.

Motion in the universe, initiated by the two types of generative power, must be regulated and suitable so as to be in accordance with principles of motion. The Creator made the universe with cosmic change and the generation of myriad things in mind. From concrete facts, we are aware that new life is the fruit of the union of *yin* and *yang* elements. Therefore, the generative power of the cosmos must be made up of two types-to be able to generate new things--which fuse together and which neither negate nor destroy each other. If husband and wife oppose each other and do not achieve union, how can they procreate? Therefore, the first principle of change of the two types of generative powers is collaborative union. This must also be evident in the myriad things. Darwin's "survival of the fittest" is not the principle of evolution. It is only one manifestation of the survival of the myriad things, and a principle showing the hierarchy of life forms and their mutual provision. When a species of plant or animal becomes extinct, it must be due to a living environment unsuitable for life. Conversely, the appearance of a new species of plant or animal results from the appearance of a living environment suitable for this life form. In this case, the generative power has generated a new kind of living thing.

The second principle of motion of the two types of generative power is the *chung-yung* (golden mean). The golden mean means appropriateness or the so-called "regulated and suitable" (*chung-chieh*). That is, the combination of the two forces must be regulated and suitable not only in the thing itself but also in its external environment. The divinatory changes in the *I Ching* must be in harmony with timing and position, a condition referred to in the *I Ching* as the "centrality and rightness" (*chung-cheng*). Thus, a well-regulated and suitable change indicates harmony. Chinese thinkers and artists have particularly lauded the natural harmony existing in the universe likening it to heavenly music (*T'ien-yueh* or *T'ien-lai*). Similarly, in appreciation of the order in the natural world, saints of the Catholic Church praised the wonders of the Creator.

In Chinese philosophy, cosmic changes are said to be cyclic or "repeating in cycle" (*chou erh fu shih*). Human events and history also follow a cyclical pattern. Isn't there a cycle of night and day? Isn't there an annual cycle of the four seasons? The principle of change of the two generative powers is continuous progress. The universe is in a process of evolution, not devolution. However, progress faces many limitations. For instance, two forces always proceeding on a parallel direction will never meet and unite. Therefore, a cyclical motion is necessary for mutual collaboration. When the two types of generative power change, they meet cyclically to cause small changes. Greater changes result from continuous progress ahead, that is, advancement within the cyclic process.

Furthermore, the myriad things in the cosmos are material in nature. Only man's soul is spiritual. In the process of change, material things suffer wear and tear. Speaking in general, there is the so-called "conservation of matter." However, all matter does not always remain conserved. Thus, we can say that although the evolution of the universe is generally considered as constant progress ahead, the process may be a devolution, speaking in a material sense. Thus, it may be possible that global changes could lead to conditions unsuitable for human life, whereupon the human race may be wiped out from the face of the earth.

The two types of generative power can bring forth other types of power in the course of their changes. These new powers also change and participate as causes in the generation of things. The *I Ching* says: "*Yin* and *yang* gave rise to the four forms which in turn led to the eight trigrams." However, Han Dynasty Confucianists and Sung dynasty rationalists propose that "*Yin* and *yang* gave rise to the five agents. The five agents generated male and female elements which in turn led to the myriad things." The concept of the four forms was abandoned by the time of the Han Dynasty. Han Dynasty philosophy on the five agents, on the other hand, enjoyed considerable popularity even in latter periods. The concept of the five agents, accepted as the cause of the myriad things in Chinese philosophical thought on the cosmos and human life, exerted a tremendous impact on Chinese culture. I think that the use of numbers four and five is too dull and numerative. Cosmic changes are mysterious and esoteric and therefore, no rigid rules can be applied to their forms. When the two generative powers unite, other new powers may result. Thus, the generation of myriad things in the universe is not solely attributed to *yin* and *yang*. Other powers derived from the two generative powers also participate as causes of the generation of things. To cite an example, the causes of a fetus are of course a spermatozoa and an ovum. But inherent in these two are other powers which form the fetus together. We thus conclude that the four forms and five agents in Chinese philosophy are in principle valid. Numerically, however, both are prosaic and erroneous.

Appendix: The Tao of Physics

Both Aristotle and St. Thomas Aquinas propose that the human intellect has its origins in sensation. Concepts are formulated based on sense impression. Therefore, philosophy is not a baseless fantasy. Neither does it stop at abstract concepts but rather seeks proof in the world of concrete realities. When I explain philosophy of life, I deal with being based on actual existence. There is, therefore, a need to turn to the natural sciences and look to physics for corroboration. In the following appendix, I have quoted the views of physicists.

1. The Universe

When we study the universe as a whole, with its millions of galaxies, we have reached the largest scale of space and time; and again, at that cosmic level, we discover that the universe is not static--it is expanding! This has been one of the most important discoveries in modern astronomy. A detailed analysis of the light received from distant galaxies has shown that the whole swarm of galaxies expands and that it does so in a well orchestrated way; the recession velocity of any galaxy we observe is proportional to the galaxy's distance. The more distant the galaxy, the faster it moves away from us; at double the distance, the recession velocity will also double. (Capra 217)

From the world of the very large, from the expanding cosmos, let us now return to the world of the infinitely small. . . This exploration of the submicroscopic world has been motivated by one basic question which has occupied and stimulated human thought throughout the ages: what is matter made of? Ever since the beginning of natural philosophy, men and women have speculated about this question, trying to find the "basic stuff" of which all matter is made; but only in our century has it been possible to seek an answer by undertaking experiments. With the help of a highly sophisticated technology, physicists were able to explore first the structure of atoms, finding that they consisted of nuclei and electrons, and then the structure of the atomic nuclei which were found to consist of protons and neutrons, commonly called nucleons. In the last two decades, they have gone yet another step farther and have begun to investigate the structure of the nucleons--the constituents of the atomic nuclei--which, again, do not seem to be ultimate elementary particles, but seem to be composed of other entities. (Capra 220-221)

Energy is one of the most important concepts used in the description of natural phenomena. As in everyday life, we say that a body has energy when it has the capacity for doing work...The mass of a body, on the other hand, is a measure of its weight, i.e. of the pull of gravity on the body... Now, relativity theory tells us that mass is nothing but a form of energy. . . Once it is seen to be a form of energy, mass is no longer required to be indestructible, but can be transformed into other forms of energy. This can happen when subatomic particles collide with one another. (Capra 222-223)

2.   The Cosmic Dance

The exploration of the subatomic world in the twentieth century has revealed that intrinsically dynamic nature of matter. It has shown that the constituents of atoms, the subatomic particles, are dynamic patterns which do not exist as isolated entities, but as integral parts of an inseparable network of interactions. These interactions involve a ceaseless flow of energy manifesting itself as the exchange of particles; a dynamic interplay in which particles are created and destroyed without end in a continual variation of energy patterns. The particle interactions give rise to the stable structures which build up the material world, which again do not remain static, but oscillate in rhythmic movements. The whole universe is thus engaged in endless motion and activity; in a continual cosmic dance of energy.

This dance involves an enormous variety of patterns but, surprisingly, they fall into few distinct categories. The study of the subatomic particles and their interactions thus reveals a great deal of order. All atoms, and consequently all forms of matter in our environment, are composed of only three massive particles: the proton, the neutron and the electron. A fourth particle, the photon, is massless and represents the unit of electromagnetic radiation. The proton, the electron and the photon are all stable particles, which means they live for ever unless they become involved in a collision process where they can be annihilated. The neutron, on the other hand, can disintegrate spontaneously. This disintegration is called a 1 ' beta decay' and is the basic process of a certain type of radioactivity. It involves the transformation of the neutron into a proton, accompanied by the creation of an electron and a new type of massless particle, called the neutrino. Like the proton and the electron, the neutrino is also stable. It is commonly denoted by the Greek letter υ (nu), and the process of beta decay is symbolically written as

$$n \rightarrow p + e^{'-} + \upsilon$$

The transformation of neutrons into protons in the atoms of a radioactive substance entails a transformation of these atoms into atoms of an entirely different kind. The electrons which are created in the process are emitted as a powerful radiation which is widely used in biology, medicine and industry. The neutrinos, on the other hand, although emitted in equal number, are very difficult to detect because they have neither mass nor electric charge. (Capra 249-250)

All these particles can be created and annihilated in collision processes; each one can also be exchanged as a virtual particle and thus contribute to the interaction between other particles. This would see, to result in a vast number of different particle interactions, but fortunately, although we do not yet know why, all these interactions seem to fall into four categories with markedly different interaction strengths:

The strong interactions

The electromagnetic interactions

The weak interactions

The gravitational interactions

Among them, the electromagnetic and gravitational interactions are the most familiar, because they are experienced in the large-scale world. The gravitational interaction acts between all particles, but is so weak it cannot be detected experimentally. In the macroscopic world, however, the huge number of particles making up massive bodies combine their gravitational interaction to produce the force of gravity which is the dominating force in the universe at large. Electromagnetic interactions take place between all charged particles. They are responsible for the chemical processes, and the formation of all atomic and molecular structures. The strong interactions hold the protons and the neutrons together in the atomic nucleus. They constitute the nuclear force, by far the strongest of all forces in nature. Electrons, for example, are bound to the atomic nuclei by the electromagnetic force with energies of about ten units (called electron volts), whereas the nuclear force holds protons and neutrons together with energies of about ten million units!

The nucleons are not the only particles interacting through the strong interactions. In fact, the overwhelming majority are strongly interacting particles. Of all the particles known today, only five (and their antiparticles) do not participate in the strong interactions. These are the photon and the four ' leptons' listed in the top part of the table. Thus all the particles fall into two broad groups: leptons and ' hadrons', or strongly interacting particles. The hadrons are further divided into ' mesons' and ' baryons' which differ in various ways, one of them being that all baryons have distinct antiparticles, whereas a meson can be its own antiparticle. (Capra 182)

The following paragraphs were quoted from Gary Zukav's *The Dancing Wu Li Masters.*

3. Matter is Energy

The distinction between organic and inorganic is a conceptual prejudice. It becomes even harder to maintain as we advance into quantum mechanics. Something is organic, according to our definition, if it can respond to processed information. The astounding discovery awaiting newcomers to physics is that the evidence gathered in the development of quantum mechanics indicates that subatomic "particles" constantly appear to be making decisions! More than that, the decisions they seem to make are based on decisions made elsewhere. Subatomic particles seem to know instantaneously what decisions are made elsewhere, and elsewhere can be as far away as another galaxy! (Zukav 47)

If there is any ultimate stuff of the universe, it is pure energy, but subatomic particles are not "made of" energy, they are energy. This is what Einstein theorized in 1905. Subatomic interactions, therefore, are interactions of energy with energy. At the subatomic level there is no longer a clear distinction between what is and what happens, between the actor and the action. At the subatomic level the dancer and the dance are one.

According to particle physics, the world is fundamentally dancing energy; energy that is everywhere and incessantly assuming this form and then that. (Zukav 193)

The world view of particle physics is that of a world without "stuff," where what is = what happens, and where an unending tumultuous dance of creation, annihilation and transformation runs unabated within a framework of conservation laws and probability. (Zukav 195)

When physicists refer to the mass of a particle, unless they indicate otherwise, they are referring to the mass of the particle when it is at rest. The mass of a particle at rest is called its rest mass. Any mass other than a rest mass is called a relativistic mass. Since the mass of any particle increases with velocity, a particle can have any number of relativistic masses. . . The masses of particles, whether at rest or in motion, are measured in electron volts. An electron volt has nothing to do with electrons. An electron volt is a unit of energy. (Zukav 202)

A special characteristic of quantum mechanics lies in its proposition that there exists no matter in this universe, only energy, constantly moving energy. What causes the formation of matter's subatomic particles is not matter itself but moving force. When studied, this moving force engaged in constant change does not necessarily exist. Whether or not the particle one is studying is the always same particle also poses a problem. This condition is comparable to that of river water. When you step into the river, the water continues to flow. The water you intended to step on has already flowed away.

Quantum mechanics views subatomic particles as "tendencies to exist" or "tendencies to happen." How strong these tendencies are is expressed in terms of probabilities. A subatomic particle is a quantum," which means a quantity of something. What that something is, however, is a matter of speculation. . . At the subatomic level, mass and energy change unceasingly into each other. (Zukav 32)

In the absence of an objective reality, all realities are observed subjectively. Without observation, there would not be any reality.

The new physics, quantum mechanics, tells us clearly that it is not possible to observe reality without changing it. If we observe certain particle collision experiment, not only do we have a way of proving that the result would have been the same if we had not been watching it, all that we know indicates that it would not have been the same, because the result that we got was affected by the fact that we were looking for it. (Zukav 30-31)

4. Constant Motion

The basic elements of matter, subatomic particles, are constantly in motion which physicists playfully call a "dance."

Subatomic particles forever partake of this unceasing dance of annihilation and creation. In fact, subatomic particles are this unceasing dance of annihilation and creation. This twentieth-century discovery, with all its psychedelic implications, is not a new concept. In fact, it is very similar to the way that much of the earth's population, including the Hindus and the Buddhists, view their reality. (Zukav 217)

Subatomic particles do not just sit around being subatomic particles. They are beehives of activity. An electron, for example, constantly is emitting and absorbing photons. These photons are not full-fledged photons, however. They are a now-you-see-it-now-you-don't variety. They are exactly like real photons except that they don't fly off on their own. They are re-absorbed by the electron almost as soon as they are emitted. Therefore, they are called "virtual" photons. (Zukav 222)

Virtual photons, even if they were charged particles, would not be visible in a bubble chamber because of their extremely short lives. Their existence is inferred mathematically. Therefore, this extraordinary theory, that particles exert a force on each other by exchanging other particles, clearly is a "free creation" of the human mind.

5. Dual Elements

The second characteristic of a subatomic particle is its charge. Every subatomic particle has a positive, a negative, or a neutral charge. Its charge determines how the particle will behave in the presence of other particles. If a particle has a neutral charge, it is utterly indifferent to other particles regardless of what charge they may have. Particles with positive and negative charges, however, behave quite differently toward each other. Positively and negatively charged particles are attracted to particles with the opposite sign and repelled by particles with the same sign. Two positively charged particles, for example, find each other's company quite repulsive and immediately put as much distance between themselves as possible. The same is true of two negatively charged particles. A negatively charged particle and a positively charged particle, on the other hand, are irresistibly attracted to each other, and they immediately move toward one another if they are able to do so. (Zukav 206)

6. Conclusion

The two books on physics quoted above both emphasize the highly mystical nature of the cosmos as contemplated in the oriental philosophies of India and China which, however, find some corroboration in modern physics. Cosmic movement, change and unity are obvious facts. In one of these books, Capra says the following comments about the *I Ching*:

The *Changes* is a book from which one may not hold aloof. Its tao is forever changing--alteration, movement without rest, flowing through the six empty places, rising and sinking without fixed law, firm and yielding transform each other. They cannot be confined within a rule. It is only change that is at work here. (123)

Works Cited

Capra, Fritjof. *The Tao of Physics: An exploration of the parallels between modern physics and Eastern mysticism.* London: Fontan a Paperbacks, 1985.

Chan, Wing-tsit. *A Source Book in Chinese Philosophy.* Princeton: Princeton UP, 1963.

Chiang Kai-shek. *Chung-li chih-nan-hsing-yi hsüeh-shuo yü yang-ming chih-hsing-he-yi che-hsüeh chih tsung-he yen-chiu. Chiang-kung ch' üan-chi* [Chiang Kai-shek Collection]. Vol. 2. Ed. Chang Ch'i-yun. Taipei.

---. *Hsing te tao-li .Chiang-kung ch' üan-chi* [Chiang Kai-shek Collection]. Vol. 2. Ed. Chang Ch'i-yun. Taipei.

Zukav, Gary. *The Dancing Wu Li Masters: An Overview of the New Physics.* New York: Bantam, 1979.

Translated by Carlos Tee

Chapter VIII

The Basis of One

I. The One of Realities

In philosophy, ordinary concepts in society often become profound issues. *Being* is a word often said in daily life, even by children. In philosophy, however, *being* becomes the focus of metaphysical studies. It is a topic that belongs to the highest philosophical level. Similarly, *one* is a word used in everyday language. But in philosophy, the same word constitutes a profound topic in metaphysics. It is an issue debated upon by philosophers, but they hardly reached a conclusion on its meaning.

I would like to discuss three issues about one.[1] First, how can a reality become one? Second, since realities are constantly in the process of change, what makes them constantly one? The third is a problem related to *persona*. What are the basic constituents of a *persona*? All these questions are interrelated.

What makes a reality *one*?

What makes a table one table and not many? Why is it that a *one* must have its components together? Why is a person one person? and a tree one tree?

---

(1) In Greek philosophy, the *one* is regarded by Plato as a conceptual *one*. The multiple is a sharing of this concept. Aristotle divided *unum* into two: *logical*, as a phrase to explain a subject; and *substantial*, explaining substance as having four different possibilities: *First*, as a means to explain inalienable action; *Second*, as referring to a substance; *Third*, as a way to express category; *Foruth*, as a way to express an indivisible concept.

In explaining the unique character of God, Catholic theologians substantially equate *one* and *being*. Truth and Good are likewise equated with being.

Kant stressed *one* as a category of knowledge while Hegel used *one* as the starting point of his dialectics. Contemporary western philosophers often analyze *one* using mathematics and psychology as tools of their study.

The reason why a table is a table is that the plan combined the different parts into one table. A house is a house because the construction plan joined all parts together to form a house. This is evident to all. Materials are needed to create a table or a house. In addition, a construction plan is needed. The material is corporeal matter (*chih*) and the plan is the principle (*li*) or the shape. Matter can be compared to material force (*ch'i*) and form to principle (*li*). Things are made up of matter and form, or of *li* and *ch'i*. A table or a house is one because of its shape. A thing is one because of its form or *li*.

Speaking in an abstract, theoretical manner, a plan for a house or a table joins different parts into something in the shape of a house or table. In practical terms, however, the plan can only delineate the position of each component. It cannot make all parts form one single table or house. In my discussion of substance, I have already said that matter (*chih*) and principle (*li*) together form nature." Nature and existence together form a concrete being. Theoretically, it is possible to say that nature and existence form the substance. In practical terms, existence requires a generative power to be able to unite with nature so as to form a substance. Therefore, the cause of a substance is mainly existence. Existence itself is power--generative power. Generative power is life itself.

Man is a rational animal. A rational animal is "existing" if this person exists. This person exists because he lives. If he is not living, then he does not exist at all. Immediately after death, a person may appear like any rational animal, but he no longer is a man because he's dead and no longer rational. Therefore, man's existence is life itself. Of course, one may say that rationality is man's form or man's formal *li*. The form of man is the soul. Hence the soul is the reason why man "exists," not because of the life of the generative power. If rationality, as the form of man, is but an abstract form, then it must not be able to cause man's "existence." If the soul is man's formal *li*, then the soul must not be abstract, but must be a concretely living soul that causes human life. Once the soul leaves, man loses life and no longer exists. Man's existence is life itself and life is man's soul. Man *is* because of the soul and through it man becomes one. The soul is itself man's generative power.

The soul makes man's every component unite and form one person. It unites and encompasses each component. Every part of man has life. A limb or a finger that loses its functions has no life and therefore separates from the body.

A tree or a flowering plant becomes one because of its life. A trunk of a tree or a leaf of a flowering plant unites to become one because of the life of the tree or plant. A thing exists because of its life. If a branch or a leaf dries up and loses life, it separates from the one body. If the tree or the plant itself dries up and dies, its branches and leaves also separate and die. The life of the tree or of the plant is itself the generative power of that tree or plant.

A stone or a mountain is made up of many components bound together by an inner force. This force also causes inner changes to happen within this piece of stone or this mountain. Although this force does not compare with those of animals or plants which circulate freely within the body, it likewise reaches every component part of the whole. If not, that component would be detached from the whole. The ancient Chinese often said that each mountain has its own veins. Improper cultivation of mountains destroys these veins and causes avalanches. Inanimate objects also possess generative power and exhibit immanent action. Thus, Chinese philosophy recognizes that there is life in them.

Every concrete reality is a subsistent because of its existence. Every subsistent is one and is so because of its existence. Existence is an active presence. It is life or creative power itself.

II. Generative Power Forms the Basis of the Identity of Concrete Realities

In philosophy, two questions arise from the concept of one concrete reality. The first is related to the question of how the same type of objects becomes a multiple. For instance, in a number of persons, what makes a person one? The second is related to identity.[2] What makes one person the same *one* from his birth to old age?

Scholastic philosophy explains the causation of the "individual" through the concept of matter. The same types of things share the same form. What makes an individual is matter's function of making the "potency" of form quantifiable in actual objects. Examples include how high a person's intelligent quotient is, or a person's body weight and height, skin color, and the relative positions of one's eyes, ears, nose and mouth. All these characteristics are derived from matter. That is, matter limits the quantity of form's potency, which in turn affects the number of individuals. The Chinese philosopher Chu Hsi, proposes that an individual is derived from material force (*ch'i*). *Li* is the material principle while *ch'i* is the material form. Individuals differ not because of the material principle but because of material form. In turn, material form depends on the clarity or turbidity of the *ch'i* (material force).

Since matter or material force (*ch'i*) limits the principle (*li*) or nature, from where does the quantity or clarity of an individual's material force (*ch'i*) arise? That is to say, why is it that my intelligence is this much and why is my external appearance like this? Chinese philosophy says that it is because of life. Mencius himself talked about nature and life. A person's human nature is determined by the Mandate of Heaven (*t'ien-ming*). A person's characteristics, or what Chu Hsi called the nature of *ch'i* and *chih*, are also determined by the Mandate of Heaven, because *ch'i* cannot determine its own clarity. Human ch'i

---

(2) Locke discussed identity in Chapter 27 of his essay *"Concerning Human Understanding"*. He proposed that identity is related to the body's physiological structure. Nevertheless, he admitted that man has a spirit from which comes memory. For him, therefore memory must be part of the concept of identity. In Book One Chapter 6 of his *Treaties on Human Nature*, Hume proposed the use of psychology to explain human identity. He said that society's substance constantly changes although it remains the same substance throughout.

is much purer than that of material objects. That is because man has a human nature. Differences in the clarity of persons' *ch'i* are determined by the Mandate of Heaven. Although matter or *ch'i* limits physical nature (or *li*) and forms human nature into personal characteristics, what determines the quantity of matter or the clarity and turbidity of *ch'i* is not chance as Chu Hsi proposes.

In his *Classified Conversations* (*Chu-tzu yü lei*), Chu Hsi writes:

> Those endowed with refined and brilliant material force will become sages and men of virtue, and will be enabled to acquire a comprehensive and correct principle. Those endowed with clear and bright material force will become talented and forthright. Those endowed with simple and rich material force will become mild. Those endowed with pure and lofty material force will become noble. Those endowed with full and thick material force will become rich. Those endowed with long lasting material force will live long. Those endowed with thin and turbid material force will become foolish, unworthy, poor, humble, and short-lived.

> He further says: Although nature is the same in all men, it is inevitable that in most cases the various elements in their material endowment are unbalanced. (*Chu-tzu yü-lei*, Book 1, *Jen-wu chih hsing* [The Nature of Things and Men], *Ch'i-chih chih hsing* [The Nature of Material Force and Matter])

> Someone asked him: "*Yin* and *yang* are supposed to be balanced. But why is it that the wise and the unwise do not come in the right proportion? Why is it that gentlemen are few and bad men all too many?" He answered: "That's because what they have are complicated. How do you expect them to come in a balanced proportion?"

> Again, someone asked: "Are sages then born by chance and not by a will of heaven?" He answered: "Heaven and earth never said that they will deliberately cause a sage to be born some

place. Sages are born where *ch'i* goes by chance." (*Chu-tzu yü-lei*, Book 1, [The Nature of Things and Men], [The Nature of Material Force and Matter])

Since the quantity of *ch'i* is determined by the Mandate of Heaven, we cannot say that the Mandate is influenced by chance. The Mandate of Heaven is not derived from nature but is the will of heaven. Nature is but a tool of heaven. In Scholastic philosophy, this is referred to by St. Thomas as God, the Providence who created the universe and the ruler of everything in it. This providence is also called continued creation. God created everything in the universe with His creative power. This creative power causes generative power. Thus, this generative power continuously causes change in the universe in its act of creation. The Mandate of Heaven is exactly this generative activity of providing the nature and characteristics of things through the action of generative power. Therefore, by the action of generative power, nature and characteristics come from the Mandate of Heaven derived from the Creator. As such, formally speaking, what makes an individual an individual is matter or *ch'i*, or in actual terms, generative power.

Both Confucius and Mencius agreed that life has a human nature and human characteristics. They even accepted destiny in life. Mencius once said: "It was the will of Heaven that I should not meet the Marquis of Lu. How can this fellow Tsang stop me from it?" (*Meng-tzu, Liang-hui wang,* Part 2) Human life continues to go on, always experiencing events big or small, which are affected by human affairs and the natural environment. As the Creator holds the myriad of things in the universe, he allows man and natural environment to proceed unimpeded. However, for some events that are important for a person, human society or nation, the Creator acts with his providence. This providence is likewise carried out through generative power. Supernaturally, the providence of God is directly carried out by the Holy Spirit. Concrete realities are individuals continuously undergoing change while remaining the same individual realities. For human beings, this is referred to as "self." From youth to old age, a person is one "self." No matter how the body, intelligence or character change, a "self" remains to be itself. How exactly is the "self" created?

We all know that "self" must not be viewed in terms of the collective because our bodies often change. Neither can "self" be viewed in terms of the spirit as its manifestations, such as intelligence and character, always undergo change. Some philosophers have suggested that memory makes a person remember who he was before. This explanation does not hold water. A person who loses his memory remains the same person. Even a person who retains his memory, but does not use it, remains the same person as before. Still other philosophers have claimed that it is self-awareness that creates the "self," since each person is aware that he is the same person as he has always been. This too does not hold true for it presents the same problem as the explanation using "memory"; in fact, even more. Not only do I know that I am the same person as before, I also know others are the same persons as before. A dog, flower or stone remains the same dog, flower or stone. Anything existing retains its body as before. This is also true with spiritual beings. An angel remains the same angel as before. The Creator remains the same Creator as before. Thus, it is evident that identity cannot be explained in terms of the spirit but through substance.

Scholastic philosophy explains the concept of identity using the idea of substance. The substance of a concrete reality remains constant, although its accidents may change. The reason why I remain I is that my substance remains the same. Only my accidents change. When I explain the concept of concrete realities, I always say that these realities are integral. The "oneness" of an integral reality depends upon generative power, or existence or life. Substance is an abstract concept like "nature" and "existence." The abstract substance becomes a concrete reality through the action of generative power. Actual concrete realities also often change because of generative power. Although generative power is constantly moving, it remains the same generative power in a concrete reality whose nature it endows. The generative power of a concrete reality is nothing but the existence of this concrete reality. The generative power of a concrete reality remains always the same. An actual concrete reality always remains the same reality.

What makes "me" always remain the same "me" is my existence or my life. Life makes me become a concrete being that is unique and that constitutes an individual "me." As long as this concrete being exists, it remains *is*. "Me" is an integral "me," a concrete being and not an abstract one. The integral me is me because of my life that remains the same as long as I live. Once I cease living, I also cease being me.

A flower or a dog remains the same flower or dog because each has the same life or generative power all along. Similarly, a rock, a table or a pen always remain the same rock, table or pen not because they do not undergo change but rather because of the generative power inherent in them. This generative power makes them one and capable of inner changes, thus making them moving subsistents. As long as their innate generative power remains the same, they always remain the same one being.

Simply stated, the scholastic philosophical principle of identity is based on substance, an abstract reality. The "identity" I propose is based on generative power which is both a concrete substance and an integral actual reality. Scholastic philosophy explains the concept of being in an abstract manner while I have used traditional Chinese philosophy to discuss the concept of concrete being.

III. Persona [3]

In contemporary language, the word identity refers to a person's "role" in society. Confucius himself stressed personal identity. Thus

---

(3) On Persona:

St. John Damascene said: "Persona is the expression of oneself through one's own actions and characteristics. It is differentiated from the subject's existence." (Dialect. c. 43 in Migne P.G. 94. cal.613)

St. Augustine defined it as: *"Singulus quisque homo, qui... secundum suam mentem imago Dei dicitur, una persona est et imago Trinitatis in mentem."* (De Trinitate, XV, 7, 11) (Each person is rationally the image of God. Persona is the image of the Blessed Trinity.)

Boetius' definition says: "*Persona est naturae rationalis individua substantia.*" (An individual substance of a rational nature.) (De duabus naturis et una substantia Christi. c.3 in Migne P.L.64, Col. 1345) father, son, emperor, official, and so on each represent a type of identity to which specific rights and duties are attached. These names are abstract. In Chinese opera, concrete identities are represented by operatic masks[4], each one identifying individual roles. In today's society, "personal status" refers to how one is perceived by others or what a person does professionally. For instance, in the case of a missionary priest, "personal status" refers to his distinguishing characteristics. In addition, personality also refers to social status. Thus, specific social status correspond to persons with different professions.

It is a social phenomenon for personal status to be perceived through one's profession and social standing. As such, it should be studied from a social viewpoint and not analyzed as a philosophical issue. However, the root of social status can be traced to the philosophical concept of persona. This can be explained by the fact that the basis of social standing is a person's self. A person is perceived by others through his own "self" by which he gains others' respect.

Once a person gains others' respect, another term applies--integrity. Each person believes he has his own integrity that others cannot insult or denigrate. In the past, young people, workers and women were often placed under the jurisdiction of others. Now, they stress their own integrity and demand respect from their parents, or employers, or from men.

There exists another type of "integrity" preferred by young people nowadays--personal character. They insist on being different from others, claiming to have a different character, hobbies and special talents. Young people in the United States and Europe who expressed dislike for the enjoyments money can buy opted for a return to primitive lifestyles. Thus, the hippies were born. Nietzsche once talked about the "superior man." Contemporary society gave birth to the women's liberationists and to political strong men. The special

---

(4) [Translator's Note] In Chinese opera, the so-called *lien-p'u* are facial makeups, each one representing specific characters in the play.

characteristics of these people represent their character and manifest their own selves.

In terms of moral ethics, integrity represents a person's virtues or moral character. A person's level of integrity shows the extent of a person's moral upbringing. Thus a person with good moral character is called virtuous, while someone with bad morals is mocked as a person without integrity.

Although the words status, role, character, virtues, and integrity differ in meaning, they are fundamentally based on "one's own self." Society or other people evaluate a person by applying social, psychological and moral standards to his words or actions. At the center of this evaluation is an integral and individual person.

Personality or persona in western philosophy is defined by Boetius[5] as "an individual substance of a rational nature." There are two important components in this definition: *rational* and *individual*. Something that is not rational cannot have a persona. Without it, that something cannot be one. Man is rational and therefore "persona" is applied to him. God and angels are likewise rational, and therefore also possess persona.

Rationality is a shared concept applicable to many concrete beings, at least to men, angels and God. Yet, although rationality is important to the concept of persona, it is not a decisive component. Persona is not determined by rationality but rather by the *individual*. A persona must always be a concrete being. Rationality is related to nature while individuality is a function of existence. In a substance, persona is not determined by nature but by existence. Human beings are human beings. An *individual* refers to this or that man.

Since an individual person is a persona (with character and indi-

---

(5) [Translator's Note] Anicius Manlius Severinus Boethius (c480-525), Roman philosopher, statesman and Christian theologian. His works were a major source of Classical thought for medieval Scholastic philosophers.

viduality), what then differentiates the individual from the persona? Or are they totally identical and do not really differ? Theoretically, the individuality of a person is a rational one. It is identical with the persona. Both refer to a person. In reality however, the contents of the two do not totally overlap. The individual person, in reality, refers to a specific person who is integral but whose characteristics are not taken into consideration. Persona, on the other hand, in reality stresses his characteristics. He exists in his own way that is different from others. In the grammar of Western languages, there are the first, second and third persons. These refer to individual persons' manners of being, which are dependent on existence. From the legal point of view, the persona represents rights. A person is the subject of rights, thus the term "natural person." A group bestowed with rights is called a legal entity. Thus, an individual with a persona must refer to an integral person together with all his characteristics. He exists as an integral person.

Catholic theology assigns a particular role to "persona" in explaining the dogma of the Blessed Trinity. Since "persona" is not explained ontologically, God is said to have one nature. His existence is also one or else God would be multiple. But *he* exists in three ways, representing three sets of "interpersonal" relationships among the three persons of the Trinity. These relationships are mysteries of the most unfathomable nature.

Scholastic philosophy of recent years has emphasized three points regarding the persona: First, that the persona is *one*. This one refers to a living individual, not an abstract concept. It is not made up of component parts, but instead causes components to make up a whole. Second, Scholastic philosophy has emphasized that the persona is autonomous. It is an independent "self" conscious of itself. Third, Scholastic philosophy has stressed that the persona is self-governing. It is the master of its own actions whose objective is the persona itself. From the above, we see that the persona is a rational individual with an integral manner of existence. This integral manner of existence refers to the three points mentioned above.

Appendix

In his work *Aesthetics*, Hegel stressed that artistic beauty consists in the incorporation of vitality; that the object of beauty has life as its basis for unity.

> . . . the beautiful itself must be grasped as Idea. Now the Idea as such is nothing but the Concept, the real existence of the Concept, and the unity of the two... But it is only when it is present in its real existence and placed in unity therewith that the Concept is the Idea...the first existence of the Idea is nature, and beauty begins as the beauty of nature. (Hegel, *Aesthetics* 106)

> . . . higher natural objects set free the distinctions of the Concept, so that now each of them outside the others is there for itself independently. Here alone appears the true nature of objectivity. For objectivity is precisely this independent dispersal of the Concept's distinctions. Now at this stage the Concept asserts itself in this way: since it is the totality of its determinacies which makes itself real, the particular bodies, though each possesses as independent existence of its own, close together into one and the same system. One example of this kind of thing is the solar system. (116)

> . . . so we do find the Concept itself becomes real, with the totality of its distinction made explicit... but even here the Concept still remains sunk in its real existence; it does not come forth as the ideality and the inner independence thereof. The decisive form of its existence remains the independent mutual externality of its different factors.

> But what the true existence of the Concept requires is that the real differences (namely the reality of the independent differences and their equally independently objectified unity as such)

be themselves brought back into unity; i.e. that such a whole of natural differences should on the one hand make the Concept explicit as a real mutual externality of its specific determinations, and yet on the other hand set down as canceled in every particular thing its self-enclosed independence; and now make the ideality, in which the differences are turned back into subjective unity, emerge in them as their universal animating soul. In that event, they are no longer merely parts hanging together and related to one another, but members; i.e. they are no longer sundered, existing independently, but they have genuine existence only in their ideal unity. Only in such an organic articulation does there dwell in the members the ideal unity of the Concept which is their support and their immanent soul. The Concept remains no longer sunk in reality but emerges into existence in it as the inner identity and universality which constitute its own essence.

The third mode of natural appearance alone is an existence of the Idea, the idea in natural form as Life. Dead, inorganic nature is not adequate to the Idea, and only the living organism is an actuality of the Idea. For in life, in the first place, the reality of the Concept's distinctions is present as real; secondly, however, there is the negation of these as merely real distinctions, in that the ideal subjectivity of the Concept subdues this reality to itself; thirdly, there is the soulful *qua* the affirmative appearance of the Concept in its corporeality, i.e. *qua* infinite form which has the power to maintain itself, as form, in its content. (118)

For the power of life, and still more the might of the spirit, consists precisely in positing contradiction in itself, enduring it, and overcoming it. This positing and resolving of the contradiction between the ideal unity and the real separatedness of the members constitutes the constant process of life, and life *is* only by being a *process*.

The process of life comprises a double activity: on the one

hand, that of bringing steadily into existence perceptibly the real differences of all the members and specific characteristics of the organism, but, on the other hand, that of asserting in them their universal ideality (which is their animation) if they try to persist in independent severance from one another and isolate themselves in fixed differences from one another. This is the idealism of life. For philosophy is not at all the only example of idealism; nature, as life, already makes a matter of fact what idealist philosophy brings to completion in its own spiritual field. --But only these two activities in one--the constant transfer of the specific characteristics of the organism into realities, and the putting of these real existents ideally into their subjective unity--constitute the complete process of life. (120)

If we ask further by what indications the Idea of life in actual living individuals can be known, the answer is as follows: Life must first be real as a totality of a bodily organism, but, secondly, as an organism which does not appear as something stubborn, but as an inherent continual process of idealizing, in which the living soul displays itself. Thirdly, this totality is not determined from without and alterable; it shapes itself outwardly from within; it is in process, and therein is continually related to itself as a subjective unity and an end in itself. (122)

Hegel takes beauty as *Concept* which is the actuality of an Idea. Concept and actuality together directly form life. Life unites all parts of an object into one body, eliminating their differences. Life is the basis of one integral body. For Hegel, life is only present in an organic body. There is no real unity in inorganic bodies. Therefore, for him natural things have no beauty. I disagree with this idea. I believe that nature has unity and is beautiful. The unity of a natural thing is its existence. Existence is power, life and generative power.

Works Cited

Hegel, Georg W. F., *Aesthetics: Lectures on Fine Art*. Trans T.M. Knox. London: Oxford UP, 1988.

"Mencius." in *English Translation of The Four Books*. Taipei: Council of Cultural Rennaisance, 1979: 131-311.

Translated by Carlos Tee

Chapter IX

Integral Realities

I. Realities Become by Virtue of Power

Being is the focus of Western metaphysical studies. The study of being leads to the study of its components: *chih* and *li* or *materia* and *forma*. *Chih* and *li* unite to make up hsing or nature (*natura*). Nature and existence together form substance (*substantia*). This so-called substance is an abstract one. In contrast, realities possess accidents. Thus, realities are the union of substance and accidents. Ordinarily, however, it is the abstract substance, not the concrete accidents, that is discussed in philosophy. Substance is dealt with in Western philosophy by analysis of the subject in a quiescent mode. Studied in the abstract sense, substance is considered via nature. The so-called existence is likewise an abstract concept. Analytically, substance is formed by nature and existence combined together. How do nature and existence actually come together? In Chinese philosophy, Chu Hsi proposes that matter results from the union of *li* (principle) and *ch'i* (material force). Here, the same problem arises. How do *li* and *ch'i* unite? Aristotle thought that union is effected by an efficient cause. He posited that all changes in the universe have four causes: material cause, formal cause, efficient cause and final cause, of which the most important is efficient cause. In explaining the act of substances, however, Western metaphysics never touches on the efficient cause nor takes existence in the concrete sense. If not taken as efficient cause, existence would remain an abstract concept which could not make nature a concrete reality.

In explaining the concept of reality, we cannot afford to remain in the abstract but we must explain it in terms of the concrete reality. We know that three components make up substance: *chih* (matter), *li* (form) and power. Matter and form unite by virtue of power. Power makes it possible for matter and form to make up substance. Thus, substance exists. Existing substances continue to undergo motion because of innate power. This innate power that makes substance exist is generative power. Through it, nature becomes an existent substance. This power then is the "existence" of "nature." This existence is one that is constantly in motion. Thus, we can still adopt Scholastic Philosophy's explanation of the concept of substance, that is, substance *is* because of matter, principle and power.

The cosmos is generative power made possible through the creative power of the Creator. The generative power or cosmos possesses its own matter and form. Within the matter of the cosmos, generative power remains constantly in motion in accordance with its own form, thus leading to various changes that generate the myriad things. The becoming of each thing is effected by generative power, which initiates change in a piece of cosmic matter. Generative power bestows the form necessary for the change to occur. The necessary form comes from generative power through the creative power, not from the form of the universe, much less from cosmic matter. With matter, form and power, a thing is thus formed.

Each thing receives a piece of matter (material) from the cosmos and a form bestowed on it by generative power. It also receives power from generative power to become a concrete reality. Generative power moves constantly and initiates changes in a piece of cosmic matter, because generative power is closely united with creative power which bestows the form of things. Creative power is the spiritual power of the Creator. The concept of time does not apply to the Creator, for whom the act of creation is one. In contrast, the concept of time is applicable to the universe. The cosmos created by the Creator is a cosmos of perpetual change in time. The creative power continues in its process of creation, initiating and sustaining changes in the universe while constantly united with generative power. This is the process described by St. Thomas Aquinas as "continual creation."

In the abstract sense, substance is formed by nature and existence. However, this substance is but an abstract substance. In this case, the accidents of a reality reside outside the substance (*substantia*). This is the explanation in traditional Western philosophy, which stresses the concept of nature. In the concrete sense, substance has matter, form and power with emphasis on the latter. Power makes possible the union of matter and form and the fusion of accidents and substance. We shall deal with the concept of accidents below.

In Chinese philosophy, only Chu Hsi has explained the concept of substance in a more detailed manner by positing that the two elements of *li* and *ch'i* make up substance. However, he failed to explain accidents but instead explained the concept of substance as integral.

II. Reality is Existence

In explaining the myriad beings, Scholastic philosophy emphasizes the nature of all things. It explains "being" using the concept of nature, and takes existence as the way of the realization of being. If nature were an abstract notion, then all beings would be abstract things. Abstract things are realized by virtue of existence. What existence bestows on nature are the accidents quality and quantity. These two ways that focus on "nature" and "existence" were conceived by the human mind. St. Thomas Aquinas insisted on using this classification in explaining the relative and created character of the creation. All things are created and are relative beings; never can they be absolute beings. Duns Scotus refused to accept this classification. He instead posited that the relative and created character of things come from their existence.

For all beings to be called being, they must be existent. A non - existent being is called non-being. Existence is actual, concrete and the substance itself. Scholastic philosophy proposes that nature and existence together form substance. Nature limits existence in such a way that substances are classified into categories. Existence also limits nature, thus making the substance a concrete individual. This idea resembles Chu Hsi's theory of *li* and *ch'i*. For Chu Hsi, *li* limits *ch'i*, making possible differentiation between men and things. *Ch'i* also limits *li*, thus making persons different from one another. However, both Chang Tsai and Wang Ch'uan-shan propose that *li* resides in the *ch'i* and that *ch'i* becomes a concrete something because of the *li* residing in it. It is not that *ch'i* causes *li* but *ch'i* possesses *li*.

The substance of all beings is "existent." The existent has nature. To explain reality, one must deal with existence. Existence must be concrete because reality is concrete. A concrete existent possesses material accidents. Material things cannot enter the spiritual (soul). For a reality, spirit and intellect are but abstract notions.

However, a reality is indivisible. It is a concrete individual. The individual's accidents of quality and quantity are the components of a reality. Thus, Chu Hsi explained that humanity is a nature possessing *ch'i* and *chih*. When we talk about man, our notion of man is not an abstract notion but our concept of a concrete man. If not, we would not be able to understand what man is. The same is true with the notion of color. For us to understand "color," a concrete color must appear in our mind. Hence, a colorless and invisible substance (that is, without the accidents of quality and quantity), a pure spiritual substance, is even less comprehensible to us.

A reality is indivisible because it is one existent. Existence cannot be analyzed. There can only be "existence" or "non-existence." Once existing, a reality is integral. Any part of this integral reality cannot exist by itself. The reality of man is ego. Ego is an integral reality. I am made up of things that comprise my own self. Remove one part and I am no longer me. Ego is a reality. It is an existence. The existence of a reality cannot be an abstract universal existence. Instead, it must be "this existence" which is determined by "nature."

The reality of "this existence" cannot be analyzed. If we were to analyze a reality into nature and existence and if we were to understand it in terms of nature, the reality understood would not be an actual substance. It would only be an abstracted universal substance or "humanness." In any environment, reality in itself is indivisible. If nature and existence are made separate, the reality ceases to exist. If the accidents are analyzed, a reality is rendered incomplete. Beings is a reality, not an independent pure concept. That is the reason why

Heidegger takes being as an existent being or "this being." Being is a reality whose existence cannot be analyzed. Neither can it be analyzed in our consciousness. Instead, it must be a complete integral.

Plato thought that concept is a subsistent which exists in the realm of ideas and not an abstract notion. Aristotle reasserted the fact that the realm of ideas cannot actually exist and that concepts are abstract in nature. Contemporary Western philosophers have tried to make a breakthrough of Aristotle's theory of concepts as abstract by directly returning to the concepts of being and substance. Bergson, Heidegger, Whitehead and Husserl proceeded from their own starting points to arrive at their own philosophies but failed to achieve their goal because this fact is in itself a mystery.

III. Realities are Complex Bodies that Generate and Metamorphose

Every existing reality is complex. Of course spiritual realities possess a simple structure. The absolute subsistent reality is *actus purus* (pure act), not possessing any potency whatsoever. However, the Roman Catholic faith believes in a Triune God. The substance of God is not simple but so complex that an abstract concept of "subsistence" can never aptly represent this complex nature. Angels, which are spiritual realities, do not possess matter and are also simple. However, according to Scholastic philosophy, each angel is in itself one angelic species which is unique and cannot exist as many individuals. Nevertheless, each angel is an independent individual that cannot constitute an abstract species. How then are angels differentiated? Does this mean that the substance of angels is not simple? All creation possesses material components. These realities are of course not simple. Man is a product of the psychophysical union and is thus, even more complex. Scholastic philosophy abstracts corporeality from the components of each kind of thing to arrive at a common concept that represents its substance. What is the substance of man? Man is a "rational animal." The concept of a rational animal is not simple because of the complexity of its components. In addition, this abstract concept cannot represent man's reality at all. It only represents the abstract meaning of man's substance. In order for man to comprehend this abstract notion, a concrete person must appear in his mind. Will a deaf and blind person who has never had a concrete impression of a human being understand the term rational animal"? It is only possible by explanation, using other concrete impressions he may easily comprehend. Abstract concepts represent concrete integral realities. Without the impression of integral realities, it is impossible to acquire an abstract concept. That is why an abstract notion of substance must necessarily have a corresponding concrete reality.

A reality is concrete, complex and perpetually in the process of change. This is why in Chinese philosophy, being is described as *sheng-sheng* [perpetual renewal of life] or a continuous generation and transformation. All things in the universe are constantly changing. The ordinary man in the street is aware that living things constantly change. For example, a person is constantly changing from his birth until the very day he dies. However, the man in the street are not usually aware that non-living things are also ever-changing. Non-living things do also change, although in a manner unnoticed by the human eye. Now, the science of physics explains that atoms and electrons that composed matter are also engaged in perpetual change.

From the standpoint of the philosophical notion of substance, the substance of the myriad things in the universe is not subsistent but instead created. With his creative power, the Creator made the universe, which is itself a kind of generative power. The generative power or the universe is constantly moving and generating things. Generative power fuses with the Creator's creative power because the former is derived from the latter. All objects originally did not exist. By the action of generative power, they came into being. The being of their substance depends upon generative power to *be*. This change involving substance is called *sheng* [generation]. When a reality ceases to exist upon the action of the generative power, the process is called *mie* [annihilation]. Thus, changes of the substance are either generation or annihilation. However, if an object comes into being owing to the action of generative power, it cannot remain as a being once and for all. It constantly needs the support of generative power. This is because the being of realities is not subsistent but is derived from generative power; its being ceases to be at the very instant in which it separates from generative power. Owing to the ever-flowing spiritual power of the Creative power, generative power is also constantly flowing in all things. Generative power is not like a person holding a cup without moving, or a table on which a cup remains without falling. The action of generative power on each object is comparable to that of a movie projector or television wherein films are successively shown by the action of electricity. The movie continues to go on. Once electric power is switched off, the film stops and the story is interrupted. Each object then is like each of the films shown. The process of showing resembles the being of things. While the continuous showing of the films depends on the flow of electric current, the existence of things depends on flowing generative power. Thus, we say that the being of things is but the continuous generation process attributed to generative power.

Generative power functions in two ways in causing continuous generation in an object. On the one hand, generative power makes realities continue their being. This is an issue related to substantial change. On the other hand, it causes realities to develop. This is accidental change. For instance, a person's being is his life. If his life continues, he exists. A change in his life itself constitutes a substantial change, which can only be towards life or death. The development of a person's life consists of all types of qualitative and quantitative changes. Changes in a person's bodily growth and the acquisition of intelligence are accidental changes in man.

Scholastic philosophy affirms that substance cannot change. Once substance changes, the object itself undergoes change, whereupon the original substance ceases to exist. However, substance is not only made up of nature but is the union of nature and existence. Since it is existing, it must have a concrete being. A concrete being cannot remain quiescent but must instead continuously undergo changes.

Scholastic philosophy confirms that the myriad things cannot subsist by themselves. They must depend upon the Creator's creative power to remain a being and existing. St. Thomas Aquinas described the Creator's continuous support for all creation as continual generation. All realities do not constantly subsist by themselves after their formation through the action of generative power but are rather continually created from nothing. This continual creation from nothing is an issue related to substantial change. Since there is a change in the substance, then it is not annihilated. This is due to generative power's continuous action, which resembles the successive showing of cinematic films one by one through the movie projector. Substantial change is a change accompanied by generation or annihilation. As the substance remains a being, signs of generation or annihilation are not made visible. This, again, is comparable to the showing of cinematic film wherein signs of the junction between each film are not visible. This change in which generation and annihilation are not manifest is itself the so-called life of the *sheng-sheng* (perpetual renewal of life). In the "*I Ching*", this perpetual generative change is described as mystical and unfathomable:

> In (all these operations forming) the *I* , there is no thought and no action. It is still and without movement; but, when acted on, it penetrates forthwith to all phenomena and events under the sky. If it were not the most spirit-like thing under the sky, how could it be found doing this?" ("The Great Appendix," Section 1, Chapter X, Legge, *I Ching* 370)

For Bergson, the universe is a rich and continuous *élan vital*. For Wang Ch'uan-shan, "nature (*hsing*) grows day by day while life decreases." All of them confirm that all the myriad things constantly undergo substantial change.

Changes in the substance are changes in existence, that is, these changes involve the concepts of being or non-being and of generation or annihilation. They are not changes occurring in their nature (*hsing*). For if they do, then the substance would not remain as the original one; the whole object would transform into another.

Objects change in a process leading from potency to act. Potency (*potentia*) is potentiality and act (*actus*) is actualization. In accidental changes, all potency resides outside the substance, while all acts can be within or outside the object. At the start of substantial change, act is a potency of the being. This potency resides in another reality. For instance, the potency of man to be born resides in his parents' bodies. The potency of a table to become a table resides in the raw materials that make up the table. A tree's potency to germinate and grow resides in a germinating seed. This has led Buddhists to say that all the myriad things do not have a self-nature but are instead formed by the union of principal and subsidiary causes. Buddhism also proposes the idea of reincarnation, comparing the process to a burning flame which passes from one burnt-out candle to another. Although Buddhist explanations do not match the philosophical concept of substance, they also express substantial change and include a hazy concept of potency.

Reality *is* because of the action of generative power. For instance, after a person is born, he possesses his own reality while continuously undergoing changes of being generated, that is, he is perpetually generating and existing. His potency must reside in his substance. Since he is already a being, he can remain as a being. Generative power acts within the substance to continuously lead potency to act. This continuous function is referred to as "action" or "life." Resembling the showing of a movie film, this process allows a being to continuously proceed from its own potency to act.

IV. Reality and Function

In its treatment of the concept of substance, traditional Western philosophy is confronted by the issue of accidents. Accidents are what substances possess concretely. Man, for instance, is a rational animal. His bodily parts are accidents but his soul, as the form of man, is itself his substance. Man's intellect and will are accidents. Again citing the example of a wooden table, its accidents are the wood of which it is made of. This idea has attracted censure from contemporary Western philosophers. They ask what man possesses aside from his bodily parts and organs. What does a wooden table have other than wood materials.

? The so-called substance supports the external accidents in an interior manner. However, in addition to his human body, what does a man have within? If ever there was anything, how does it support the body? There is a need to clearly analyze this point.

Substance (*substantia*), an abstract concept, is made up of nature and existence, both of which are also abstract. When this abstract substance becomes a concrete being, it is called reality and may also be called being or concrete being.

A concrete being is an integral reality. The material it is made of has become concrete material. (A person's concrete material is his own body.) Concrete material is the substance of a reality and cannot be considered as an accident. It would thus be wrong to say that the body of a person is his accident.

This concrete being is itself existence. It is a reality and is itself this very person. His being is active and constantly in motion because his being is constantly moving generative power. A being moves because of generative power. This motion's expression and consequence, or result, is an accident. For instance, a person who is reading and writing is performing actions which are themselves accidents. The body is perpetually changing in terms of the color of the skin, body weight and height. All these characteristics are accidents. To better explain this analysis, using the Chinese philosophical terms *t'i-yung* (reality and function) would be more appropriate. Reality (*t'i*) refers to a body formed by the concretization of material. Function (*yung*) refers to all the actions and other supplementary actions of man. However, in Chinese philosophy, explanations of the concept of *t'i-yung* are disparate. I shall use the term with the meaning explained above.

The myriad things in the universe are relative non-subsistents. Their substances undergo generation and annihilation and their accidents also change. Accidental change happens when the potency of realities gradually develop. This vital movement is called substantial function (*yung*). The significance of function to substance are manifold. First, function shows development of the substance. It allows its potency gradually to be actualized. This leads to an enriched substance. Although for corporeal things, function causes wear and tear and reduction, it often causes enhancement in the spiritual sense. Second, function shows the nature of the substance. The nature of relative beings is a collection of potencies. If not manifested as a reality, potency is beyond knowing. Only when potency becomes a reality and is later known is it possible for us to know nature through potency. This explains why in Chinese philosophy, reality and function are often undifferentiated. Function is even equated with reality. Third, function shows vital activity. Things that show no function are lifeless. Ordinarily, when we say that plants and animals have functions, we infer that they have activity and that they possess life. Minerals, which show no activity, and thus have no function, are considered nonliving. However, the substances of minerals also have functions. Not a single mineral does not undergo change even infinitesimally. Minerals gradually change, often over a long period of time. This change, often unnoticed, proceeds extremely slowly and stretches over along period of time. Thus, minerals also have substantial functions and vital activity. Fourth, the relationship between function and reality comes about through corporeality. As a consequence, rationalists posit that human emotion and passion are derived from humanity. They posit that if one's emotion and passion are evil, it follows that this person's humanity is evil. It is therefore proper to say that the so-called accidents, with the exception of movement and its consequences, are not incidental additions to things. Instead, they form being together with substance. They are components of a being and are essential to it. We often think that the limbs and organs are essential to man, while skin color, height and body weight are not. For a specific human being, color, height and weight are the effects of life. They, of course, can change any time. During the process of change, this person remains the same person. However, this human being exists in a particular time and space with a certain color and physical build. In conclusion, we can say that accidents manifest and limit the being of substances.

However, although function and substance are inseparable, function is not substance, nor are they equal. Function is a part of substance. But the real subsistent being continues to move by itself because existence is a moving one. For instance, human life cannot be called function but is instead the reality of man or man's existence itself. Therefore, life and the living thing are inseparable. Nevertheless, "living" is not life but is life's manifestation. Man knows about life by living. This also explains why Chinese philosophy equates function with substance.

Some will probably ask how my explanation above differs from the standard explanation of Scholastic philosophy. Scholasticism contrasts substance with accidents. Substance is made up of nature and existence. Accidents are what the substance possesses other than nature and existence. I distinguish substance from reality. Substance is abstract while reality is concrete. All matters possessed by the concrete reality belong to the substance. They are the matter of substance. All "mmanent movements" of concrete realities--that is, changes attributed to generative power or life itself, are not accidents but the substance of realities. Manifestations and results of the immanent action of realities (which are the existing substances) are accidents. My explanation differs in some points from the concept of unseparated function and substance in Chinese philosophy. Chinese philosophy has a broad explanation of *t'i-yung*, with these notions differing from school to school.

V. Conclusions

Reality is being and being is perpetually in motion. In the absolute subsistent being, motion is pure act and does not lead to change. In relative non-self subsistent beings, motion is always accompanied by change, which leads from potency to act. The motion of beings can perhaps be called transformation (*hua*). It is interior and substantial. In the being of the absolute subsistent, action and transformation occur within himself and do not lead to addition or reduction. On the contrary, what happens within the being of relative non-self subsistents is made possible by the action of creative power through generative power, leading to substantial change and development. Chinese philosophy deals with the fulfillment of nature *(chin-hsing)* and its enhancement. Motion within the substance is itself life. The being of the absolute subsistent possesses pure life, which is itself pure act. It acts without motion and transforms without changing. This is something we humans cannot comprehend. On the contrary, the being of the non-self subsistents often changes owing to immanent motion with resultant changes of varying degrees. Changes in minerals are the weakest, the slightest and the slowest to occur. From the outside, it appears as though there is no hange at all. Ordinarily, therefore, minerals are considered non-living. The so-called living things show the greatest variety of levels. For Chu Hsi, this is called the "unity and diversity of form" wherein the principle *(li)* of life is manifested in degrees determined by the clarity and turbidity of material force *(ch'i)*. For me, classification of the myriad things is determined by their nature *(hsing)* and existence *(tsai)*. Nature is composed of substantial form *(yuan-hsing)* and prime matter *(yuan-chih)*. Nature comes from a cosmos created by the creative power through generative power. Existence proceeds from the action of generative power. All the myriad things have life. Life, which comes from generative power, makes being become a reality. This is the basis of existence. Existing realities are integral realities, made up of substance and accidents. In theory, accidents are separable from realities. In actual terms, however, once accidents are separated, the reality ceases to remain the same reality. In conclusion, we therefore say that all realities are integral realities.

Appendix: Hsiung Shih-li's New Doctrine of Consciousness-Only

Explaining Reality and Function *(T'i-yung)*:

The basic structure of the New Doctrine of Consciousness-Only is a definition of reality and function *(t'i-yung)* of which readers are still in the dark. Now let me explain these two concepts. Philosophers must have a proper understanding of fundamental issues. Otherwise, even if they can form a set of theories, it would still be far from the truth and at best only a farce. The most basic issues in philosophy are those of noumenon and phenomenon, which are referred to as *t'i* and *yung* in the New Doctrine of Consciousness-Only. *T'i* is the substance. *Yung* is a shorter term for *chuo-yung* (function) or *kung-yung* (use). Phenomenon is not called as such but is instead called *yung* (function). The "world of phenomena" is a generic term for all creation. The so-called all creation actually consists in the operations manifested by realities to which different names are given. Therefore, all creation is inseparable from functions. Actual things can also be called the world of phenomena. This explains why function is used instead of phenomenon. Reality is manifested in function. This [idea] must be properly understood. The two [reality and function] must not be taken as two things. Philosophers often confuse reality as being beyond and above the world of phenomena. It is also erroneously considered to be hidden behind the world of phenomena, using phenomenon as its basis. This is a fundamental blunder. In fact, to rectify this error is the purpose of the discussion of reality and function in the New Doctrine of Consciousness-Only.

T'i (reality) occupies no space and is formless. Nevertheless, it embodies all principles (*li*) and includes all *good*. It holds infinite possibilities. It is the only truth. This is why it is said to be unchanging.

Yung (function) is called the "flowing action" of reality. It is the manifestation of the reality. This is because reality is empty yet potent. And this is also why realities continuously generate and renew without end. This process of generation and transformation is the so-called "running current" or otherwise known as *chuo-yung* (function) and *kung-yung* (use).

An analysis of *t'i* shows that it is ultimate and absolute. It occupies no space and is formless.

Analysis of *yung* reveals that it possesses a phantasmal state. It appears in various forms and myriad manifestations.

T'i can be compared to the deep and wide ocean water.

Yung can be compared to ocean waves rising and falling incessantly.

Anyone who has traveled by sea has surely seen ocean water whose reality is manifested as the countless waves. It is not possible to look for the ocean water outside of the countless waves. Similarly, the countless waves find their reality in the ocean water. They cannot be separated from ocean water and do not have their own self-nature.

Although reality and function are not two, they are distinguished from each other. Yet, although distinct, they do not constitute two. This explains their comparison with ocean water and its many waves. Ocean water is made up of all the many waves which do not possess a self-nature of their own. This is because the countless waves and the ocean water are not two. Yet, although not two, it is possible to point out each individual wave, thus proving that ocean water is distinguished from its many waves. This is similar to *t'i* and *yung*, which are not two but are distinct. Although the shapes of the many waves are myriad, yet each one is an ocean wave. This is because all of them have ocean water as their reality. Again, this shows that the many waves and ocean water are not two. By the same token, although distinct from one another, *t'i* and *yung* are not two. The meaning of reality and function are very difficult to explain. The most convenient method of explaining them uses the ocean-water-and-wave analogy above. By this analogy, I believe that students can have a deeper understanding of the matter. Philosophers may perhaps only accept the present myriad phenomena of unceasing changes as together forming an integrated whole, which they consider as the only fact. If so, they can only know the existence of a world of phenomena, but will fail to accept the reality to which the phenomenon belongs. This situation is comparable to a young boy standing by the sea coast. He sees only the many waves and overlooks the existence of ocean water.

If philosophers take reality as a fact, they take it as above and beyond the world of phenomena or hidden behind each phenomenon. This leads to the error of a dichotomous world. In fact, the idea of reality and function as distinct but not two, or as not two but distinct, has never been explained in philosophy. This is precisely why the New

Doctrine of Consciousness-Only was written.

We have already explained *t'i* and *yung*. Now let us take *yung*. *Yung* is not a simple moving tendency but must instead be a two-way process called opening and closing (*hsi-p'i*). *P'i* is called the mind (*shen*) while *hsi* is the transformation of things. Things have limits whereas mind is not limited. The mind, circulating and operating in things, is the master of the latter. This is the usual condition. The thing can also conceal its mind as opportunities allow. This is an unusual condition. Nevertheless, the mind is still the master of things. This trend does not go against realities' formal condition at all. Since the New Doctrine of Consciousness-Only was published, readers have searched its underlying principles and patterns, and launched senseless attacks. This convinced me to write more about it.

Explaining the Constancy of Reality:

Reality is real constancy. This is what Lao-tzu called "constant way" (*ch'ang-tao*) or what the Buddhists call "true reality" (*chen-ju*). Western philosophy denies reality. This cannot be compared to my idea of a moving and changing reality. When Western philosophy explains reality as constant, there exist some similarities with Eastern philosophy's definition of real constancy. It explanations differ from one another and form different systems of thought. This was described in the *I Ching* as unity in diversity (*yi-chih erh bai-lu*). I have studied the meaning of constancy for decades. If I were to say that reality is not real constancy, then it would be false and pretentious. For if so, how is reality the origin of the myriad transformations and be named as such. If I say that the self-nature of reality is real constancy, then it merits a deeper probing. Let us realize that once we talk about reality, we mean it as not vacuous but as having a self-nature. However, this real constancy we are referring to is taken to have the meaning of being ungenerated and imperishable, unchanging and unmoving. Therefore, this reality must be something towering and firm. Real constancy contrasts with a generating, transforming, changing and moving cosmos. How then can it be said to be the reality of the cosmos. I spent decades painstakingly analyzing this issue. It was not until I almost turned fifty before I dared to suddenly announce the New Doctrine of Consciousness-Only. Those who affirm that reality and function are not two deeply realize and believe that one cannot take the self-nature of reality as something constant. Constancy is called virtue. Let me cite an example. The *k'un* trigram of the *I Ching* is referred to as the "square earth" (*ti-fang*). Successive generations of scholars dealing with the *I Ching* thought that the self-nature of the earth is square. This is an error. Squareness (*fang*) is called the virtue of the earth (*ti-teh*). The term has its roots in the phrase "supporting the *ch'ien* (heaven) without any distortion" (*ch'eng-ch'ien erh wu hsieh-ch'u*). This explains why this virtue of the earth is called beauty. From this, we can see that the terms "real" and "constant" are derived from the virtue of reality which they make manifest.

Works Cited

Legge, James. trans. The *I Ching*. 2nd ed. New York: Dover, 1963.

Translated by Carlos Tee

Chapter X

The Subject: Ego

I. Man-Relationship Between Mind and Matter

Man was created by God the Creator based on His idea of Himself. This demonstrates the extraordinary importance of man among all creation and the fact that his qualities differ from those of the rest of the universe. For this reason, both Western and Chinese philosophy recognize man as the creation *par excellence,* aptly representing all creation.

In Chinese philosophy, the *Li-chi* (Book of Rites) considers man as possessing the delicate ether of heaven and earth and the soul of all creation. Chu Hsi considered man to have been bestowed the fullness of the *li* (principle) of heaven and earth while material things possess only a fragment of it. The distinct quality of man lies in his soul. In his teachings about man, Mencius says that man possesses small and large bodies. Small bodies refer to bodily organs like eyes and ears while large bodies are the organs of thought, which are the reason why man is man. Since man possesses organs of thought, he is capable of knowing all creation, and more especially, of making a free choice. It is because of man that the whole creation is full of meaning and abounding in sentiment. God, the Creator, left the whole universe at man's disposal and under his dominion. This is why St. Paul said that the sin of man brought the whole universe into sin and that the salvation of man also brought salvation to the whole of creation.

What distinguishes man is his soul. However, man in his totality is a reality made up of body and soul. This is why man is said to be a psychophysical union. Philosophers hold varying opinions on the relationship between body and soul. Materialism posits that the soul is subtle matter sharing the same qualities as the body. These two, forming not a duality but a unity, have no so-called relationship of association. However, mainstream traditional Chinese and Western philosophies affirm the spiritual nature of the soul. The body is material and a relationship of association exists between it and the human soul. Plato proposed that the spirit, or soul, originally existed in the world of Ideas. It later united with the body to form man. For him, the human body is the prison of the soul. This idea developed into Platonism. Both Aristotle and St. Thomas Aquinas posit that the soul is form (*forma*) and the body is matter (*materia*). Together, they constitute man's dual elements. This basic idea was later followed by Scholasticism. From this idea was derived the notion that the body is a tool used by the soul in its activities. In contrast, the Chinese philosopher Chu Hsi proposed that the spirit is formed by a clear material force (*ch'i*). The material force of the body is turbid and thus, is divided into the upper and lower parts, *hun* (the spirit of man's vital force) and *p'o* (the spirit of man's physical nature). Although this sounds similar to the ideas of materialism, Chu Hsi and the Neo-Confucians affirm that a clear material force (*ch'i*) is a vacuous spirit or a non-material spirit. However, contemporary Neo-Confucianists share the same view as Han Dynasty's Wang Ch'ung who denied the spiritual nature of the soul. They reason that the actions of the soul are actualized through the body, that is, the brain. There is likewise a tendency among contemporary Western philosophers to deny the spiritual nature of the soul. They have abandoned the traditional term "soul" in favor of the term "mind."

To explain the relationship between body and soul, one cannot deny duality and only posit singularity. Singularity refers to material force (*ch'i*). How is material force in the body divided into a clear part and a turbid part? Singularity is also matter. How is matter inside the body differentiated as lightly clear and heavily turbid? How do these two relate with one another? Body and soul are two different elements. Soul is a spiritual entity while body is a material entity. They possess qualities that are different besides being non-subsistent realities. These two elements possessing different qualities unite together in existence to form a subsistent reality. The existence of man is life. In human life, body and soul join together to form one. Human life is a psychophysical life.

Man's body and soul are two elements of human life. Here, the word "element" does not have exactly the same meaning as when we normally refer to elements of things. The elements we normally refer to do not themselves possess complete forms. On the contrary, body and soul each have a complete form of their own. The body possesses a complete form. The soul is a complete spiritual form. Furthermore, the soul possesses a form that can independently exist. Once it separates from the body, the soul exists independently. These two elements in which each possesses a complete form unite to form a psychophysical man.

The psychophysical man is not a divided form but is rather united. It is not that the soul operates the body. Both of them share action. This is because body and soul unite in life to form one single life. The human life is psychophysical in nature. A person's vital actions are necessarily joint actions of both body and soul. There is no such things as a purely bodily action nor a purely spiritual (soul) action. In terms of substance, man is constantly man whether in his conscious awakened state or in his unconscious state of sleep. A conscious activity is an activity of both body and soul. The same is true with an unconscious activity. It would be wrong to say that in man's body are found a living soul, a sentient soul and a spiritual soul. Man possesses one single soul, the spiritual soul. Similarly, man possesses only one life. It is wrong to say that physiological life is not human life. The issue of being conscious or unconscious has nothing to do with substantial differentiation; it relates to functional differentiation. A comatose person remains a human being. All his actions remain those of a soul.

The fusion of body and soul is made possible by existence." Within a reality, existence is singular and indivisible. Existence is a moving one. It is life. Similarly, life is a singular reality. It is also indivisible.

Therefore, for man to think, he must use his brains. It is not that the soul is using the brains. The act of thinking is necessarily a psychophysical action. Similarly, sense activities are also jointly done with the brain. Even physiological activities are joint activities of body and soul. This point is perhaps unacceptable to many since everybody is used to saying that the soul plays no part in physiological activities. Yet, they are important activities in man's life. Without them, man could not continue to live. Man's life is singular and indivisible. As such, the soul is singular and indivisible. All activities are vital activities in which both soul and body are involved.

We therefore conclude that it is wrong to say that the soul is material in nature just because the brain is needed for mental activities. The activities of man are necessarily psychophysical. They pose no obstacle to recognizing the spiritual nature of the soul.[1]

II. The Origin of the Soul and Eternal Life

Scholars hold divergent views on the origin of the soul. Some say it comes from the physical bodies of parents, that it initially forms the flesh of the embryo then later develops into the soul. Some simply say that the soul is inherited from parents and is not of a spiritual nature. Still others say that souls originally exist in the world of Ideas then later join bodies. And there are those who say that souls are created by God.

The human soul is created by God, as Donceel writes:

> . . . Not simply in the sense that God carries the causality of the parents in the begetting of their child. For God carries every finite causality by what is called divine concurrence. Likewise

---

(1) The main opinions on the relation between body and soul:
① Body and soul are complete substances which act upon each other (interactionism).
② Body and soul are complete substances which do not act upon each other (psychophysical parallelism).
③ Body and soul ar e but two aspects of one fundamental reality (panpsy chism).
④ Only the body is a substance; what is called "soul" is only a collection of psychic phenomenon (actualism, phenomenalism).
⑤ The soul may be a substance, but we cannot demonstrate this by theoretical reason (agnosticism).
⑥ Man and only man is a complete substance. The soul is an incomplete substance; the body is a body only because of the soul (hylomorphism). (Donceel 424)

not in the sense that God makes the soul out of nothing, without any direct cooperation of the parents, for this sounds like a miraculous intervention. But in the sense that he makes the parents transcend their own powers and produce, as an effect which they are unable to produce by their own unaided powers, the soul of their child. Hence the human soul is created in the sense in which every new reality in the world is created. (441)

This is because the emergence of a new reality represents an "exceeding of Self" and an "increase of being" on the part of the source of this new reality. This extension must have its origin in God.

When is the human soul created? Donceel says:

We do not know. We are certain only that it must occur some time between the moment of conception and the moment when the child performs its first intellectual activity. We know the human soul only through its operations... St. Thomas, the Scholastic Masters, and also a slowly increasing number of modern philosophers claim that it is present only when the organs required to make such an act of reflection possible — especially the brain — are present, although they need not yet be functional. This might be some time around the third month of pregnancy. . . Only when the human embryo began to show a human outline, had developed the main human organs, the brain and the limbs, could there be a human body, hence a human soul. This is the theory of mediate animation. Nowadays the theory of immediate animation is more generally accepted. It claims that as soon as the ovum is fecundated, as soon as the embryo possesses the normal human body, it possesses a human soul, it is a human being. According to this theory, the human soul is infused at the moment of conception. (442-443)

My views on these two issues are very simple. The human soul comes from creative power, bestowed at the moment of conception upon the union of spermatozoa and ovum.

The generation or transformation of each thing in the universe represents an "exceeding of Self" and an "increase of being" of the parent object. When something prepares to transform its own material into some other thing, the generative power bestows the form through creative power (the spiritual power of God), allowing their union and eventual existence as a new being. Generative power is God's tool for continual creation. Through God's creative power, generative power obtains all that is needed for the transformation of all creation. Generative power causes spermatozoa and ovum from the parents to unite, while at the same time, bestowing the form of the union, that is, a concrete human nature. The product of this union is a human being. Man only has one form. He cannot change his nature at will. When spermatozoa and ovum join at the moment of conception, it is the conception of a human being. The embryo cannot be of a vegetative nature upon conception and transform itself into a human nature only upon the formation of human organs three or more months later. Again, Donceel writes:

> With Aquinas we might say that at first it lives only with a vegetative life, it is an autonomous growth in the mother's womb. Next it passes to sentient or animal life. Only when the essential human organs are ready does the human soul take over. This human soul, whose emergence occurs after a real "evolution" within the mother's womb, is the joint effect of the cooperation of the parents and the creative First Cause. (444)

This idea is based on the concept that function is the basis of life. Physiological life, sentient life and intellectual life are all determined by bodily organs. There is a corresponding life only when there is an organ. At the same time, there appeared the idea that man possesses a physiological soul, a sentient soul and a spiritual soul. However, life is itself existence. Human life is itself man's existence. Once a person loses life, he ceases to exist. Since life is existence, the latter can only be one. Although existence is constantly in motion and changing, it cannot lead from one specie to another specie. That is because the form of existence is unchangeable and constantly remains one kind. The human embryo formed at the moment of conception upon the union of spermatozoa and ovum receives a form that is human. It cannot originally be a vegetative form that later changes into an animal form and finally into a human form. Evolution of form within a thing is impossible. The form cannot evolve within a thing. Although this thing's existence is a moving one and is capable of change, it cannot evolve. Neither can its vital life evolve. An embryo inside a mother's womb cannot originally be vegetative in nature and later change into animal and eventually human.

Life is manifested by organic activity. Nevertheless, one cannot conclude that something exists simply on the basis of its manifestation. Existence precedes manifestation. By the same token, the absence of organs does not absolutely prevent the manifestation of life. Neither does it lead to the conclusion that the human soul is inexistent. Existence is substantial existence and function is substantial function. Substance can exist before function. Function and existence cannot be one and the same thing.

A person possesses only one life. He lives a human life right from the very start of his life. Human life is determined by form. The form of a person's life is this person's very form. The form of man is his soul. Therefore, an embryo in the mother's womb possesses a soul right from the moment of conception. It is not that the soul is infused into an embryo. Rather, the embryo exists because of the soul. The Roman Catholic Church bans abortion. It abandoned all discussions regarding the stage of fetal growth at which abortion could be considered prudent. The Church ban on abortion applies from the moment of conception. Donceel is of the opinion that this teaching poses some problems. He cited that the same ovum can lead to twins. He writes:

> [Identical twins] are caused by the splitting, soon after conception, of one fecundated ovum. According to the theory of immediate animation we would first have one human person, which would subsequently split into two equal halves and turn into two human persons. A metaphysical impossibility. (444-445)

Yet what really constitutes a metaphysical impossibility is to say that the same embryo changes from vegetative form to animal and later to a human form. Furthermore, based on their theory of indirect animation, an embryo starts either as one vegetative or one animal form. How then does it become two persons? If twins share some of the organs, it then would mean that their souls are incomplete, since these philosophers propose that without organs the soul cannot exist.

Actually, identical twins come from an embryo formed by one fecundated ovum which possesses two different existences for a pair of twins, that is, different lives, albeit not manifested. Spermatozoa and ovum are mere materials. Only with a soul can they lead to the conception of a living thing. One ovum providing material for one or two souls is not a metaphysical impossibility.

The human soul is man's form. His body is matter. These are not only abstract concepts, but actual realities. The human soul is a spiritual reality while body is a material reality. The two unite in existence to form a psychophysical entity which possesses a psychophysical existence --psychophysical life.

The spiritual soul can possess knowledge, emotion and freedom. It is the origin of human life. Because the soul is living and is man's generative power, it resides totally in the human body and in all of its parts. If there is no life in a certain part of the body, then the soul is not residing in that part. That is to say, if there is no soul, there is no life. However, this is not speaking from the "functional" point of view. It is not because a certain part of the body is unsuitable for vital life that it has no life but rather it is because there is no soul in it. That part separates from the existence of the integral entity and possesses no life.

The human soul is spiritual. A spiritual being is imperishable. It cannot destroy itself nor be destroyed by things outside itself. Only God the Creator can destroy spiritual beings. However, from God's revelation, we know that He will not destroy human souls.

However, in philosophy, the problem is not that simple. The human soul and body enter into union in existence, that is, they join together in one life. This one life disappears with death. The body ceases to exist, that is, after death, the body is no longer human body. It becomes lifeless. How then can the soul exist? Is man's existence actually the existence of the soul and the body appended to it? This concept is illogical. This is similar to Plato's concept of the *a priori* soul. However, the body is not an accident but a matter of man's substance. The human soul and body share the same existence or life to make up one subject. Existence is subjective as life is. Once the subject disappears, existence and life also disappear. How does the soul survive and continue living? Some philosophers take organic activity as the basis of the soul's existence. Since corpses do not show any activity at all, how then can the soul survive?

The human soul and body enter into union in existence to become a psychophysical life. This existence is shared between the two. The same is true with life. The human soul does not change nor split whereas the body changes and can disintegrate. If a limb dries up and is lifeless, it separates from existence. After death, the whole of man's body becomes unsuitable for life and separates from existence. On the contrary, the human soul is fit to live. It does not separate from existence but continues existing and living. The individual life of the human soul is not human life. It only constitutes life of the soul. When bodies resurrect, they will again enter into union with the soul's existence to regain human life. However, by that time, the human body will no longer be material in nature but instead non-material. Human life will instead be spiritual and no longer psychophysical.

III. Knowing the Subject

The psychophysical union of the human soul and body forms one person. A person is himself the subject of his life and of all his activities. Furthermore, he also is the master of his body and soul. Although the words "subject" and "master" differ in meaning--the former suggesting operation while the latter expressing possession--they actually have the same meaning. Both denote that this person is the basis of all his relationships.

A person is a subject, an "ego." A subject is necessarily a reality whose basis is existence. Therefore, the basis of a subject is existence, an existence that is moving and life. A subject is a reality, that is, a subsistent individual. It is a persona. Thus, a person is one persona.

Persona has a very rich meaning. It is an integral, real "ego." All that the "ego" possesses are included in the persona, including all its actions.

A subject is a subsistent reality. A subsistent reality is an autonomous existence. If it does not exist, it would not be a subsistent reality. Therefore, to talk about a subject, one must bring up existence. If a person exists and lives, then there is this person. When I say "this person," I mean that this person exists and lives. If this person dies and disappears, I can no longer say "this person." If I still say so, it would be meaningless.

It is because of existence that everything about the subject has meaning. Everything about the ego has meaning only if he is living. If the ego dies and disappears, everything about him ceases to be meaningful and no longer continues existing.

The existence of the subject therefore needs no proof. That is because ego is existence. The ego is actually a living person. There is no need to prove that I am a living person. If I no longer live, I would no longer be this person.

In Chinese philosophy, there has never been a call for proof to the existence of the subject--the existence of an "ego." You, me and him are all existence and life. If we are inexistent and not living, then there would not be you, me and him. This point needs no proof and in fact cannot be proven. Western philosophy has its objective in searching for truth. Truth is the object of the intellect. Everything uttered by man has to go through the process of knowledge. All that is unknown or unintelligible to man is inexistent. Hence, some philosophers propose that what is logical must necessarily exist.

To prove its existence, the subject/ego must be "known" through self-knowledge. When I know myself, two "ego's" appear. One is the knowing ego and the other, the known ego. Thus, the unbridgeable problem of subject and object in Western epistemology again presents itself. How do I know myself?

René Descartes said: "I think, therefore I am." Experientially, this proof is correct. Viewed from the epistemological angle, however, what relates my thinking to my existence? Here, there must be a major premise, that is, "All that thinks necessarily exists." This is acceptable to all. However, how do you prove the minor premise "I think"? We can only say that "when I speak, I am of course thinking." But how do we prove that "I am speaking"? We can only do it. When I am speaking, I am speaking. This requires no proof. This is like saying "When I exist I exist. What further proof is needed?"

With his phenomenological methods, Edmund Husserl advocated that all subjective notions or experiences are "existing but not discussed." Instead, he opted for a direct return to the thing itself--the subject. Phenomenologists use this method to know the subject-the ego. Donceel writes:

> We must penetrate more deeply into ourselves until we reach precisely that which tries to penetrate thus more deeply into ourselves, which is ultimately an act of knowing and willing: I wish to know the knower in me. We shall try to show that in the act of knowing and willing, more precisely in the act of affirming and willing, I really coincide with myself. In that same act I also coincide with being. I have probed the ultimate depths where I am rooted in being.(31)

Donceel proposes that God knows himself, undifferentiated as subject or as object, "but the luminous self-presence and self-awareness of the subject, who is entirely knowing and entirely known in the one undivided and indivisible effulgence of Pure Act"(28). Man is incapable of this knowing. However, in his judgment and will, man is united with himself. He further writes:

> The pure I is to some extent that in me which perceives, feels, imagines, remembers, solves problems. It is specifically and properly that in me which affirms and wills...the knowing and willing of these activities is no longer quasi-objective; here the subjective, originating ego is at work. (Donceel 33)

However, in knowing the subject/ego through knowing and willing, although these two overlap in the ego, the subject-object relationship between the knower and willer, and between knowing and willing still cannot be totally avoided. We must break away from the practice of knowing by knowing the subject and avoid the use of knowing to prove the subject by still proving oneself through oneself. The subject is a living existence. It is life. A living existence manifests itself. As I live I manifest my ego. My judgment or will are manners of manifesting myself. Besides, the ego is a psychophysical existence--life. Sentient activities also manifest the ego. In addition, to say that consciousness is self-manifestation is of course correct. However, consciousness is but a most direct way of manifestation. It would be wrong to say that consciousness is me and that, without it, I do not exist.

Chinese philosophy strongly emphasizes the concepts of brightness *(ming)*, penetration *(t'ung)* and identity *(yi)*. Applied to the subject/ego, the brightness of the self resembles that of a transparent crystal image and not that of a candle. It can illumine other things but not itself. If the ego's subject is bright, then the ego can directly see it with penetration and identify [be united] with it. This is true for all spiritual beings. The human soul is spiritual and is therefore, bright, penetrated and identified. However, as the ego is made up of soul and body, the ego is not transparent owing to its corporeal body. The clarity of the soul can be manifested through the body. However, the body is not totally material to totally obstruct the brightness of the soul. Man can know things outside of himself and thus the subject of the soul can also be made manifest to himself. This manifestation is not only true in introspective consciousness, for even children who do not have introspective consciousness know in a natural manner that they exist and that they are themselves. When children want something, they say "I want this or that thing." Although they do not understand "ego," they know that "I is I."

In spiritual beings, the existence and the contents of the subject are totally one. Once the subject appears, all its contents appear with it. In psychophysical beings, however, the contents are not totally manifested when the subject manifests itself. Since psychophysical beings need the body to know, and owing to the material nature of the body, the contents of the subject are not fully manifested. This is why Chuang-tzu talked about the attainment of supreme knowledge by chastising the body and cultivating a clean heart and by interpenetrating one's own *ch'i* with that of things. He called knowledge obtained with the use of the intellect and brain partial knowledge. Nevertheless, this apprehension of *ch'i* is impossible. Man can only use his intellect to comprehend the outside world and his own subject. When man manifests his subject via his psychophysical activites, some of these manifestations are exterior and some interior. Some of man's understanding of himself are intimate and almost resemble a direct observation, like, for instance, the feeling of delectation, anger, sorrow and happiness and personal judgment. Some are indirect such as one's own physical appearance and talents. In Chinese philosophy, each person's "nature," that is, human nature, it itself transparent. The contents of human nature regulate one's activities. Sages did not have private passions. Sages performed good acts during which human nature was made manifest naturally. In Chapter XX of the *Chung-yung*, it is said:

> Sincerity is the Way of Heaven. To think how to be sincere is the way of man. He who is sincere is one who hits upon what is right without effort and apprehends without thinking. He is naturally and easily in harmony with the Way. Such a man is a sage. (Chan, p. 107)

The ordinary man has private passions in his heart. This keeps his human nature from being naturally made manifest. This condition calls for control of one's passions. In the same chapter, the *Chung-yung* says: "To be sincere is the Way of man. He who tries to be sincere is one who chooses the good and holds fast to it." The manifestation of the subject as explained by the Neo-Confucianists is the manifestation of human nature. The so-called human nature refers to the principle of human life. Lu Hsiang-shan proposes that "outside the heart, there is no principle (*li*)." However, what the subject/ego possesses is not only limited to principle (*li*) but also includes accidents like personality and talents which cannot be made totally manifest through the heart. The Buddhist Ch'an vision posits that "a bright heart shows one's nature" (*ming hsin chien hsing*). A bright heart is one that is devoid of all mundane things. "Shows one's nature" means being able to see one's own real nature. Nature is the so-called true reality (*chen-ju*), which refers to the substance of myriad realities. This manifestation of the true reality as taught by Ch'an Buddhism cannot be realized in a psychophysical subject. If ever realized, it is only in the manner described by Lu Hsiang-shan as manifestation of the principle (*li*).

In terms of existence, knowledge of the subject is directly made manifest without any need for introspection or proof whatsoever. In terms of contents, the subject is known through the manifestation of the psychophysical entity. The self-nature of the subject is transparent, a special quality belonging to spiritual beings. According to Mencius, man's supreme essence is his mind. This mind is spiritual in nature. However, the mind or the soul does not make up the whole of man's subject. The subject of the mind is still the human body. We can therefore say that the self-nature of man's subject is transparent and it is so owing to the body's transparency. Bodily activities manifest the subject in varying degrees. Physiological activities manifest very little of the subject's contents while sentient activities manifest more of the subject's contents. Emotional activities manifest a large quantity and intellectual activities manifest the largest quantity of the subject's contents. In the process of knowing the subject, no differentiation can be made between subject and object. This is because in the manifestation of the subject, it is a psychophysical entity that is made manifest. Manifestation of the subject is nothing but the knowing of the subject. They share the same subject and occur in the same existence and the same life. The manifestation of my subject is also the knowledge of the subject about myself. Therefore, manifestation is nothing but knowing. Here, subject and object are undifferentiated. In the case of a spiritual subject, its transparent self-nature manifests its own self, which leads to self-knowledge. In the case of a psychophysical subject, whose manifestation is a psychophysical manifestation, the subject's knowledge of himself is also a psychophysical knowledge. In this case, manifestation and knowledge also overlap with one another. However, the subject's knowledge of things external to it depends upon the manifestation of these things to the subject. Hence, in this case, subject and object are differentiated from one another.

IV. The Three Ego's

The subject is ego. Ego is a persona comprised of human nature, personality, subsistence and accidents. Persona is itself this actual, subsistent individual. Persona is a concrete person. Since a concrete person is ego, then ego is concrete existence, or even "being," a concretely existing being. The concrete existence of the ego is a moving one. It is life. Ego is a concrete life.

A concrete life is a concrete existence. A concrete existence is then ego itself. Speaking in terms of the substance, ego is concrete existence and life. This is "substantial ego." Metaphysically, since ego is concrete existence, then ego is made manifest naturally. Ego is itself existence. Without existence, there would not be ego. This needs not be proven and cannot, in fact, be proven.

The subject/ego is integral and includes many complex components, that is, contents. The contents of the ego's subject are psychophysical. Similarly, the manifestation of the subject's contents is likewise a psychophysical manifestation. The ego manifested by a psychophysical manifestation is not integral. This ego is a manifested ego. This manifested ego is the basis of all its relationships on earth and can therefore be called the "ego of the present life." The "ego of the present life" is nothing but the life of the ego on earth. When ego leaves this world, the body separates from life, after which the ego no longer remains psychophysical. What remains is spiritual life. Since the self-nature of spiritual beings is transparent, the ego manifested by the spirit includes all the contents of the spirit. This is no longer the "ego of the present life" but the "ego of the world to come." In the present life, I know myself by the ego manifested by my mind and body. This known ego is known from the manifested ego to the subjective ego through what is ordinarily called "introspective consciousness." Introspective ego is said to be the ego's subject because the ego knows that he is the master of his actions. I think that the manifestation of the ego's subject through the psychophysical entity is itself the process of knowing. There is no subject-object differentiation between knowing and manifestation. On the contrary, introspection suggests a differentiation between subject and object. This tells us that introspective consciousness cannot be used to explain knowing of the subject, much less be taken as the subject of the ego. While the ego is living in this world, it is a psychophysical subject which is manifested through a psychophysical entity. It remains in the process of manifestation. In knowing the subject of the ego, what is known is an ego that tends towards the unlimited. None of its relations in the world can satisfy the ego, which constantly searches ahead. This is true not only for material things but also for the so-called spiritual goods: true, good and beautiful. The Taoist philosopher Chuang-tzu advocates a reclusive lifestyle characterized by the cultivation of a pure mind. The Buddhists talk about a cleansed life of eternal bliss in the state of nirvana. Although the Neo-Confucianists teach about a life within the world, they likewise search for a lifestyle that is united with the virtue of Heaven and Earth. Actually, all these teachings search for a coming world because of the impossibility of realizing objectives in the present world. We can thus conclude that the ego known through its manifestation is an ego in "search of the coming world."

The "substanial ego" is the actual existence and life of the ego. Ego is itself life. Ego is living.

The "ego of the present life" is an ego manifested by the human body and soul. It is nothing but the life of the ego in this present world. Viewed from tne angle of the ego itself, all the facets of the life of the ego manifest itself. All the facets of the ego's life belong to his life. They all manifest his persona. The ego's physiological life is based on the ego's physical structure. It differs from the physiological life of other persons. Although for all human beings, common points on physiological life exist, the overall physiological life differs from person to person. The same is true with sentient life. Each person lives according to one's sensory organs. Emotional life manifests character in a special way. It clearly manifests the ego's persona. Intellectual life shows a psychophysical ego. It shows the ego as subject.

The ego does not live a solitary existence. The ego lives together with the myriad things in the universe. Since existence involves a living life, the myriad things enter into relationship with others. The ego manifested as a psychophysical ego is the subject of all the different relationships in the world. The ego's relationship with the outside world can be active or passive. These relationshps are decided by and at the same time determined by an ego manifested by the human soul and body or the "ego in the present world." The ego's knowledge of the outside world, its feelings for it, its sensitive response to the exterior things, even its physiological acceptance (digestion) of the things outside, are all determined by the "ego of the present life." The ego's life in this world is determined by this "ego of the present world."

The "ego of the coming world," described in terms of its breadth, is characterized by a search for the acquisiton of all things in the universe without attaining satisfaction. Mencius taught that flood-like *ch'i* is stuck between Heaven and Earth. Chang Tsai expounded on the "Englargement of the mind" which he described as accommodation of the myriad things in the universe inside one's mind. This spirit abounds in the works of Chuang-tzu. The "vision" of the Buddhist *Hua-yen* and *Tien-t'ai* schools says that one is within the many, the many are within the one and the many within the many (Chan 423). The "ego of the coming world," described in terms of its depth, is characterized by man's search for eternity. The Taoists have their *hsien-jen* [saints], the Buddhist their nirvana and world of eternal bliss and the Catholics have their eternal life after death. Although the Neo-Confucians do not mention an afterlife, they search for fulfillment of nature (*chin-shing*) in the present life. Chapter XXII of the *Chung-yung* talks about how fully developing the nature of things can make one assist in the transforming and nourishing process of Heaven and Earth (Chan 108).

The existence of the ego is a living existence. It is life itself. Life's substance is infinite, not in the sense of the present but in the sense of a search toward the infinite. In the present life, what the ego attains is limited, thus leading to constant dissatisfaction and feelings of depression and inadequacy. Since the ego is a psychophysical entity, what is can come into contact with in the present life are material things and psychophysical entities, all of which are limited. The ego cannot directly come into contact with spiritual entities. Only after death when the soul exists alone or after the resurrection when the ego already turns into a non-material spiritual being can it directly come into contact with the Absolute Reality--God, the Creator. Only then can the ego be satisfied and be really happy.

The "ego of the next life" is hidden and not manifest. The "substantial ego" is made manifest naturally. This needs no proof. The "ego of this present world" is made manifest through the psychophysical entity. It is at the same time the knowing of the psychophysical entity. The ego known by the ego is itself the same ego. The ego and persona referred to ordinarily point to the "ego of the present world." The "ego of the next life" is not made manifest exteriorly but is instead manifested inside our hearts. It is a personal experience. The ego feels dissatisfied with he outside world and itself, an experience which always makes it feel that the present it [ego] is not the real it [ego]. It thinks its real self is the future it [ego]. Hence, this ego often takes the ideal ego as its real ego. However, the ideal ego often does not attain the moment of realization. It is always engaged in some kind of a search. Even if it already attains the objects ego, it is never satisfied. It always has further ideals coming. Hence, the ego cannot take the ideal ego as the final objective in this present life. It is a kind of endless search. On the contrary, the "ego of the next life" lies hidden in one's heart. It cannot be clearly known or described. Ordinarily it is said that knowledge of the ego is mysterious and beyond description. This mystery of self-knowledge is often associated with the "ego of the next life."

Works Cited

Chan, Wing-tsit. *A Source Book in Chinese Philosophy*. Princeton: Princeton UP,1963.

Donceel, J. F. *Philosophical Anthropology*. Taipei: Hsien-chih, 1974.

Translated by Carlos Tee

Chapter XI

One Universe

I. One Universe in Ecology

Physics has developed Quantum Mechanics thereby allowing the possibility of probing the oneness of the universe. In his book, *The Tao of Physics*, Capra writes:

> The basic oneness of the universe is not only the central characteristic of the mystical experience, but is also one of the most important revelations of modern physics. It becomes apparent at the atomic level and manifests itself more and more as one penetrates deeper into matter, down into the realm of subatomic particles. The unity of all things and events will be a recurring theme throughout our comparison of modern physics and Eastern philosophy. (142)

Physicists hold the idea that the cosmos resembles a spider web whose parts are all joined together. Within this network, dynamic changes occur to mutually affect each part of the whole. As Commoner writes:

> The science that studies these relationships and the processes linking each living thing to the physical and chemical environment is ecology. It is the science of planetary housekeeping. For the environment is, so to speak, the house created on the earth by living things for living things. It is a young science and much of what it teaches has been learned from only small segments of the whole network of life on the earth. (32)

From its study of things, ecology formulated three laws, as follows:

The First Law of Ecology: Everything is Connected to Everything Else. This law points out the existence of a mutual relationship among all things on earth. This relationship resembles a network wherein things are interconnected. One type of living thing depends upon another for existence. This other type of living thing in turn depends upon the first type of living thing. They mutually maintain a balance. Consider, for example, the fresh-water ecological cycle: fish -- organic waste -- bacteria of decay -- inorganic products -- algae--fish. Suppose that due to unusually warm summer weather there is a rapid growth of algae. This unusual weather would deplete the supply of inorganic nutrients so that two sectors of the cycle, algae and nutrients, would become out of balance. The excess in algae would increase the ease with which fish can feed on them; this would reduce the algal population, increase fish waste production, and the levels of algae and nutrients would tend to return to their original balanced position.

These balanced cyclic reactions naturally occur in natural environments. If, due to the action of an exterior force, one of these cycles is damaged, the cycle of ecosystem equilibrium collapses. Such a collapse is precisely the peril faced by the ecosystem in present times due to pollution.

Among the different life forms, animals depend on plants for life. Larger animals depend on smaller ones for life. However, the relationship in this system is far from simple. The cycle of the ecosystem is not a simple loop. In this cycle, interconnecting branches are found, which together form a network structure that can better withstand the stress of collapse. The present environmental crisis has resulted from the cutting off of the cycles in the web-like structure by man-made activities. With the ecosystem thus impaired, the risk of collapse presents itself (Commoner 32-35).

The Second Law of Ecology: Everything Must Go Somewhere. The problem of wastes besets many governments. There is no such thing as waste in the world of nature. Waste matter excreted by organic bodies are absorbed as food by other organic bodies. The carbon dioxide exhaled by animals serves as food for green plants. Oxygen gas given off by plants is consumed by animals. Waste matter excreted by animals nourishes bacteria and decay bacteria serve as algal nutrients. However, owing to man's actions, these wastes often do not reach their destined places. Instead, they pile up and cause harm. For instance, when mercury-containing dry-cell batteries thrown into the garbage are incinerated, the mercury is carried off with water vapor. When precipitated as rain, the mercury-bearing steam finds its ways into rivers where the metal is absorbed by fish. When caught and taken by man, the mercury-bearing fish thus introduces the toxic metal to humans (40).

The Third Law of Ecology: Nature Knows Best. In the natural ecosystem, when a part of nature loses it balance, the system naturally relieves it. When an unwanted factor appears in a part of the ecosystem, it is eliminated in a natural way. This is why we say "Nature knows best." The addition of an artificial factor into the ecosystem by man usually leads to harm. For instance, improper use of insecticides and agricultural chemicals necessarily causes harm. This situation is similar to the use of artificial organs. If they do not match natural conditions, they cannot be of practical use at all (41).

The Fourth Law of Ecology: There Is No Such Thing as a Free Lunch. When natural resources are depleted, they must be replenished. Man cannot freely take [from nature] as though someone else is paying for his lunch. If forests are denuded, replanting of trees is necessary to keep the ecosystem from getting damaged. The earth's ecosystem makes one integral whole. Not any single object can suddenly pop up in the whole or disappear from it. If any part of the whole is taken away by man, it needs a replacement by something else (45-46).

However, in today's world, the needs of the human race have ballooned to levels that are beyond control. Man employs massive technical power to effect an increase in production. Oftentimes, the technological methods he uses damage the ecology and are often self-destroying. "The present course of human civilization is suicidal" (295). On this, Ashby writes:

> No one can predict the full consequences of tinkering with any part of an ecosystem. Even the non-living environment has

properties without which life as we know it would be inconceivable. The idea of man as lord of nature is, in the minds of scientists, replaced by the idea of man in symbiosis with nature. Hamlet's comment "We fat all creatures else to fat us, and we fat ourselves for maggots" is a curt but accurate summary of man's place in the biosphere. (82-83)

II. One Universe: The Neo-Confucian Idea

The idea of one universe can be considered indigenous to the religions and philosophies of India and China. Both Hinduism and Buddhism do not differentiate between man and the cosmos. The Buddhist sects of *T'ien-t'ai* and *Hua-yen* share the view that "one is within the many and the many are within the one." Both propose the congruence of the myriad dharmas. The real man (*chen-jen*) proposed by the Taoist Chuang-tzu is envisaged to inter-penetrate with the primeval ether (*ch'i*) of Heaven and Earth, with which he exists in harmony forever. The Neo-Confucians stress the role of moral virtues by saying:

> The character of the great man is identical with that of Heaven and Earth; his brilliance is identical with that of the sun and the moon; his order is identical with that of the four seasons, and his good and evil fortunes are identical with those of spiritual beings. ("*I Ching*, Hexagram No. 1, *Ch'ien*, Chan 264)

The Neo-Confucian vision of the cosmos, as reflected by ideas in the *I Ching*, is that of a unity between the universe and man. The *I Ching* was originally a book on divination used to foretell good fortune or ill-fate. The book employs as tools changes in the hexagrams which follow the principles of cosmic change. In the eyes of the designer of the hexagrams, cosmic change is a change that occurs in the whole. The whole refers to the cosmos represented by Heaven, earth and man. Heaven and earth each symbolize one element while man represents the myriad things formed by the two elements. The element of Heaven is *yang* or *ch'ien* while that of earth is *yin* or *k'un*.

"The successive movement of *yin* and *yang* constitutes the way (*Tao*). What issues from the Way is good, and that which realizes it is the individual nature" (Appended Remarks, Ch. V, Chan 266). The whole cosmos is but the operation of *yin* and *yang*.

The *I Ching* propounded by Han Dynasty scholars, referred to as the *hsiang-shu* scholarship of the *I* (change), boils down to the concept of *ch'i*. For them, cosmic change results from the operation of *ch'i* following a certain pathway called *ch'i-yun*. The central idea of Hsien-wei is based on *ch'i-y*un as well as the concept of Five Agents (*wu-hsing*). Expressed in terms of time, cosmic *ch'i-yun* is shown by the four seasons. In terms of space, it is manifested by the four directions. These concepts of four seasons, four directions and five agents are represented by four hexagrams. Then, the ideas of twelve months, twenty four sections (*chieh*), three hundred sixty-five days and sixty-four hexagrams are integrated to form one integral body — the cosmos.

Tung Chung-shu not only adopted the idea of mutual succession and restriction among the five agents, but also compared the human body to a micro-cosmos whose structure he said runs parallel to that of the universe.

Reflecting Neo-Confucian philosophical thought, the *yueh-ling* [monthly decrees] of the *Book of Rites* (*Li chi*) affirms that an emperor governing the four seas resembles one who controls Heaven and Earth. If an emperor were to govern the state which is referred to as *t'ien-hsia* , palace objects must be arranged in conformity with the seasons and directions. Spirits of each season must also be honored. This way of doing things was referred to as the governance of one universe. In fact, even ritual music also followed divine principles and *ch'i-yun*. There was also the so-called *wu-te chung-shih* [immutable five virtues] which regulates the succession of dynastic emperors. The concept of interaction between man and Heaven (*t'ien-jen kan-ying*), which spells out the ideas of auspicious reward and ill punishment, was also based on the concept of *ch'i-yun*.

By the waning years of the Han Dynasty, the Taoists adopted the study of *ch'i-yun* to formulate the art of longevity. They proposed imbibition of the primeval *ch'i* or concoction of the golden pills (*chin-tan*) as means to extend one's life.

Chou Tun-i, a Sung Dynasty rationalist, borrowed the Taoist Diagram of the Great Ultimate to design his own. In his work, *T'ai-chi t'u-shuo* (Explanation of the Diagram of the Great Ultimate), Chou pointed out that the Great Ultimate or the Non-ultimate generates *yin* and *yang,* which give rise to the Five Agents. The Five Agents engender male and female, both of which generate the myriad things. He explained the process of generation of the myriad things in terms of the operation of *ch'i.* The whole cosmos and the myriad things in it undergo change through the *yin* and *yang* of one *ch'i.* Shao Yung[1] employed this idea to explain the cosmic cycle. In his *Huang-chi ching-shih* [Supreme Principles Governing the World], Shao Yung calculated the chronological timing of the cosmic cycle based on the sixty-four hexagrams of the *I Ching.*

In contrast, Chang Tsai explained the *I Ching's T'ai-chi* (Great Ultimate) in terms of the *T'ai-hsu* (Great Vacuity) which he equated with the substance of *ch'i.* In turn, the substance of the Great Vacuity is the Great Harmony. He writes:

> The Great Harmony is called the Way (Tao). It embraces the nature which underlies all counter processes of floating and sinking, rising and falling, and motion and rest. It is the origin of the process of fusion and intermingling, of overcoming and being overcome, and of expansion and contraction." (*Cheng-meng t'ai-he pien* [Correcting Youthful Ignorance, Ch. I: Great Harmony], Chan 500)

Chang Tsai further writes:

---

(1) [Translator's Note] Shao Yung (1011-1077) was a neo-Confucianist who received training from a Taoist. He served as a keeper of records in the Board of public Works and as a militia judge. His principal writing is the *Supreme Principles Governing the World.*

As the Great Vacuity, material force is extensive and vague. Yet it ascends and descends and moves in all ways without ever ceasing. This is what is called in the *Book of Changes* ' fusion and intermingling' and in the *Chuang Tzu* ' fleeting forces moving in all directions while all living beings blow against one another with their breath.' Here lies the subtle, incipient activation of reality and unreality, of motion and rest, and the beginning of *yin* and *yang*, as well as the elements of strength and weakness. (*Tai-he* [Great Harmony], Chan 503)

Changes in *yin* and *yang* engender the myriad things. The myriad things in the universe together form one body within the changes of the *ch'i*. Thus, in his life, man needs to experience this one linkage. For him to experience this, his heart must be sincere. "The Doctrine of the Mean calls sincerity the capacity to generate. Mencius described it as expansion and generation. Both take its character as embodying *yin* and *yang*, and in harmony with Heaven and Earth with which it interfuses totally" (*Shen Hua*).

In his work *Hsi-ming* (Western Inscription), Chang Tsai explained the experience of sharing the same body with Heaven and earth.

Heaven is my father and Earth is my mother, and even such a small creature as I find an intimate place in their midst. Therefore that which fills the universe I regard as my body and that which directs the universe I consider my nature. All people are my brothers and sisters, and all things are my companions. (Chan 497)

The heart of man needs to experience the myriad things. Chang Tsai further said:

By enlarging one's mind, one can enter into all the things in the world [to examine and understand their principle.] As long as anything is not yet entered into, there is still something outside

the mind. The mind of ordinary people is limited to the narrow-
ness of what is seen and what is heard. The sage, however,
fully develops his nature and does not allow what is seen or
heard to fetter his mind. He regards everything in the world to
be his own self. This is why Mencius said that if one exerts his
mind to the utmost, he can know nature and Heaven. Heaven is
so vast that there is nothing outside of it. Therefore the mind
that leaves something outside is not capable of uniting itself
with the mind of Heaven. Knowledge coming from seeing and
hearing is knowledge obtained through contact with things. It
is not knowledge obtained through one's moral nature. Knowledge obtained through one's moral nature does not originate
from seeing or hearing. (*Cheng-meng* [Correcting Youthful
Ignorance], *Ta-hsin* [Enlarging One's Mind])

Mencius, however, explained the concept of experiencing the myriad
things through the virtue of kindness. He said: "[The superior man]
care for his next of kin, is charitable to people and loving to creatures." (*Chin-hsin*, Part 1, Chan 515)

Ch'eng Hao's views reflect the spirit of Mencius. Ch'eng once
said: "Wthin Heaven and Earth, man interacts with the myriad things.
When did Heaven ever distinguish between man and things?" (*Erh-
Ch'eng yi-lu* 2A, Complete Work of the Two Ch'eng's, Surviving
Works 2A) He further writes:

The reason why it is said that all things form one body is that
all have this principle, simply because they all have come from
it. ' Change means production and reproduction.' In production, once a thing is produced, it possesses this principle
complete. Man can extend this principle to others, but because
their material force with which they are endowed is dark,
things cannot do so. But we must say that they do not share
principle with others."(*Erh Ch'eng yi-lu* 2A [Complete Work
of the Two Ch'eng's] Surviving Works 2A, Chan 533)

The myriad things share the same principle. This principle is the same principle of production and reproduction. Production and reproduction are defined as humanity (*jen*). When humanity resides in the heart of man, he feels happy and contented. Ch'eng composed a poem that reads:

> Placid and serenely at leisure,
>
> Sound asleep 'til the eastern sun is high.
>
> Calmly gaze and see through myriad things,
>
> And relish with delight the joy of seasons changing.
>
> When all creation with form the Tao transcends,
>
> Then into the world of whirling change the mind enters.
>
> Sobriety in fortune or joy in humble poverty,
>
> Distinguishes the man of heroic dignity. (*Erh Ch'eng ch'üan-shu, Min-tao wen-chi, Ch'iu-ji ou-ch'eng* [Complete Work of the Two Ch'eng's V, Mingtao Collection] 3)

Following the Two *Ch'eng's* idea of "the unity and diversity of principle." Chu Hsi affirms that the whole universe and the myriad things share the same principle of production and reproduction. Yet, because of the differences in the clarity or turbidity of the material force, the principle of things differ from one another. He thus emphasized that the center of Heaven and Earth is the production of things. For him, production is nothing but humanity (*jen*). Since man possesses the mind of Heaven and Earth, then the mind of man is also humanity (*jen*). Because of this humanity (*jen*), the human mind is capable of thoroughly penetrating the myriad things.

Wang Yang-ming propounds that "the man of humanity regards Heaven and Earth and all things as one body." "For at bottom, Heaven, Earth, the myriad things, and man form one body. The point at which this unity manifests in its most refined and excellent form is the clear intelligence of the human mind. Wind, rain, dew, thunder, sun and moon, stars, animals and plants, mountains and rivers, earth and stones are essentially of one body with man. It is for this reason that such things as the grains and animals can nourish man and that such things as medicine and minerals can heal diseases. Since they share the same material force, they enter into one another." (*Wang wen-ch'eng-kung ch'üan-shu, chuan 4, Ch'uan-hsi lu* C [Complete Works of Wang Yang-ming, Vol. 3, Part 2], Chan 685) The human mind is endowed with clear intelligence. It can interfuse with the myriad things. The same is true with the humanity of man. This explains the phrase "the man of humanity regards Heaven and earth and all things as one body."

Deeply convinced by the ideas of Chang Tsai, Wang Ch'uan-shan wrote the *Cheng-meng chu* [Annotations on 'Correcting Youthful Ignorance'], in which he expressed approval of Chang Tsai's idea of a unified cosmos. In the chapter entitled *Ta-hsin* [Enlarging One's Mind] of his work "Correcting Youthful Ignorance," Chang Tsai said"

> Things have Tao as their body. This is basic to the Tao. A man becomes immensely useful once his body has Tao as its body. If his body is taken as an object and is utilized by Tao, then he becomes great as a result. In contrast, he becomes ignoble if his body is not utilized by Tao and instead becomes his obsession.

In his commentary, Wang Ch'uan-shan explained:

> The reason why the myriad things are self-generating and subsistent, and the reason why eyes and ears can see and hear, and why the mind can look through things is all because they have one body with the Tao. Only when the Tao is known can one reach all things and fulfill one's own self. If not, it would be attaining the purpose while forgetting the fundamental.

The Tao mentioned by Wang is similar to princile (*li*) as explained by Chu Hsi. That is, within Tao, the myriad things share the same body.

Starting from the writing of the *I Ching* up to the Ch'ing Dynasty, Confucianists always proposed a unity between the cosmos and the myriad things in it. The unity of man and Heaven is the objective of spiritual life. The path leading to this unity lies in the union of man's humanity with the mind of Heaven and Earth to generate things. Such a union is a praise to the generation and procreation by Heaven and Earth.

III. One Universe in the Philosophy of Life

Philosophy of Life explains the universe as one.

The universe was created by the Creator. With His creative power, the Creator brought forth generative power which is itself the universe. From astronomy, we know that the primeval universe was described as a cloud of gaseous matter containing limitless power. By an explosion within the cloud of gas, the galaxies and stars were gradually formed. Tens of millions of galaxies, hundreds of millions of light years apart yet joined to each other by energy, together form one universe. Physics explains cosmic galaxies and stars as sharing the same elements, now known as subatomic particles. "Philosophy of Life" proposes that the universe is itself the generative power. It possesses matter and form and continuously undergoes change.

Generative power possesses a tremendous motivating power which serves as the efficient cause of all the myriad changes in the cosmos. Generative power possesses matter. Viewed in terms of the whole cosmos, it also possesses its own form. Hence, generative power forms one universe. Cosmic generative power is perpetually in the process of change during which its matter is split. Matter, together with the form bestowed by the Creator through His creative power, engenders new things. In the material sense, new things are made from matter derived from the cosmos. However, in terms of the form, they are created by the Creator. As such, when cosmic generative power continues generating myriad things, it is actually the continual creation of the Creator.

In the process of the continual creation of myriad things, although their matter is derived from the matter of the same universe, the forms endowed by the Creator differ from one another. Thus, the matter of myriad things also differ from one another. However, the substance of matter is still the same matter from the one same universe. In the material sense, the myriad things are one. For instance, the human body and the body of animals are materially the same. In terms of physics and chemistry, animals, plants, minerals share the same matter.

The form of the myriad things differ from each other. Not only is the form of things different from one species to another, the form of each thing within the same species is likewise different. Man's form differs from that of animals. Each person's form is also different from others'. Mencius once said that the principle (*li*) of man is human nature, that each person's principle is life itself. Chu Hsi considered man's principle as the nature of the Mandate of Heaven (*T'ien-ming*). For him, each person's principle is itself the nature of material force (*ch'i*) and matter (*chih*). However, although the principles of things differ from one another, their matter is all identified with the matter of the cosmos. As such, they are mutually linked with one another.

The generation and metamorphosis of the myriad things in the universe result from the motion of the generative power. Similarly, the existence of these myriad things is also made possible by the motion of the generative power. That is to say, cosmic generative power acts as the efficient cause that generates the myriad things. After their generation, the myriad things exist in a way that can be described as continuous motion. This continuous motion, itself the motion of generative power, occurs within things. It is life itself. Since the motion of the myriad things in the universe is itself the motion of the generative power, we can say that they share the same life.

Chu Hsi and the Two Ch'eng's affirmed that the myriad things in the universe share the same living principle and the same life. Nevertheless, they proposed a "unity and diversity of forms," wherein the form (*li*) differs according to the clarity and turbidity of material force (*ch'i*). Therefore, the life of the myriad things also differs. Chu Hsi posited that man is endowed with the fullness of the form of life while material things, only a portion of it.

In its operation, the generative power generates and engenders the myriad things. The form endowed to each thing comes from creative power or what the Chinese call *ming* (fate), which differs from person to person. Great differences in the form are observed between species while smaller differences are found among individual members of the same species. As such, we can also say that the life of things differ from one another. Things belonging to the lowest level only have interior actions that are not manifest. They cannot add to their self-nature. This is the life of the minerals. Things belonging to a higher level, the plants, have interior actions. They are capable of adding to their self-nature and their life is manifest exteriorly. These are ordinarily called primary living things. Classified one rung higher, the animals have interior actions and are capable of adding to their self-nature. They are sentient forms of life. Still one level higher is human life. Psychophysical in nature, human life includes interior action, sensitivity, consciousness and creativity. One level higher than human life is the life of the spiritual beings. After death, the human soul survives and lives the life of a spiritual being, sharing it with angels and devils. Among spiritual beings, there is only act. There is no change whatsoever. The highest form of life is that of the absolute spiritual being who is pure and perfect act.

In biology, we know that a cell can divide to form another cell, in this way extending its own life. A contemporary writer, Prof. Su Hsüeh-lin has written:

> Living things, regardless of their size and type, must have a circulatory system and a nervous system. They must be able to protect themselves, launch an attack, eat, drink, behave atrociously, get old, become sick and die. Do stones in the manure pit possess these characteristics? The atoms of stones are able to find and unite with opposite atoms. This is nothing but some form of a chemical reaction and therefore, cannot be called life. (Su)

These explanations about life only deal with the life of things in the universe but miss spiritual forms transcendent of the universe. For philosophers, an explanation on the spiritual forms is a necessity. Life is the existence of immanent actions in realities. Existence is itself the generative power of each thing. For instance, man is generated because of the cosmic generative power. After birth, man lives. Life is motion and motion is generative power. Human life is itself generative power. Once he ceases to live, a person stops existing. The generation and the existence of the myriad things in the universe are themselves the one same generative power.

Every person is unique in terms of his form as well as his matter. Each person is an integral persona. In life, each integral persona bears characteristics and talents different from others'. Yet, far from isolating themselves, these persons need to associate with each other. Human life is "cosmic life." It is linked with the cosmos and the myriad things in it.

All things in the universe become and exist by virtue of generative power. In theory, each thing is a subsistent reality that does not rely on other things. In actual terms, however, they are linked together and rely on one another because actual existence is continuous motion whose motive force resides in the mutual influences existing among things. Concretely, in the natural world, soil, plants, animals, water and air are interrelated. If one part is damaged, the other parts are also jointly damaged. Such a condition is what is now known as the environmental crisis.

In its operation to generate and sustain the myriad things, the generative power follows a natural order that proceeds from one thing to another. This order naturally faces obstacles occasionally which generative power restores in a natural manner. If man-made activities destroy this natural order, human efforts are necessary to restore it. If not, the generative power's operation will be obstructed to the detriment of universe in all its totality.

Among the myriad things in the universe, only man possesses intellect. While man can decide his own actions, other things act on the basis of their material nature. The *Chung-yung* says: "Sincerity is the Way of Heaven. To think how to be sincere is the way of man" (Chan 107). Things in the natural world do not destroy the order existing in it but instead constantly conserve its balance. Man's desires to exploit natural resources with the purpose of creating different types of technology. However, the application of these technologies destroys the balance in nature. Consequently, the relationship among things in the universe suffers damage.

The moral objective of Confucianists lies in "praising the generation and procreation by Heaven and Earth." This objective proposes that man must assist the myriad things in their natural procreation. That is, man must not only refrain from damaging the order in the generation of the myriad things by Heaven and Earth. He must also assist in this process. The Roman Catholic Faith teaches that God created all things for mankind. All things are left at man's disposal. However, the usual management ideas suggest that the administration of things must be based on the nature of the things themselves. In addition, the administered things themselves must gain benefit. God left all things at man's disposal. It is only proper that man should use it rationally and not abuse it. These two concepts are both related to humanity (*jen*).

That the myriad things in the universe are linked together and that they are one are objective facts about nature. However, only man can perceive this fact. Only man has the power to make this objective natural fact become a conscious reality. The human mind is endowed with clear intelligence. His intelligence can be applied to factual phenomena in the natural world.

Answering a student's question on the human mind's identity with things, Wang Yang-ming said:

> We know, then, in all that fills Heaven and earth there is but this clear intelligence. It is only because of their physical forms and bodies that men are separated. My clear intelligence is the master of heaven and earth and spiritual being. If heaven is deprived of my clear intelligence, who is going to look into is height? If earth is deprived of my clear intelligence, who is going to look into its height? If spiritual beings are deprived of my clear intelligence, who is going to distinguish their good

and evil fortune or the calamities and blessings that they will bring? Separated from my clear intelligence, there will be no heaven, earth, spiritual beings, or myriad things, and separated from these, there will not be my clear intelligence. Thus they are all permeated with one material force. How can they be separated?" Then, another asked further: "Heaven, earth, spiritual beings, and the myriad things have existed from great antiquity. Why should it be that if my clear intelligence is gone, they will cease to exist?" Wang Yang-ming answered: "Consider the dead man. His spirit has drifted away and dispersed. Where are his heaven and earth and myriad things? (*Wang Wen-ch'eng kung ch'üan-shu, chüan 3, Ch'uan-hsi lu C* [Complete Works of Wang Yang-ming, Vol. 3], Chan 690)

This is Wang Yang-ming's idea of the unity between knowledge and action. It proceeds from the unity of knowledge and action in the realm of conscience to the area of all knowledge. In the gnosiological sense, things unknown to the mind do not exist. Regarding this point, we agree with the idea of Wang Yang-ming. However, viewed in terms of ontology, we do not accept that things exist owing to the human mind. The existence of things that exist not because of the human mind is unconscious. The oneness of the universe remains an unconscious oneness without the human mind. The human mind makes oneness of the universe become a conscious oneness. The human mind is capable of knowing and loving. As such, man is capable of knowing the oneness of the universe as well as capable of loving it. In this way, what St. Paul said about all creation participating as adopted sons in the glory of God can be realized:

> The whole creation is eagerly waiting for God to reveal his sons. It was not for any fault on the part of creation that it was made unable to attain its purpose, it was made so by God; but creation still retains the hope of being freed, like us, from its slavery to decadence, to enjoy the same freedom and glory as the children of God. (Romans 8:19-21)

Mankind was redeemed by Jesus Christ to become sons and daughters of God. With mankind's restoration to Christ, the myriad things at the disposal of man are also restored to Christ. With Christ, they are restored to God, the Father. As St. Paul also said: "Paul, Apollos, Cephas, the world, life and death, the present and the future, are all your servants; but you belong to Christ and Christ belongs to God." (1 Corinthians 3:21-23)

Appendix: Nature and Life: Alfred North Whitehead

Source: White, Morton (ed.). *The Age of Analysis*. New York: The New American Library, 1959: 86-88.

The familiar testimony is finally buttressed by the statement of a much more powerful and respected figure — the twentieth-century scientist — who not only drives the last nail into the coffin of common sense but also launches Whitehead into his activistic philosophy of process. The doctrine of empty space has been eliminated by modern physics, Whitehead says, and replaced by the idea of field of force, a field of incessant activity. Moreover, "Matter has been identified with energy, and energy is sheer activity." Since any local agitation shakes the whole universe there is no point in treating anything as local, detached existence. The environment enters into the very nature of each thing. The common-sense and older scientific view of self-contained particles of matter is an abstraction, and a useless one when are plumbing the depths of the universe. It may suffice for lawyers and ignorant philosophers, Whitehead says, but it prevents us from seeing that the basic fact of modern physics is activity. However, this figure of activity that the modern physicist places at the center of his picture of the universe is what Whitehead calls "bare activity," and it remains for the philosopher to veil it decently with the answers to the very large questions: "Activity for what, producing what, Activity involving what?" To this exacting task Whitehead turns his attention in the selection that follows. It is an abridgment, with omissions indicated, of Lecture Eight, "Nature Alive," of Whitehead's *Modes of Thought* (1938).

[The status of life in nature. . . is the modern problem of philosophy and of science. Indeed it is the central meeting point of all the strains of systematic thought, humanistic, naturalistic, philosophic. The very meaning of life is in doubt. When we understand it, we shall also understand its status in the world. But its essence and its status are alike baffling. . .

The doctrine that I am maintaining is that neither physical nature nor life can be understood unless we fuse them together as essential factors in the composition of "really real" things whose interconnections and individual characters constitute the universe.

The first step in the argument must be to form some concept of what life can mean. Also we require that the deficiencies in our concept of physical nature should be supplied by its fusion with life. And we require that, on the other hand, the notion of life should involve the notion of physical nature.

Now as a first approximation the notion of life implies a certain absoluteness of self-enjoyment. This must mean a certain immediate individuality, which is a complex process of appropriating into a unity of existence the many data presented as relevant by the physical processes of nature. Life implies the absolute, individual self-enjoyment arising out of this process of appropriation. I have, in my recent writings, used the word "prehension" to express this process of appropriation. Also I have termed each individual act of immediate self-enjoyment an "occasion of experience." I hold that these unities of existence, these occasions of experience, are the really real things which in their collective unity composed the evolving universe, ever plunging into the creative advance...

This concept of self-enjoyment does not exhaust that aspect of process here termed "life." Process for its intelligibility involves the notion of a creative activity belonging to the very essence of each occasion. It is the process of eliciting into actual being factors in the universe which antecedently to that process exist only in the mode of unrealized potentialities. The process of self-creation is the transformation of the potential into the actual, and the fact of such transformation includes the immediacy of self-enjoyment.

Thus in conceiving the function of life in an occasion of experience, we must discriminate the actualized data presented by the antecedent world, the non-actualized potentialities which lie ready to promote their fusion into a new unity of experience, and the immediacy of self-enjoyment which belongs to the creative fusion of those data with those potentialities. This is the doctrine of the creative advance whereby it belongs to the essence of the universe, that it passes into a future. It is nonsense to conceive of nature as a static fact, even for an instant devoid of duration. There is no nature apart from temporal duration. This is the reason why the notion of an instant of time, conceived as a primary simple fact, is nonsense.

But even yet we have not exhausted the notion of creation which is essential to the understanding of nature. We must add yet another character tom our description of life. This missing characteristic is "aim." By this term "aim" is meant the exclusion of the boundless wealth of alternative potentiality, and the inclusion of that definite factor of novelty which constitutes the selected way of entertaining those data in that process of unification. The aim is at that complex of feeling which is enjoyment of those data in that way. "The way of enjoyment" is selected from the boundless wealth of alternatives. It has been aimed at for actualization in that process. . .

Works Cited

Ashby, Eric. *Reconciling Man with the Environment.* Stanford: Stanford UP, 1978.

Capra, Fritjof. *The Tao of Physics: An exploration of the parallels between modern physics and Eastern mysticism.* London: Fontana, 1978.

Chan, Wing-tsit. *A Source Book in Chinese Philosophy.* Princeton: Princeton UP, 1963.

Commoner, Barry. *The Closing Circle: Nature, Man and Technology.* New York: Knopf, 1972.

Su, Hsüeh-lin. "Yi-p'ien hsuan-k'e chih chan ya-chen te wen-chang." *Chung-yang ji-pao* (Taipei: Central Daily News). 28 August, 1991.

Translated by Carlos Tee

Chapter XII

Time and Memory in the Philosophy of Life

I. Time

Different schools of philosophy have a consensus regarding "time," that is, being is a dynamic being, not a stationary one. Although Heidegger did not clearly refer to this dynamism, the manner of existence of his Being [*das Sein*] also involves processes that are dynamic in nature. I consider time as the dynamism of matter. Without motion, there would not be the concept of time.

Thus, the common consensus is that time is derived from motion. Without motion there is no time. Whether viewed from the perspective of the natural sciences or philosophy, time represents motion.

In Philosophy of Life, existence is motion in the general sense. Since existence is life, then life necessarily also involves motion. However, since the significance of life is not identical for realities belonging to different levels, the relationship of time and life also differs. As a consequence, the meaning of time likewise varies.

1. The Time of Existing Substances

In its widest sense, time represents motion. It is not motion itself but an attribute of motion. Upon hearing the word motion, we usually associate it with duration or transience. The duration or transience of motion is a simple vertical extension of the issue of time. They do not explain the characteristics of motion or its intensity. Rather, they only describe the vertical extension of a motion. It is like the concept of space being explained as a simple extension of a plane.

Human cognition is a psychophysical activity. All our knowing are coursed through sense organs. They carry a certain materiality, and thus, involve "quantity." Furthermore, since all matters in the universe are material in nature, they cannot exist in the same place at the same time. This is because "quantity" makes a material component to be extraneous to another component. They thus lead to the concept of space, which is the simple extension of a plane. Similarly, we are aware of the concept of motion. We divide motion into smaller components. Each component of motion cannot exist at the same time with another component of motion. Thus, time becomes a simple vertical extension. If we combine the concepts of time and space, time acquires the attributes of space. In such a case, time means the order of motion. This time is called "cosmic time."

Defining time through its meaning per se, time represents pure motion. It does not represents a "before and after." In this way, time is associated with life. In fact, time represents life. This is pure time or the very essence of time.

2. Only Pure Time is Applicable to the Absolute Life

Absolute life is the life of God. It is pure act. It involves no motion or change.

We usually say that God is transcednent to time, that the life of God is not subject to time and space. This statement is true. God's life has neither "before" nor "after." It involves no duration or transient. It has no position and direction. However, we also often say that God's life is forever or that God is eternal. St. Thomas defined "eternity" as *"interminabilis vitae tota simul et perfecta possesio"* (Aquinas, I.q.X.a.I.c). It is infinite, has no beginning and end, neither having an origin nor a terminus. Therefore, an infinite life excludes the idea of succession, and instead involves a simultaneous and perfect possession. Eternity is simultaneous and perfect possession while time is a succession. [*Differt aeternitas a tempore quod ea est tota simul, tempus vero successivum.*]

In terms of time, eternity is a perfect "now," possessing neither past nor future. It resembles a circle. Every point along the circle is equidistant to its center. Eternity is comparable to the center of the circle and time resembles the circumference. Eternity, in comparison with time, has no "before" and "after." It is interminable.

3. Substantial Existence Possesses Substantial Time

Substantial time is itself time and possesses the meaning of time itself. Substantial time represents motion in the general sense or represents life itself. It is indistinguishable. It cannot be compared to each of the points making a straight line or a circumference. A substance's motion is pure motion. It cannot be distinguished into its attributes; neither can motion's succession be distinguished. Substantial time refers to the motion of the substance of material things. The motion of the substance is existence or life itself.

The existence of all realities is a dynamic existence. They all are life. Based on this, the existence of realities includes substantial time.

God, the Absolute Existence, is eternity. It is a perfect "now". A perfect "now" is not *durée* which as we know involves simple succession. In contrast, eternity does not involve succession. It is a simultaneous perfection and a perfect now. Eternity is a perfect substantial time.

The relative existents — realities — may be spiritual, material or psychophysical. The spiritual realities, the angels, have an existence that has a beginning but no end. It involves no change whatsoever. Angels' existence is *durée*. It is not a perfect now and includes the concept of succession. However, the existence of angels is indistinguishable. It cannot be involved with space. Thus, the existence of angels possesses substantial time.

For St. Thomas, the concepts of eternity and time also include aevum. Eternity is the time of the Absolute Existent. Aevum is the time corresponding to spiritual realities and time belongs to material beings. Aevum has a beginning but no end. Although angels' substance does not change, their actions, such as intellectual cognition and emotion, all possess a beginning and an end. St. Thomas explained that aevum partially possesses attributes of both eternity and time. *Aevum ipsum est medium inter aeternitatem et tempus, utroque participans* (Aquinas, I.q.X.a.5.c.). The existence of angels possesses a beginning but no end. Their substance does not change although their motions change. Their time is aevum which is *durée*.

Since man is a psychophysical being, his existence is also

psychophysical in nature. Similarly, man's life is a psychophysical life. Man's life exists together with those of the myriad things in the universe. Since the myriad things in the universe are material beings, then the life of man involves "cosmic time." However, viewed from the existence of man's substance, his existence possesses substantial time. Because the existence of the substance is life and since life is immanent motion, it is proper to say that this immanent motion does not manifest the attributes of motion but instead its significance. Therefore, man's life involves "cosmic time." The human soul possesses "cosmic time" together with the body when that person is still living. After death, the soul exists alone. This time, the existence of the soul has the same attributes as that of angels' existence. The separated souls time is also aevum.

Similarly, all the myriad things in the universe also possess substantial time.

4. Cosmic Time

Cosmic time is the way of reckoning time among the myriad things in the universe. It has a beginning and an end, a "before and after." Divided into past, present and future, it always involves succession.

All the myriad things in the universe are material beings. They are made up of components extraneous to one another. They occupy space. When material things move, the moving force proceeds from one component part to another. Therefore, the motion of material things always involves before and after. Only the human soul, as a spiritual substance, is present in the whole body at the same time. Furthermore, changes in a material being proceed from potency to act (realization) and also involve a "before and after." This is because the potencies of matter cannot be actualized all at the same time. The existence of the myriad things in the universe is itself in time. Aside from having substantial time, they also possess "cosmic time."

A standard for reckoning "before and after" in cosmic time must be some kind of a simple, successive movement. In ancient China, for example, the passage of time was measured by copper vessels filled with water that was supposed to drip. However, to measure universal time, the standard must be based on a universal successive movment. This explains why time is calculated using the relationship between the earth and the sun. In ancient times, the sun was thought to have revolved around the earth. It was later proved otherwise. This terrestrial revolution is shared and identical for all in this world. It thus became the universal standard for measuring time. Certainly, it is not as Bergson explained that the sun was adopted as the standard for measuring time because men work during daytime when the sun is out.

To measure "cosmic time," the standard must be a simple, unified movemer.t. It must also be a cyclic movement. Because the earth moves in a cyclic manner, with alternating day and night and a repeating cycle of four seasons, the adoption of a simple, unified but forward movement as standard for measuring time will not allow designation of the time of the occurrence of events. In the case of the ancient Chinese copper vessels used for telling time, it can only tell the passage of day and night. It cannot be used for reckoning number of days, months or years. The more detailed issues of calendar making and accuracy are technological issues beyond our scope of discussion here.

5. Time is Only Now

Cosmic time is divided into past, present and future. St. Augustine pointed out that this method of classification is actually untenable, past being past and no longer existent while future has not yet arrived and is also inexistent. Only the present instant is existing. St. Augustine said that the past must be memory and the future must be expectation. Both of them are mental ideas, not objective realities.

Time, whether substantial or cosmic, is not the existence of objective realities. Rather, it is an attribute of realities. Thus, eternity is an attribute of the Absolute Reality. Aevum is an attribute of relative realities. Time is an attribute belonging to material beings. The Absolute Reality cannot have accidents. All his attributes form part of his substance. Therefore, eternity is itself his nature and substance. It is a perfect existence. Aevum is an attribute belonging to relative realities.

Although spiritual beings move, they do not change. Only their work possess "before and after." The existence of spiritual beings is *durée*. It cannot be terminated and involves no before and after. It is a simple now. The myriad things in the universe possess a chronological "before and after." This is because their substance, made up of components, is a "quantity." This is also the reason why cosmic time has spatial attributes, that is, it is quantified. The quantity of matter forbids component parts from occupying the same space at the same time, or one movement overlapping with another movement at the same time. Component parts of a reality share the same existence of the reality. Although they cannot occupy the same location, they can exist at the same time in different locations. Only the currently on-going movement is attached to the existence of the reality. The past and the future do not actually exist. This explains why motion manifests a realitys existence. The existence of motion is a divided but successive existence. What is divisible, or rather, what division manifests is the existence of the present motion. Such an existence is an existence in the present time. We can therefore say that cosmic time is only now.

Although the "present" of cosmic time is the time corresponding to the present motion, the existence of the motion is an accident of the reality's existence. The existence of a reality is substantial existence. Thus, the existence of present motion is manifested at the present instant of the motion. This "present instant" still is a manifestation of "substantial time." As a substantial existence, it is manifested as the existence of present motion. The past and the future are mental concepts. As St. Augustine said, they are memory and expectation respectively. "Substantial time," not "cosmic time," is used to reckon the time of man's life. This is because man unites the time of his life based on the duration of his life. Cosmic time cannot be united. In contrast, substantial time is *durée*. It is endless.

II. Memory

In his philosophy, St. Augustine stressed the concept of memory. He cited the role of this faculty in seeing God and in recalling one's own life. Time, or specifically, substantial time, shows the duration of each person's life and existence. It is a simple mark to reckon man's life. In comparison, memory actually shows the life of each person and his existence.

1. Memory Resides in the Mind

Bergson was against psychology's adoption of the human brain as the foundation of memory. He disagreed with the way psychology points out each part of the brain as the storehouse of memory. For Bergson, this method erroneously applies the concept of container and contents in the issue of memory. Instead, Bergson propounds that memory resides in the human mind.

Indeed, contemporary psychology often assigns certain areas of the brain as the storehouse of human memory. If that part of the brain suffers damage, the person loses his memory. This is not accepted in the academic sense. How does the brains nervous system retain memory? Since the nervous system is material in nature, then it has quantity. Quantity forbids different components to remain in the same location at the same time. Although it is tenable that the quantitative character of the nervous system can retain impression in a way similar to photographic film's retention of an image, the latter is different since each film can only retain an image once. Lets say it is possible to take pictures of different images using the same film, then the original image would be clattered by the other images. Everything will appear blurred. How is man's memory containing numerous details of his lifetime retained by the brain? Besides these sense impressions, there are also intellectual knowledge, feelings and emotions. How are they retained in the human brain? Memory finds its basis in the mind. It is retained in the mind. The Chinese philosopher Hsun-tzu once said: "The human mind is empty but sharp." It can retain an infinite volume of knowledge. Memory is retained in the mind. In this process, the brain acts as the functioning organ much as it is used in all of man's intellectual processes.

2. Memory Is Not Man's Ego

Contemporary Western philosophy studies man's persona and deals with the integrity of the ego. It asks the questions: "Why do I always remain the same I? Why do I remain the same person in youth and in old age?" Some philosophers propound that the integrity of the ego depends upon memory. Because of memory, I can remain the same person. If I lose my memory, I also lose myself. Although this may be acceptable in psychology, it is untenable in ontology. In fact, a person who loses his memory remains the same person, the same ego. Memory is one of the faculties of man. It does not form man's substance. Man's ego is his very substance.

3. Memory Represents Man's Life

Man's life is a kind of *durée*, not a perfect now. The *durée* of man's life comes about through successive motion and endless changes. The substance of man's body continues its successive changes. Similarly, the activities of the soul also undergo successive changes. The duration of life only suggests that life continues its successive motion. It does not say what changes life undergoes. In fact, it is memory that joins together all changes in man's life into an actual *durée* of life. Through memory, the life of a person, is actually joined into one in a chronological manner, with the succession of events clearly marked out. If a person loses his memory, all changes in his life cannot be joined together. His life then becomes "cosmic time" in which there is only the present instant. In such a case, life is split. This explains why memory is valuable.

4. Memory Is Not Merely A Mental Idea

St. Augustine's philosophy virtually considers time passed as inexistent. Events of the past are also not existing. They only exist in the mind. Contemporary Western Idealism propounds that historical events are things of the past and do not exist. It teaches that events of the past only exist in the minds of the analysts of history. History only exists in these people's minds, and therefore, it totally loses its objectivity.

Although past events have already elapsed, they actually existed in those times. Time already elapsed but events that had happened are not erased as a consequence. Thus, memory turns events of the past into the "present" in time. This "present" is not my own mental fiction created at will. Instead, it is presenting once again things of the past. It is therefore proper to say that memory is not a mental imagination. Rather, it is a re-emergence of things of the past. What is presented is the idea of past events, the "present" of the life already gone. This "present" appears mentally in the "present" of the person who recalls.

Life is the existence of immanent motion. This immanent motion is manifested outside. It shows changes attributed to existence. In his work *"De Quantitate Animae,"* St. Augustine says that the human body experiences immanent changes while the soul does not. The movement of the matter making up the human body causes these changes. Since material changes necessarily happen following a certain sequence, then the existence of material beings includes the feature of time. Time records changes and represents existence. Spiritual beings have immanent actions but experience no immanent changes. They do not include the feature of time. Instead, they either include the feature of perfect "now" or aevum characterized by *durée*. However, substance is life and activity and therefore, also represents time, which is action in the general sense. This type of "time" is not cosmic time, which has no before and after, only now. All "now," be it perfect now or the now of *durée,* are substantial time.

Works Cited

Aquinas, St. Thomas. *Summa Theologica.*

Translated by Carlos Tee

Chapter XIII

Towards a Satisfactory Epistemology

I. The Premise for Confirmation

In recent centuries, Western philosophy showed very little room for development in its discussion of reality. Western philosophy is comparable to Western oil painting whose objective expression of beauty reached its zenith during the Renaissance. In the last few centuries, the art of Western oil painting can no longer tread the path of tradition. As a consequence, first came Impressionist works, followed by Abstract, Futuristic and Idealistic paintings, in all their strange varieties and styles. Similarly, during the Ming Dynasty, Chinese landscape, flower and bird paintings failed to surpass the works of Sung and Yuan masters. Consequently, Ming painters were left to imitate Sung and Yuan works. In recent times, Western philosophy studied the issue of knowledge starting from Descartes. Until now, Western philosophy still follows the epistemological path. Edmund Husserl criticized modern philosophy by calling it erroneous epistemology. Citing Descartes' philosophy, he commented that it entered the road of dualism between mind and matter in such a way that a deep chasm was cut between the two. Husserl also pointed out that Geulincx's Occasionalism views mind and matter as two synchronized clocks. Berkeley took existence as experience while Kant thought that the pure rationality of the subject can only recognize phenomena and is incapable of reaching the noumenon. Husserl himself proposed phenomenology, which affirms a direct cognition of essence. He established the concept of the pure ego and pure consciousness. However, the logical positivists returned to linguistic structure and denied the universality of concepts. Whitehead proposed an eternal, universal object and thus affirmed the value of knowledge. The latest philosophical school, Structuralism, dropped all ideas about substance and essence, only concerning itself with matter *per se* and relationships between material things. Heidegger's Existentialism attempted to grasp an ontological substance, yet it only reached as far as discussing the manner of "being" and thus, was gradually forgotten.

Epistemology, itself the first issue in philosophy, is a topic that opens many doors. In fact, through cognition, man learns about the existence of the universe, all creation and its contents. What man does not know is tantamount to nonexistent. Countless stars and galaxies remain unknown to man at present. For man, they are taken as nonexistent and vice-versa because man needs "cognition" to act regarding his own self or things external to him, with the exception of his own physiological actions. Cognition necessarily means knowledge. This knowledge can be about himself or things external in a manner similar to what Buddhism calls the grasping of oneself and things" (*wo-chih he wu-chih*). Within the consciousness of man, his own self and external things are both interior knowledge, thus making it proper to say that the so-called universe and all creation--or better, what man calls universe and all creation--are the universe and all creation in his consciousness. However, we cannot as such say that the universe and all creation are created by the human mind in the sense of the "myriad dharmas only emanate from the heart" or that the "myriad dharmas only emanate from the mind." The universe and all creation in the human consciousness are the "existence" of this exterior universe and all creation in the human mind. This "existence" is objective as it is factual.

Modern Western philosophy has been attempting to solve this problem of cognition. Man's cognition is the object of philosophical studies. Is this cognition objectively factual? Or is it only a figment of subjective thought? Western philosophy often employs scientific analytical methods in its search for attributes of truth. Everything needs to be supported by evidence. In epistemology, proof showing the subjective rationality of cognitive power is sought for. Proof about the knowability of the object is sought for, as well as evidence showing how subject and object overlap. After going in circles for more than four centuries, philosophers are finding themselves more and more in a hopeless tangle concerning these three issues. Husserl attempted to use pure consciousness, a concept that forms part of the theory of the "existent yet undiscussed" of his phenomenology, to establish a solid epistemology. However, his phenomenology is also a form of "philosophical assumption." Similar to assumptions made in the natural sciences, Husserl's philosophical assumption is not itself truth but rather something that can be readily modified or abandoned by others. The present Structuralism that has newly emerged is in fact another type of opposing "philosophical assumption."

This scholastic phenomenon is a necessary one. Human cognition arises from the intellect. Similarly, sensation by sense organs also requires confirmation by the intellect. The *Ta-hsüeh* says: ". . . we look but do not see, listen but do not hear, and eat but do not know the taste of the food" (*Ta-hsüeh*, Chapter VII, Chan 90). Since cognition arises from the intellect, then it must be a product of the intellect. Outside the intellect, man has no other sense of cognition. The first issue in Western epistemology is concerned with whether or not the intellect is capable of knowing. To answer this question, man can but only use his intellect. In this way, it uses the intellect itself to prove its ability to answer this question. The intellect cannot prove itself. Rather, it is only capable of affirming that it possesses cognitive ability because responding that it cannot know is itself a form of cognition action. It is possible to prove sense experience. This possibility is due to the fact that the intellect is above the sense organs. Furthermore, as sense organs are material in nature, their actions can be proven using material instruments. However, we have no way of showing evidence about the intellect. We must certainly affirm the premise that the intellect can know its own object. It is capable of knowing. This affirmation factual and not baseless. A natural organic function can necessarily act based on its innate principles to arrive at its own objectives. A pair of eyes can naturally see, ears can naturally hear, a stomach can naturally digest and a heart can naturally circulate blood. As to whether or not these organs can function totally or be fully effective depends upon the integrity of the organic structure. By the same token, the intellect is man's natural cognitive sense. It must be able to know its own object.

Descartes' skepticism casts no doubt about intellectual functions but instead suggests doubting every affirmation made. Every affirmation must be clearly presented before the intellect, which sees it with clarity before it is accepted as truth. Descartes pointed out his first affirmation in the statement "*Cogito, ergo sum,*" believing that this affirmation is naturally clear and requires no other evidence whatsoever. *Cogito* means "I think." "My thoughts" and "I am thinking" of course exist. If I do not exist, my thoughts would of course be nonexistent. Moreover, everything about me should be viewed as nonexistent. However, my existence cannot be used as proof that the intellect is capable of knowing because in Western philosophy, "existence" is but a concept that does not include everything belonging to an actually existent reality. What Descartes wanted to say is that in making a deduction, there must be basic principles established as assumed premises which need not be proven. "*Cogito, ergo sum*" is precisely a premise that requires no proof. We must also add that the premise "The intellect is capable of knowing" is likewise a basic principle that needs not and cannot be proven.

The second issue in Western epistemology is concerned with whether or not the subject and object of knowing can overlap. Only when they can overlap is knowing possible. Western epistemology distinguished between subject and object. It later engaged itself in studying the possibility of bridging that chasm. In fact, Western philosophers have been going around this same circle in recent centuries. In comparison, Chinese philosophy never had this same problem Western philosophers deliberately got themselves into. However, Chinese philosophers never explained why there is no gap between subject and object. They only explained that humanity (*jen*) is intuition by the human mind. Furthermore, Chinese philosophy affirms that intuition cannot explain all the knowledge of man because man mutually penetrates with the myriad things owing to material force (*ch'i*). As Liang Shu-ming said: "Without experience, how can there be knowledge? Without memory, how can there be experience? And without intuition, how can there be memory?"(72) Chuang -tzu affirms the mutual penetration of material force (*ch'i*) among the myriad things and the possibility of intuitive knowledge.

II. The "Spiritual Cognition" of Chuang-Tzu

> "Make your will one! Don't listen with your ears, listen with your mind. No, don't listen with your mind, but listen with your spirit [material force, *ch'i*]. Listening stops with the ears, the mind stops with recognition, but spirit [material force] is empty and waits on all things. The Way gathers in emptiness alone. Emptiness is the fasting of the mind." (*Chuang Tzu*, Chapter IV: *Jen-chien shih* [In The World of Men], Watson 57)

> "You have only to comprehend the one breath that is the world. The sage never ceases to value oneness." (Chapter XXII: *Chih pei you* [Knowledge Wandered North], Watson 236)

> "I cast aside my limbs, discard my intelligence, detach from both body and mind, and become one with Great Universal (Tao). This is called sitting down and forgetting everything." (Chapter VI: *Ta tsung -shih* [The Great Teacher], Chan 201)

Chuang-tzu proposes the nurturing of life (*yang-sheng*). Human life is derived from material force (*ch'i*). The accumulation of material force (*ch'i*) means life and its dissipation means death. This accumulation and dissipation of material force (*ch'i*) follow nature. Nature, in turn, is the recipient of the operations of material force. By "nature" is meant heaven. Chuang-tzu's exposition on nurturing for life proposes taking no action and following the natural course. He discourages being self clever and suggests setting regulations for behavior. If not, he warned of mental and physical fatigue that cause a short life span.

Man is intelligent. He is capable of knowing. Chuang-tzu explained that man is endowed with cognition of sense, mind and material force (*ch'i*). Before man can act, there must first be knowledge. Both sense cognition and mental cognition require man to use his body and mind. In his teachings, Chuang-tzu dissuaded men from using the senses and the mind by saying: "Don't listen with your ears. . . No, don't listen with your mind, but listen with your spirit." This spirit, within man, is the spirit of Heaven and Earth. Regarding spirit, Chuang-tzu affirms that the original spirit shows in the human mind. On the human mind, he said that it is "empty and waits on all things." Hsün-tzu also once proposed that the "mind is empty and quiescent" (*hsin-hsü erh ching*) and that "the mind aspires for knowledge" (*hsin you cheng chih*). Hsün-tzu explained "aspiring for knowledge" as an activity or behavior of the mind. In contrast, Chuang-tzu affirms that for the mind to know, it must not take any action. There is no need for it to contemplate on things but rather it must "sit and forget" (*tsuo wang*) by "detaching from both body and mind." If the mind refrains from contemplating, it naturally penetrates things. In the phrase "becoming one with Great Universal," "Great Universal" applies not only in its physiological sense but also in its cognitive sense. External forms and things penetrate human eyes and ears. External things penetrate the human mind. Things are derived from material force (*ch'i*) which is the substance of things. Since the material force of things penetrate the human mind, then things also penetrate the mind. And since the human mind is empty and potent as a mirror, then the substance of things appears before the human mind. As such, the human mind naturally apprehends. What it apprehends is the substance of things. Substance is the basis or the Tao of things. Not only things are apprehended by the human mind, the essence of the whole universe also appears before the human mind through material force(*ch'i*). It is in this way that the human mind apprehends. On this point, Chuang-tzu said:

The mind of the perfect man is like a mirror. It does not lean forward or backward in its response to things. It responds to things but conceals nothing of its own. Therefore, it is able to deal with things without injury to [its reality]. (Chapter VII: *Ying ti-wang* [Fit For Emperors And Kings], Chan 207)

Sages use their mind with naturalness and no action, both in terms of emotions and desires. Their mind, resembling a mirror, allows knowledge to naturally appear, that is, without exerting the mind to seek knowledge. Thus, Chuang-tzu wrote:

"You have only to rest in inaction and things will transform themselves. Smash your form and body, spit out hearing and eyesight, forget you are a thing among other things, and you may join in great unity with the deep and boundless. Undo the mind, slough off spirit, be blank and soulless, and the ten thousand things one by one will return to the root--return to the root and not know why. Dark and undifferentiated chaos--to the end of life none will depart from it. Do not ask what its name is, do not try to observe its form. Things will live naturally and of themselves." (Chapter XI: *Tsai you* [Let It Be, Leave It Alone], Watson 122)

Chuang-tzu explained nurturing for life (*yang sheng*) as taking no action and having no desires. For him, it is making man's material force (*ch'i*) unite with the material force of things without making oneself think of having desires or action. Furthermore, it requires no planning by oneself but is instead done naturally while forgetting oneself and external things. Man and things will transform themselves in "a dark and undifferentiated chaos." Man, not separated from things, will return to the root of life. If one thinks about himself or the things around him, then he is differentiated from things. However, human life is a life of knowledge. In this life of common transformation with things, although the mind does not move, knowing is still possible. This type of knowing is spiritual cognition (*ch'i-chih*) wherein the substance of the human mind and those of things join together. That is, the substance of things appears in the human mind.

In the chapter entitled *Yang-sheng chu* [Principle of Life Nurture] , Chuang-tzu told the story of how Pao Ting[1] employed spiritual cognition in carving a bull:

> What I care about is the Way [Tao], which goes beyond skill. When I first began cutting up oxen, all I could see was the ox itself. After three years I no longer saw the whole ox. And now- -now I go at it by spirit and don't look with my eyes. Perception and understanding have come to a stop and spirit moves where it wants. I go along with the natural makeup, strike in the big hollows, guide the knife through the big openings, and follow things as they are. So I never touch the smallest ligament or tendon, much less a main joint. (Watson 50-51)

In cutting the bull, Pao Ting did not use his eyes to see nor his thoughts to infer. Instead, by apprehending with the soul (*shen-hui*), he makes his knife reach the parts of the bull in such manner that the blade does not touch any bone. The so-called "apprehension with the soul," meaning that the material force (*ch'i*) of Pao Ting and the material force of the bull fuse together, allows Pao Ting to realize directly which spot to work on. There are spaces between the joints, and the blade of the knife has really no thickness. If you insert what has no thickness into such spaces, then there's plenty of room--more than enough for the blade to play about it" (Watson 51).

Chuang-tzu further writes:

> In the midst of darkness, he alone sees the dawn; in the midst of the soundless, he alone hears a harmony. Therefore, in depth piled upon depth he can spy out the thing; in spirituality piled upon spirituality he can discover the essence. So in his dealings with the ten thousand things he supplies all their wants out of total nothingness." (Chapter XII: *T'ien-ti* [Heaven and Earth], Watson 128)

---

(1) [Translator's Note] Pao Ting was a cook of King Hui of Wei (Watson 50).

In this passage, Chuang-tzu refers to Tao and virtue. In an earlier passage, he said:

> Pervading Heaven and earth: that is the Way [Tao]. Moving among the ten thousand things: that is Virtue. Superiors governing the men below them: that is called administration. Ability finding trained expression: that is called skill. Skill is subsumed in administration; administration in duty; duty in Virtue; Virtue in the Way [Tao]; and the Way in Heaven. . . To act through inaction is called Heaven. To speak through inaction is called Virtue. . . The Master said: The Way [Tao]--how deep its dwelling!" (Chapter XII: T'ien-ti [Heaven and Earth], Watson 126, 127, 128)

For Chuang-tzu, Tao resides deep in things. That is, the essence of things is Tao. To know Tao, one must obtain it in the midst of darkness, formlessness and soundlessness. Only by reaching the essence of things can things be known as suggested by the phrase "in depth piled upon depth he can spy out the thing." Man's spirit (*shen*) is the original spirit (*yüan-ch'i*) found in his mind. When this original spirit in the mind of man joins with the myriad things, sense organs and inference are not necessary to obtain "all their wants out of total nothingness." Nothing [total nothingness] is needed to make the myriad things appear in the human mind. Man gets to know the nature of myriad things and "all their wants" in this way.

In the chapter entitled *Ta tsung shih* [The Great Teacher], Chuang-tzu expounds on the Way of Nurturing for life (*yang-sheng*). He says:

> So I began explaining and kept at him for three days, and after that he was able to put the world outside himself. When he had put the world outside himself, I kept at him for seven days more, and after that he was able to put things outside himself. When he had put things outside himself, I kept at him for nine days more, and after that he was able to put life outside himself. After he had put life outside himself, he was able to achieve the brightness of dawn, and when he had achieved the

brightness of dawn, he could see his own aloneness. After he had managed to see his own aloneness, he could do away with past and present, and after he had done away with past and present, he was able to enter where there is no life and no death. That which kills life does not die; that which gives life to life does not live. (Watson 82-83)

To do away with worries about life and death, one must be able to rid himself of the sense of time. To achieve this, one must only pay attention to one point--seeing oneness (*chien-tu*). If everything is done away with, one only knows that he exists. One's existence transcends Heaven and Earth, all the myriad things, life and death because "This is the kind of thing it is: there is nothing it doesn't send off, nothing it doesn't welcome, nothing it doesn't destroy, nothing it doesn't complete. Its name is Peace-in-Strife'" (Watson 83). When one's existence fuses with the existence of myriad things, "nothing it doesn't send off, nothing it doesn't welcome, nothing it doesn't destroy, nothing it doesn't complete" based on the nature of things, one's mind attains the state of "Peace-in-Strife." As Kuo Hsiang's[2] commentary says: "I and the things are in darkness. If things shine, I also shine. And never does it lead to lack of peace." In this darkness together with things, man's spirit joins with the spirit of things. In the midst of darkness, "he alone sees the dawn" and attains knowledge in a direct manner.

In the conclusion of the chapter entitled *Ch'iu-shui* [Autumn Floods], Chuang-tzu tells the story of how he and Hui-tzu were strolling along the bank of the river one day when they saw and envied how fish were swimming happily and leisurely. He wrote:

"You are not a fish, "said Hui-tzu, "How do you know its happiness?" "You are not I," said Chuang-tzu. "How do you know that I do not know the happiness of fish?" Hui-tzu said, "Of

---

(2) [Translator's Note] Kuo Hsiang (3rd-4th cent. A.D.) was a neo-Taoist philosopher. He is known for his *Commentary on the Chuang-tzu.*

course I do not know, since I am not you. But you are not the fish, and it is perfectly clear that you do not know the happiness of fish." Chuang-tzu said, "Let us get at the bottom of the matter. When you asked how I knew the happiness of the fish, you already knew that I knew the happiness of the fish but asked how. I knew it along the river." (Chan 209-210)

In his annotation on this passage, Kuo Hsiang writes:

Let us get at the bottom of Hui-tzu's position. He said that it is not possible to know [the happiness] of the fish unless one is a fish. I am not Chuang-tzu, yet I can also say that when you asked how I knew the happiness of the fish, you knew that I am not a fish. You know that I am not fish. Those who mutually know each other can know things about each other. Therefore, there is no need to become a fish in order to know fish. . . [Chuang-tzu] said that he knew the fish while walking along the river. He did not have to enter the water in order to know. I and things have a permanent congenital nature which Heaven and Earth cannot alter. *Yin* and *yang* cannot reverse what they have done. Hence, for [a creature] born on land to know the happiness of what is born in the water is not at all an astounding thing. Chuang-tzu's answer to Hui-tzu, "Let us get at the bottom of the matter." He says: "You are not me, how can you say that since I am not fish, I cannot know the happiness of fish? If I cannot know [a] fish, you cannot know me either. Since you think that you know I cannot know the happiness of fish, then you think by yourself that you know me. You are not me, but you can know me. Similarly, I am not a fish, but I can also know fish. Besides, persons and things are basically joined together. I know my happiness and the happiness of fish." Here, Chuang-tzu still uses his own principle, that is, you have only to comprehend the one breath that is the world." (Chapter XXII: *Chih pei you* [Knowledge Wandered North], Watson 236)

Owing to its interpenetration [*t'ung*] with material force (*ch'i*), the human mind naturally knows the nature of myriad things without the need for inference. In the chapter entitled *Ta sheng* [Mastering Life], Chuang-tzu wrote about a lumberjack who went up the mountain in search of trees to cut. He wrote:

> After that, I go into the mountain forest and examine the Heavenly nature of the trees. If I find one of the superlative form, and I can see a bell stand there, I put my hand to the job of carving; if not, I let go. This way I am simply matching up a ' Heaven' with ' Heaven.' That's probably the reason that people wonder if the results were not made by spirits! (Watson 206)

The phrase "matching up Heaven with Heaven" shows that Chuang-tzu's principle for nurturing life is the very same principle he applied to his epistemology. That is, not to use and exert the mind but instead keep the mind empty. An empty mind accumulates Tao. When the Tao of myriad things accumulates in the mind, man naturally knows the essence of things.

III. A Logical and Satisfactory Epistemology

We cannot accept the epistemology of Chuang-tzu. His entire system of thought was established on one sentence: "You have only to comprehend the one breath that is the world" (*T'ien-ti yi ch'i erh*). This is both illogical and unrealistic. His epistemology, based on the mutual penetration of the mind's material force (*ch'i*) with the material force of things and the mind's natural and direct knowing of the Tao of things, is equally absurd and unrealistic. Nevertheless, the epistemology of Chuang-tzu enunciates a few principles on research which can be of assistance in our search for solutions to the problem of cognition. First, Chuang-tzu took the universe and all creation as mutually joined and penetrating. Second, the principle (*li*) of things can be directly made manifest in the human mind. Let us draw out these two points from the epistemology of Chuang-tzu to serve as our principles in solving the problem of cognition.

Let us discuss the first point: The object and subject of cognition are joined mutually and penetrating in such manner that there exists no unbrideagable chasm between the two.

The universe and all creation are all derived from the action of the generative power. They continue to exist through the operation of the generative power. Again, owing to the generative power, they are mutually joined together and penetrating. The shape and color of a thing naturally join with the human eyes upon the action of light. A sound joins naturally with the ears when its sonic vibrations in the air reach the ears. Mencius said:

> When our senses of sight and hearing are used without thought and are thereby obscured by material things, the material things act on the material senses and lead them astray. That is all. (*Kao-tzu*, Part I, Chan 59)

Eyes and ears are material as shapes, colors and sounds are. Eyes and ears are inborn organs. Bodily organs and their objects, that is, shapes, colors and sounds, must naturally join together. If not, eyes and ears would not be functional. If congenital functions cannot be achieved, it would be like a stomach failing to digest or a heart incapable of circulating blood. Why then does nature provide these organs? Since the eyes and ears, shapes, colors and sounds are material, how they function can be tested using material instruments. Everybody accepts the fact that sense organs and their objects join together.

As for the intellect, problems arise in philosophy because of the absence of a way to prove its cognitive processes. This absence led many philosophers to affirm that a deep chasm divides the intellect from its objects, isolating them from each other and preventing their mutual union. However, theoretically and factually, there is no single reality in the universe that is isolated from the rest. Things are linked with things by a nexus of "power." Spiritual beings, too, are mutually linked. The bond that joins spiritual beings together is spiritual power (*Ching-shen li*). This bond of power, derived from the substance of things, has one direction representing repulsion and the other attraction. On the one hand, the actual power of a thing is divided into components that repel one another and occupy their own positions. They form an area or an interior space. On the other hand, they exert mutual attraction to form one united power, that is, the power of the substance which causes the "oneness" of the thing. This substantial power of a thing radiates outward, thereby repelling other things and keeping them away from its own interior space. It also absorbs other things, mutually linked in terms of power. In contrast, the mutual relationship between the power of spiritual beings is one of mutual manifestation. Resembling lighted lamps, the power of spiritual beings each manifest themselves. What is ordinarily called feelings is a release of power either through repulsion or attraction. Physiological operations are likewise operations of power.

Man is a psychophysical reality. His body and soul unite to form one. Physiological life, needed for maintaining and developing the body, is the body's only activity by itself. The rest of man's activities are jointly operated by his body and soul. Activities of the sense organs, mainly operated by the organs, need to pass through the soul. This need to pass through the soul is described in the *Ta-hsüeh as ."* . .we look but do not see, listen but do not hear, and eat but do not know the taste of the food" (Chapter VII, Chan 90). The body's feelings of pain and joy also need to pass through the soul or else they would not be felt at all. The activities of the soul also need to be conducted through the body. The soul borrows the brain's sensory nerve in its activities. Knowledge and feelings of the mind are made active through the nervous system.

Cognition is an intellectual activity of the mind. It requires the body's operation in order to know its internal object as well as its external object. For an external object to enter the mind, it must pass through sense organs. Similarly, when the mind expresses thoughts outwardly, it also requires passing through sense organs.

The "existence" of realities is an integral existence. When a reality gets into contact with another reality, the degree and effects of contact are determined by the attributes of both realities. When two rocks come into contact, they mutually repel each other to keep their own space. When both sides (or at least one side) have sentient activities, their contact leads to sense reactions in the form of sense impression. Man possesses a mind which makes possible a life of intellect, will and emotion. When an external object gets into contact with man, it is an integral object that gets into contact with an integral man. Here, the integral object gets into contact with man's body as well as his mind. Since man is a psychophysical integral body, contact from an external object means contact with both the human body and soul. If any of these two is lacking, contact cannot be realized. To cite an example, when a spiritual reality only gets into contact with man's body and not with his mind, man would not be able to see nor hear it. It would appear to be no contact at all. Similarly, a spiritual reality cannot get into contact with the human mind alone because it cannot be possible for the mind to rid itself from the body and enter into contact with the spiritual reality.

Man's cognitive actions are integral actions. They are actions of the psychophysical unity. The mind, that is, the intellect, is involved in sense cognition. In intellectual cognition, the senses are involved through the nervous system. At the same time, cognitive actions are actions of the whole subject. When I see, it is the whole me that sees. When I think, it is the whole me that thinks. Similarly, the object known is likewise an integral reality. When I see color, I see the reality, for example, a table or a flower, possessing that color. We can therefore say that cognitive actions involve relationships between integral realities. The action, the subject and the object are all integral. All cognition start from sensation. A sense cognition is at the same time an intellectual cognition. When I see a table, my eyes see its outer form. At the same time, the intellect knows that it is a table. When I hear sound, my intellect knows what type of sound it is. What I now feel is felt by my whole person. When I make an inference, the whole of me is thinking. When the object faces the knowing subject, it shows as an integral object. Therefore, the process of cognition cannot be analyzed as a pure sense cognition or as a pure intellectual cognition. Both types of cognition are always united in one movement. In this one movement, sense and intellect obtain their respective objects. There exists no great division between subject and object.

Cognitive action is an integral action. During cognition, it is not possible to distinguish between sense cognition and intellectual cognition. Both actions run and end simultaneously. In cognition, the knowing subject is an integral psychophysical reality who employs both his sense organs and his mind. To cite and example, when I see a red flower, I see red and, at the same time, know that it is a flower. Similarly, the object known is also an integral reality. A flower is known in its entirety as flower and not first known as color and later known as flower. We can neither say that if I am not aware that it is a flower, then I cannot tell that it is a flower upon seeing its color. In cognition, the flower and its color are distinguishable. However, if you do not know what "color" is, you will not know that it is color even if you come to see it. This distinction is not a distinction between object and subject *per se*, but rather arises out of the subject's lack of normal psychophysical unity.

We can therefore say that in cognition, contact between subject and object is integral. That is, the object is made manifest in its entirety to the subject. Similarly, the subject's reception of the object is also an integral function. It is a psychophysical cognitive function wherein the sense organs grasp the object's outer form and the intellect grasps the object's substance.

Analytical studies in Western philosophy separate sense organ cognition from intellectual cognition. This analysis is abstract and academic, not factual. In actual terms, these two types of cognition are always united. That is because they both are human vital activities. Human vital activities are inseparable.

Cognition by the union of mind and matter is a preliminary step. It is further analyzed by the intellect after which ideas are created. Then, definitions of things and events are established. These are activities of the mind. However, corporeal imagination also often accompanies intellectual activities. We never have a purely mental idea that absolutely is not derived with the help of imagination. Neither is it possible to comprehend a theory that is absolutely inconceivable.

Both the issues of the unbridgeability of the subject-object division of Western epistemology and the incapability of the subject's intellect to detach itself from the subject and enter the object are not factual problems but are abstract ones.

The second point from the epistemology of Chuang-tzu that can serve as our principle in solving the problem of cognition is that the human mind resembles a clear mirror.

Western epistemology often accepted the idea that the intellect cannot detach itself from the subject and reach the object during the process of intellectual cognition. In Chinese philosophy, the human mind is always taken as empty and clear (*hsu-ming*). In the first chapter of the *Ta-hsüeh*, it says: "The Way [Tao] of learning to be great consists in manifesting the clear character" (Chan 86). In the Chinese text, the character ming appears twice. The first character functions as a verb, meaning "to make manifest." The second Chinese character (*ming*) functions as an adjective which describes the character as clear. Here, "character" (*te* [virtue]) refers to human nature which, is goodness (*shan*). The opening chapter of the Chung-yung says: "What Heaven imparts to man is called human nature. To follow our nature is called the Way (*Tao*)" (Chan 98). Human nature means goodness. It is a virtue. Sung and Ming Dynasty Rationalists referred to nature as *li* (principle, form). The virtue of human nature is itself the principle of human nature. It is a clear and manifest principle that is made obvious naturally. Human nature, an abstract principle, is, concretely, nothing but the human mind. Sung and Ming Dynasty Rationalists often overlapped the terms "principle," "nature" and "mind." Hsun-tzu once affirmed that the human mind is empty and potent. Chu Hsi himself made the same affirmation. Wang Yang-ming compared the human mind to a mirror. For Wang, the human mind manifests not only the principle (*li*) of human nature but also the principle of things. Lu Hsiang-shan believed that when man stares at his own mind, he sees the principle of the myriad phenomena without any effort. Chu Hsi affirmed that man needs to study the principle of external things. After various types of study, however, knowledge naturally dawns on the human mind. Both Chu Hsi and Lu Hsiang-shan affirmed that there exists one single principle in Heaven and Earth. Chu Hsi further proposed the "unity and diversity of principle." In addition, the principles (*li*) dealt with in Chinese philosophy are all principles pertaining to human life. They all are principles related to morality and the concepts of good and evil.

The principle (*li*) I am about to explain is the corporeal principle (*wu-li*) of every object. Corporeal principle is the principle of the existence of things, or the principle that makes a thing what it is. Whenever a thing comes into contact with me, it is the integral reality of that thing coming into contact with the integral me. Its outer shape is made manifest to my sense organs and its corporeal principle appears in my mind, which is both empty and clear. When the corporeal principle is made manifest to my mind, my intellect gets to know its principle. This cognition, preliminary and general in nature, is what Scholasticism calls "passive intellectual impression." Then, it is further analyzed by my intellect which results in the formation of an abstract idea. This is referred to in Scholastic philosophy as active intellectual movement. The intellect further compares the established idea with other ideas. Thus, inference is carried out and scholarly knowledge becomes a consequence. In Buddhism, mental cognition is called *liao pie shih* [knowledge by understanding and differentiation] or *pi liang* [quantitative comparison].

Chuang-tzu affirmed that Heaven and Earth and the myriad things, joined together and mutually penetrating, share the same material force (*ch'i*). I believe that Heaven and Earth and the myriad things are moved by the same power derived from generative power and, thus, are mutually linked and penetrating. Wang Yang-ming explained his concept of "the unity of *jen*" in terms of physiological life. In his life, man needs to eat animal flesh, vegetables, fruits and drug of mineral origin. This need shows the mutual penetration of life. In terms of emotional life, man's feelings also interpenetrate with the myriad things. Poets and artists have both experience and their creation. In terms of the intellect, man and the myriad things must likewise interpenetrate. The myriad things are made manifest to the mind of man whose intellect is capable of knowing corporeal principles.

In actual terms, there are many conditions when things are made manifest to the human mind, just as when things are made manifest to man's sense organs. Thus, man's intellectual life differs from person to person. Intellectual ability is classified into different levels. There are weak and strong abilities to concentrate. Methods of research have distinctions of superiority or inferiority. Emotional desires lead to both positive and negative consequences. The adage "Spectators see the chess game better than the players" precisely refers to the effects of human passion and emotion.

In summary, cognition is part of the intellectual life of man. Intellectual life is a vital [life] activity of man. Vital activity is always an activity of an integral reality. In man, integral activity is a psychophysical activity. Mind and matter simultaneously reach the object of their own movements. I call this kind of epistemology logical and satisfactory.

Works Cited

Chan, Wing-tsit. *A Source Book in Chinese Philosophy*. Princeton: Princeton UP, 1963.

Liang, Shu-ming. *Jen-hsin yü jen-sheng* [*The Human Mind and Human Life*]. Taipei: Ku-feng Publications.

Waley, Arthur. *Three Ways of Thought in Ancient China*. Lanham, Maryland: Rowman, 1964.

Watson, Burton. Chuang Tzu. New York: Columbia University Press, 1968.

Translated by Carlos Tee

Chapter XIV

Epistemology in the Philosophy of Life

Philosophy of Life focuses on life. Man's activities are also life. Cognition, being a human activity, is then also based on life. Since man's life is psychophysical, then human cognition is also a psychophysical activity.

I.   Man's cognitive activities are not limited to knowing the way (Tao) of human life. They must also be extended to things in the natural sciences, and even, to the substance of metaphysical beings. The Tao of human life is the center of human knowledge. Since human life is itself human living, then living is the activity of life, which in turn is the existence of man. Man thus, naturally, must know his own way of existence. Besides, all activities of man must be rooted in existence. In fact, they all are related to existence. Man engages in activities for his own survival. All his activities are geared toward his own survival.

In Western philosophy, the way of human life is not dealt with not because of lack of emphasis but rather because it is a topic discussed under religion. Western countries were all Catholic until some one-third later turned to Protestantism. Both Roman Catholicism and Protestantism take religious faith as the overall rule in man's life. By tradition, both religions did not advocate separation between Church and State. It was only in recent times when public life broke away from its religious affiliation. This explains why way of life is dealt with in terms of religion in the West. In Western countries, children are required to attend catechism and ethics classes in churches until now. Although ethics classes do not necessarily work in these children, people in society reach a common consensus on what is right or wrong. By tradition, Chinese families stress moral education. In the old-style private schools, teachers always made it a point to explain the way of human life through the Four Books [*Ssu-shu*]. In present times, not only families are lacking in basic ethical education, schools too are neglecting education on life in favor of preparations for entrance examinations. There is, therefore, a need to once again emphasize ethical education in both the family and educational institutions. Contemporary formal education has shifted its educational objectives to imparting scientific knowledge, with much stress on Western educational policies. In present times, receiving education no longer means studying the way of human life but rather an understanding of the principles governing things in the natural world. Therefore, the epistemology of Confucianism requires an expansion. The objectives of Confucian epistemology lie in the search for the development of life. These objectives remain as they are. The way of human life in fact is geared toward the development of life. The knowledge in natural sciences is, directly or otherwise, beneficial to the development of human life. In contrast, metaphysics is the principle underlying the way of human life and the natural sciences. It is also the principle governing their application. At present, research in Chinese philosophy has also deviated from the traditional, and has in fact, followed the path of Western philosophy. It is now more directed toward the pursuit of practical truths and not those on the way of human life.

II.   Research methods for different disciplines vary. Progress in the natural sciences during the past two centuries in Europe has made their research methods into something universal for all disciplines. Traditional metaphysics was virtually overturned. In the last half century, however, metaphysics has again gradually recovered its place, although its research methods have largely been changed. Metaphysics has now followed the trend in the natural sciences were stress is placed on actual things. By tradition, philosophy only studied universal concepts and principles while the natural sciences focused on concrete, individual realities. This century, however, witnessed Western philosophy's shift to actual things. Existentialism studied a concretely existing "ego" while Whitehead focused his attention to actual realities. Still, there are even schools of philosophy which study man's actual experience in life and actual persons.

The debate between Chu Hsi and Lu Hsiang-shan in Sung Dynasty

China centered precisely around philosophical research methods. Traditional Western philosophy belonged to the theoretical level. The research method proposed by Lu Hsiang-shan was based on the interior and the psychological, or in other words, the theoretical level. In contrast, Chu Hsi's proposed research method paid equal importance to the theoretical and the practical. He propounds that both material principle (*li*) and material force (*ch'i*) are equally significant, with material principle corresponding to the theoretical and material force to the practical. However, the emphasis on the actual by both philosophy and the natural sciences corresponds only in terms of their material object. They differ in their formal objects. Philosophy stresses the actual from the point of view of the existence of the concrete reality. It studies the principle of existence of the actual reality. In the natural sciences, actual realities are studied as they are.

III. Studying the way of human life is a process of reflection of one's own heart. The principles of the way of human life are inscribed by the Creator in human nature. One's human nature is made manifest through one's heart, which is empty and clear. By reflecting on one's own heart, it is possible to know the way of human life. This process is often discussed in Chinese philosophy. For Lu Hsiang-shan, the heart is itself material principle (*li*). For him, "there is no principle outside the human heart." Wang Yang-ming went a step further. For him, conscience is itself the heart or the principle. In the West, St. Augustine once propounded that the principles of things were placed by the Creator in the hearts of men. When someone sees things external, it triggers off all principles residing in his heart, and in so doing, gets to know the things around him. St. Augustine's "idea" sounds very similar to that proposed by the doctrine of innate ideas, which as Plato explained, are concepts belonging to the human soul's *a priori* knowledge. After union of the soul and body, contact with external things triggers off the souls *a priori* knowledge. St. Augustine rejected Plato's idea of the independent existence of concepts. Instead, he considered concepts as God's ideas in his act of creation. When God created man, he informed these concepts in man, i.e., making them inborn in him. St. Thomas did not accept St. Augustines proposal. For

St. Thomas, concepts are man's knowledge and are created by man's knowing action. However, if explained in terms of the way of human life, the principles of the ways of human life are inborn knowledge hidden in the human heart, known as "human natural law." They are naturally obvious and are referred to in the *Ta-hsueh* [Great Learning] as "bright virtues" [*ming teh*]. Human passion can be suppressed. A person has to control his passion. In the *Ta-hsueh,* this process is called "manifesting bright virtues" [*ming ming teh*]. Both the Confucian concept of "manifesting" [*ming*] and Chuang-tzu's "interpenetration" [*t'ung*] refer to the controlling of passion. Western philosophy also deals with conscience, which includes the concept of intuitive knowledge, a natural way of knowing inborn moral principles. This point overlaps with Confucian philosophy.

Philosophy of Life takes the ways of human life as the first objects of knowing. The ways of human life are the path of life's development. Although human life is psychophysical, spiritual life ranks highest. In fact, it also forms the basis of human life. If spiritual life is able to develop reasonably, the human heart feels relieved and, as a consequence, man's life is made happy. The soul has an inborn knowledge of the principles of spiritual life. If the soul is virtually proficient, the inborn principles are naturally made manifest. With the soul virtually proficient and able to know, it necessarily can directly know the ways of spiritual life.

The lives of the universe and all the myriad things are interconnected. Man's life is psychophysical. The relationship between spirit and body, other than the physiological, is outside man's consciousness, and which the soul cannot directly experience. Man's intellectual and emotional lives are directly experienced by the soul, and even, can be put into introspection. The relationship of external matters with life or with man's life, with the exception of the physiological, can be directly experienced by the soul. This is what Chuang-tzu referred to as penetration [*t'ung*]. However, it is not an "interpenetration between material force" but rather one related to generative power. Chinese poets and writers have always manifested this interpenetration between their own feelings with things in the natural world through their poems and other literary works, such as in the following lines:

"This feeling left the flowers moist with tears,

the birds frightened by the sad separation."

In fact, Chinese traditional art has often emphasized this interpenetration with the belief that art objects must evoke a certain vivid spirit [*sheng ch'i*] and must not appear dull. Chuang-tzu once mentioned "heavenly music" and "human music." For him, the former meant the music of the natural world which man hears deep in his heart. The Confucianists also talked about "heavenly music," defining it as the harmony existing in nature. The *I Ching* proposes what is central and right in terms of time and disposition while Confucius stressed the golden mean. All these are in pursuit of a balance between the life of man and the myriad things of the universe, which when achieved, would mean making the universe a harmonious whole.

IV. Intellectual cognition is psychophysical cognition, not achieved in a direct manner but rather through the formation of concepts which are abstracted from experience. Concepts are objects of cognition, which, in the human mind, form a type of intentional existence with the intellect.

Things in the universe, with the exception of man, are all material in nature. Every material things possesses a principle that causes its existential. This existential principle is naturally manifest in each thing. For instance, a table's existential principle is naturally shown in its structure. A painting or a carving has its meaning naturally shown in the thing itself. This is true not only for man-made things but for things created by the Creator in the natural world as well. Some things have simple principles while others have more complicated ones. For instance, the meaning behind some modern art works is difficult to discern. The principle of a thing is its existential principle. Existence is itself a principle and things have principles of action. In Scholasticism, there is the saying "*Ratio essendi est ratio operandi.*" (Existential principle is itself the principle of action.) An active existence is life itself. Action is living. Living necessarily finds its principle of action in life. Thus, to say that man is a rational animal is using action to explain why man is man. In Chinese philosophy, it is often said that "reality (substance) and function are one." Epistemologically, this saying is correct. Ontologically, however, this statement is false. This is because ontologically, a reality is a reality, and a function is a function. They differ. In actual terms, however, the two are indistinguishable.

The principle of each thing in the universe is naturally manifested in its own structure and action. Things are composed of matter. Their actions are also material. To know these things, one needs sense organs, which get an impression of the components or actions of things. These impressions of the material or action of things, such as color and sound, are not ordinary color and sound, but are perceived as component elements of a material or an action. They are subjected to the limitations of the principle of the material or action. This limiting principle is actually the principle that makes up the thing itself. Therefore, these sense impressions bear with them material principle. When a sense impression enters the mind, the mind's intellect actively knows the material principle inherent in the impression. The intellect then knows the principle of the impression, which unites with the intellect to form a concept. Concepts are not abstracted from impressions and separated from external things just as Plato explained it by saying that a concept unites with the model concept existing in the realm of concepts, thus becoming a type of unreal, symbolic sign. Rather, the forms in the intellect and the impression unite to arrive at an actual being--an objective external thing. Through intellectual cognitive power, it forms an "intentional existent" known as concept.

How can an objective external things enter the human mind? This question has always been the subject of debate in recent centuries by philosophers in the West.

Man is a psychophysical integral consisting of body and soul. External actions of the body require the use of bodily organs whose actions, in turn, are coursed through the soul's (mind's) consciousness. This is how actions are completed. In this process, the sense impressions derived through the action of bodily organs naturally enter the human mind. If not, one will not be able to see, for instance. The sense impressions that enter the mind are the joining of things and sense organs. It is the fusion of the sense organs with the object external thing and the matter and principle the latter consists of. Man's mental actions must also pass through the body using the nervous system. Any contact between mental actions and external things is always coursed through bodily organs. This contact is a natural process determined by the Creator. Just like the other natural processes composed of different types of actions, this process always achieves its purpose. For instance, natural physiological processes all reach their objectives. If not, abnormal conditions appear. The process of knowing occurs when an external object enters the human mind through sense organs in the form of sense impression. This sense impression includes the form of the thing, which unites with the intellect to form a concept. This concept is then the "intentional existence" of external objects in the human mind, or, the intellect's knowledge of the external object. The entry of external things into a subject through the action of knowing represents the interconnection of the lives of myriad things in the universe. They are interconnected in their physiological life as well as their spiritual lives. Since for knowing to occur, the external object must unite with the human intellect, then the knowing action is the natural way in which human life and external things unite. This natural way requires external things to enter the mind. A question may be asked: why so? The only answer to this question is that the process was determined by the Creator. It is a type of natural law. Why is it that a particular type of thing is edible and others not? The natural sciences could only say that the material characteristics of both are compatible or incompatible. If a further question is asked why, the answer would most likely be that nature made it that way.

The ultimate reason why the lives of the myriad things in the universe are joined together lies in the fact that they share the same generative power. This generative power pervades the universe and everything in it, and triggers off all actions. In ancient Chinese philosophy, it says that a "Great Transformation" [*Ta-hua*] occurs in the universe, causing a continued generation of life. It can be said that this "Great Transformation" must refer to the universal generative power designed by the Creator.

Man sometimes makes mistakes in knowing. Since concepts are derived from external objects, where do errors in knowing come from? We have discussed above that forms of external objects may be simple or complex. A simple form is very obvious while a complex one requires further study. An error does not mean an error of the concept in question. Rather, it could be due to mistakes in analyzing or explaining the concept.

This conclusion resembles that proposed by Jacques Maritain, except that the idea of the interconnected character of the life of myriad inherent to the Philosophy of Life was used as a fundamental theoretical basis.

V. Man does not have direct intuition of external objects. Since man's knowing action is psychophysical, then it must be carried out through the sense organs. The "spiritual knowledge" proposed by Chuang-tzu, the Buddhists' "seeing things' nature through the Zen vision" and the Roman Catholic "direct vision" are all impossible. This is explained by the fact that body cannot be separated from the spirit, a condition that would lead to death. However, in the history of the Roman Catholic Church, there have been incidents of "direct vision" which can only be explained as God's special favor. During "direct vision," more properly known as "Beatific vision," God, through his omnipotent power, makes a person temporarily leave the body, with his soul being in action on its own. In this process, the body is tantamount to being dead, with all its consciousness lost although the body remains alive. The soul directly faces God. After return to normal conditions, the person cannot recall details about the "direct vision" owing to the absence of corresponding concepts.

After death, only the soul remains existing. The soul, without sense organs, cannot get into contact with the material world. It cannot see, hear or speak. It can only know things in the world through God.

The soul, which retains the ability to know the form of things, cannot know things in the world without union with God.

Jacques Maritain's "mystical experience" [*experience mystique*] is not the "direct vision" explained above but is instead a type of spiritual experience characterized by the direct experiencing of God's presence, which leaves the soul extremely satisfied. St. John of the Cross once preached that man's love for God, if exercised to the fullest, surpasses the level of intellectual knowing. With help from the Holy Spirit, the soul actually lives in the holy love of God that transcends all things in the universe. Without having a vision of God, without directly knowing Him, and in the absence of sense or intellectual knowledge, the soul experiences His presence.

This mystical experience has been used to explain Indian Mysticism and Buddhist Zen vision. Facing an absolute and highest being, the soul only directly experiences it in the darkness of his intellect, without seeing or hearing it. Yet, the soul is filled with light and experiences extreme satisfaction.

On man's consciousness, the Philosophy of Life explains that man has an eternal consciousness. It proposes that the human heart always aspires for eternal life. Maritain said that metaphysics represents a hope for a transcendence from intellect. Because of this aspiration for eternity, the human soul can attain a "mystical experience."

In conclusion, the epistemology of the Philosophy of Life can be summarized into the following points:

1. The way of human life is the first object of knowing. The way of human life is clearly manifested in man's heart. By introspection of one's heart, the way of human life can be known.

2. The natural sciences and philosophy differ in their methods regarding knowledge of external things.

3. The form of things is naturally made manifest in the structure and actions of things. This is the so-called "unity between reality and function."

4. Through sense organs, external things enter the mind, thereby

creating sense impressions. Through the sense impression, reason actively knows the form of things, thus creating concepts.

5. Concepts are the fusion of external things with the intellect. They are the "intentional existence" of external things. Concept is itself the external thing.

6. The entry of external things into the human mind is the natural process of knowing, accomplished by generative power.

7. It is possible for man to receive a "mystical experience" from the highest absolute being who transcends the universe.

Translated by Carlos Tee

Chapter XV

Ethics, Morality and Life

I. Ethics and Life

Ethics is the regulation of life. Man lives a communal or social life. It is so because man's existence, that is, human life, is not and cannot be a solitary one. The existence of man is a life of activity in which life continues to flourish, and the life of other things are interlinked. The flourishing of life, therefore, must follow certain laws if conflicts and friction are to be avoided.

In its discussion of the Tao of the perpetual renewal of life, the *I Ching* mentions that common principles govern changes in the cosmos and the myriad things. The most fundamental of these principles is embodied in the passage "The successive movement of *yin* and *yang* constitutes the Way [*Tao*]." Arising from this Tao of the movement of *yin* and *yang* are the principles governing motion and rest, progression and regression. Then, there are the standards of time and location, which regulate the "centrality and rightness" of all changes. Chapter X of the Appended Remarks (Part I) of the Commentaries on the *I Ching* says:

> The *I Ching* is a book of wide comprehension and great scope, embracing everything. There are in it the way of heaven, the way of man, and the way of earth. It then takes (the lines representing) those three Powers, and doubles them till they amount to six. What these six lines show is simply this--the Way of the three Powers. (Legge 402)

The *I Ching* discusses laws governing changes in Heaven and Earth and man. Although vestiges of changes involving Heaven and earth are visible, they are complex and intricate in nature. The *I Ching* says:

The system of change is tantamount to Heaven and Earth, and therefore can always handle and adjust the way of Heaven and Earth. Looking up, we observe the pattern of the heavens; looking down, we examine the order of the earth. Thus we know the causes of what is hidden and what is manifest. If we investigate the cycle of things, we shall understand the concepts of life and death. The refined material force (ch'i) [integrates] to become things. [As it disintegrates] the wandering away of its spirit (force) becomes change. From this we know that the characteristics and conditions of spiritual being are similar to those of Heaven and earth and therefore there is no disagreement between them. The knowledge [of spirit] embraces all things and its way helps all under heaven, and therefore there is no mistake. It operates freely and does not go off course. It rejoices in Nature (T'ien, Heaven) and understands destiny. Therefore there is no worry. As [things] are contented in their stations and earnest in practising kindness, there can be love. It molds and encompasses all transformations of Heaven and earth without mistake, and it stoops to bring things into completion without missing any. It penetrates to a knowledge of the course of day and night. Therefore spirit has no spatial restriction and Change has no physical form. (Hsi-tz'u shang [Appended Remarks], Part I, Ch. IV, Chan 117-118)

The I Ch'uan [Commentaries on the I Ching] explains that by delving into astronomy and geography, one comes to know the Tao of the perpetual renewal of life in the cosmos, whose results are deeply mysterious. In their study of this Tao of generation and metamorphosis, sages "came to understand all the myriad things and learned that Tao pervades the whole world." The sages first designed the pa-kua as "the sage was able to survey all the complex phenomena under the sky. He then considered in his mind how they could be figured, and (by means of the diagrams) represented their material forms and their character. Hence these (diagrams) are denominated Semblances (or emblematic figures, the Hsiang)." (Hsi-tz'u [Appended Remarks], Part I, Chapter VIII, Legge 360) The pa-kua was used for divining good or bad luck on which behaviors are based. Consequently, divination became the standards of behavior. Later, when people gradually improved their knowledge, they realized that good and evil cannot be solely judged from good or evil fortune. Realizing the need to adopt their own principles, the sage kings designed rites and guidelines based on the heavenly principles. The *Chung-yung* says:

> Although a man occupies the throne, if he has not the corresponding virtue, he may not dare to institute systems of music and ceremony. Although a man has the virtue, if he does not occupy the throne, he may not dare to institute systems of music and ceremony either. (Ch. XXVIII, Chan 111)

After their establishment, the rites became the ethical norms. Confucius said:

> Do not look at what is contrary to propriety, do not listen to what is contrary to propriety, do not speak what is contrary to propriety, and do not make any movement which is contrary to propriety." *The Analects, Yen Yuan*, Chan 38)

The principle of Heaven is found within the cosmos and the myriad things. Since man forms part of the myriad things, the Tao of man's life must also be found within man. The *Chung-yung* says: What Heaven (*T'ien*, Nature) imparts to man is called human nature. To follow our nature is called the Way (Tao). Cultivating the Way is called education." (Ch. I, Chan 98) Laws governing man's activities in life are found in his nature. When man lives according to his human nature, it is good. The *Chung-yung* explains "sincerity" (*ch'eng*) as nothing but the "following of one's nature." Hence, Sung Dynasty Idealists affirmed that "nature" is itself *li* (principle). For man to cultivate his moral character, he must know his nature and principle.

The existence of each thing is based on its corporeal nature. This existence is an active existence. It is a life characterized by immanent activity. Activities in life are but the development of existence. This development must necessarily be based on corporeal nature. We can therefore say that the laws governing life are themselves the corporeal nature of things. Things in the natural world do not possess rationality. Things are unable to act on themselves. All their activities are done naturally. These natural movements are naturally based on their corporeal nature. This is why the *Chung-yung* says: "Sincerity is the Way of Heaven" (Ch. XX, Chan 107).

Man is endowed with a rational mind able to know and decide. Man is aware of his human nature and Heavenly principles. He knows that he can live according to his human nature and Heavenly principles. Hence, the *Chung-yung* says: "To think how to be sincere is the Way [Tao] of man" (Ch. XX, Chan 107). For man to be sincere and follow his nature, he needs to act. Human action is an action of the mind which comes about through one's own decision. In contrast, physiological activities, not based on man's own decision, naturally follow Heavenly principles. Acts following man's own decisions may or may not be in conformity with his human nature and heavenly principles, in this way forming good and evil. Good and evil actions are judged based on their conformity with human nature and heavenly principles. The *Chung-yung* says: "When feelings are aroused and each and all attain due measure and degree, it is called harmony" (Ch. I, Chan 98). If man's actions attain due measure and degree, then they are in conformity with human nature, and thus, his life attains development. If his actions fail to attain due measure and degree, his life bears damage. Not only are good and evil the relationship between behavior and regulation, they also are the consequences of man's actions. To cite an example, if a flowering plant lives in accordance with its corporeal nature, then it can attain growth. If hampered by an outside factor preventing the plant from living in accordance with its corporeal nature, the plant dries up. Human life is a psychophysical life. Man's mental life can represent human life. That is because the physical life of man does not significantly differ from that of beasts. Therefore, good and evil actions are actions of the mind. They are actions following man's own decisions, and influence the life of the mind. The *Chung-yung* says that only those who are absolutely sincere can fully develop their nature (Chan 107). Ethical laws are the laws governing the development of human life.

In Western philosophy, ethical laws governing good and evil include the supernatural law, natural law and man-made laws. The supernatural law, a set of laws directly established by God for man, are the so-called "Ten Commandments" in the *Old Testament*. Natural law, also established by God, includes all the laws concerning man's nature. Man-made laws are legislated by men, by the power of the state or those made by following popular customs. These three-tiered ethical laws are maintained in traditional Western ethics. Fused with religious faith, they determine whether an action is good or evil. However, contemporary and modern Western philosophies oppose this tradition. They solely accept man-made ethical laws and believe that ethical laws must only regulate social relations among men and bear no links with life at all. Laws governing social relationship are established by man. They change following changes in the social environment. In modern Western philosophies, ethical laws are relative in nature. Once standards of social relationships are determined by man, he usually sets laws based on his own vested interests. In ancient Greek philosophy, there was Epicureanism, a school of thought founded by Epicureus (341-270 B.C.), whose ethical standards are based on human material enjoyment. In the past three millennia, Epicureanism was often adopted as a sense of value. Now, Epicureanism coupled with Eudemonism is the most prevalent in European and American societies. In the 19th Century, Utilitarianism was started in England by Jeremy Bentham (1749-1832) and James Mill (1773-1836) using utility as an ethical standard. Also in the 19th Century, Pragmatism developed in the United States with Charles Pierce (1839-1914), William James (1842-1912) and John Dewey (1859-1952), who adopted ethical standards based on actual results. The Twentieth Century saw the rise of communism, with means of production adopted as ethical standards. In contrast to these thoughts favoring material things as standards of ethics, there were those which proposed the suppression of passion as their standard. In Greece, Aristiphus (435-350 B.C.) proposed that happiness consists in being contented with the present, an idea later known as Asceticism. Later, in the 18th Century, the pessimist philosopher Arthur Schopenhauer (1768-1860) proposed an ethical standard characterized by living a life of relief from pain through abstention from desire. This is an off-shoot of Asceticism.

After the rise of Existentialism in the 20th century, ethical standards once again returned to the idea of existence. The ethics of Existentialism can be considered to have been adopted from Kant's ideas. Kant affirmed that man is a rational subject whose actions are always oriented towards objectives. These objectives lie in the pursuit of happiness. Here, Kant employed an unqualified *a priori* method of realization called *postula*. This type of assumption cannot be proven by reason nor attested by experience. Rather, they fulfill the demands of reason. To live following these demands assures one of the objectives of life. In contrast, Heidegger explained the purpose of life via the existence of the ego. The ego stands "out from the crowd," departs from "an untrustworthy existence" and "steps into" its own ego. There, he lives a trustworthy existence enjoying the significance of the ego in infinite truth (Chou 156). Sartre, an atheist, proposed the creation of all based on one's own freedom. However, to avoid an extremely irrational Solipsism, he proposed that freedom must work for the good of both the ego and others.

Traditional Western ethics is preserved within Scholasticism. Scholasticism, on the basis of the Roman Catholic faith, affirms the existence of a supernatural law, natural law and later man-made laws in ethics. Ethical laws are the basis of man's spiritual life. They allow man to reach the objective of "unity between Heaven and man." On this point, Scholasticism converges with Confucian ideals. The *Chung-yung* says:

> Equilibrium is the great foundation of the world, and harmony its universal path. When equilibrium and harmony are realized to the highest degree, heaven and earth will attain their proper order and all things will flourish. (Ch. I, Chan 98)

II. Morality and Life

If man follows ethical laws and does good deeds, he cultivates the virtue of goodness. This good virtue is a moral virtue, the fruit of ethical laws.

Hsiung Shih-li, a contemporary scholar, explains virtue (*te*):

> The word *te* (virtue) means training (*hsūn*). When you say virtue, you mean acquiring (*te*) it. When you say that a white object possesses the virtue of whiteness, you mean that its whiteness is what makes that object a thing. Nowadays, we ascribe ' real constancy' and other virtues to realities. Yet, ' real constancy' and other virtues are what makes realities [substances] become realities [substances] in this universe. If not for the different virtues, how could the myriad transformations have generated and formed the myriad things? If not, the term reality would not have been coined. The word virtue has two meanings. One is *te-hsing*. The other is *te-yung*. The character *hsing* in *te-hsing* cannot be translated directly as the English ' nature' (*hsing*). This character (*hsing*) has quite a flexible meaning. Similarly, the *yung* in *te-yung* cannot be translated as the English ' power' or ' function' as the character is also very flexible. On the contrary, these terms must be considered thoughtfully and not casually disposed of.

The *te-hsing* discussed by Hsiung must be the "characteristics" (*t'e-hsing*) of realities such as the whiteness of white objects. Hsiung thinks that an object's characteristics make it what it is. The *yung* in his so-called *te-yung* must be the *yung* in *t'i-yung* (reality and function) mentioned by ancient Chinese. *Yung* means the "manifestation" or "action" of a substance. Hsiung affirms that virtue is the characteristic of a reality. It makes the nature of things manifest. Virtue is explained ontologically and not studied in terms of ethics. Chuang-tzu once said:

> In the Great Beginning, there was nonbeing; there was no being, no name. Out of it arose One; there was One, but it had no form. Things got hold of it and came to life, and it was called Virtue. (*T'ien-ti* [Heaven and Earth], Watson 131)

Furthermore, he said:

> If the nature is trained, you may return to Virtue, and virtue at its highest peak is identical with the Beginning. Being identical you will be empty. . .This is called Dark Virtue. Rude and unwittingly, you take part in the Great Submission." (Watson 132)

Chu Hsi once also explained virtue (*te*) as "acquiring" (*te*). In his commentary on the *Shu-erh* of the *Analects*, he explained the phrase "a will set towards the Tao while founded on virtue" (*chih yü tao, chü yü te*) by writing: "The character *chü* means grasping and abiding while *te* implies acquiring. Acquiring means having Tao in one's heart and not losing it." In another commentary on Chou Tun-i's *T'ung-shu* [Penetrating The Book of Changes] (Chapter V: *Shen-tung* [Caution about Activity]), Chu Hsi wrote the following about the passage "when operations are harmonized, we have virtue": The reason why operations become harmonized is because one possesses Tao within oneself, not outside." Chu Hsi further said: "Virtue means possessing the way of Tao in one's mind. Cultivation refers to the proper nurturing of virtue" (*Chu-tzu yu-lei* [Classified Conversations of Chu Hsi], Bk. 34). Again, in a commentary on a passage in the *Analects* (*Li-jen*) that reads "a Gentleman contemplates on cultivation of virtues while a petty man contemplates on increase in land property," Chu Hsi" wrote: "The character *huai* means to contemplate on something. Contemplating virtue means nurturing one's own goodness."

> In his *Ssu-shu hsun-yi* [Commentary on the Four Books], Wang Ch'uan-shan wrote about the passage "gentleman contemplating about virtue" in the *Analects* (*Li-jen*) as follows: The gentleman finds peace in his nature without which his conduct will have no basis. That is to say, when he performs something, he always remembers and ponders it in his heart...It is a different case with what the gentleman contemplates. The gentleman must necessarily seek virtues. And when he has obtained a virtue, it necessarily will not be lost. Instead, it grows day by day. (*Ssu-shu hsün-yi*, Vol.VIII, on Chapter IV of the *Analects*)

In another commentary on the *Analects* (*Shu-erh*) on the line "heaven produced the virtue that is in me," Wang wrote: "I was born with a life bestowed by the *li* (principle) of heaven. I then solidified it into virtue. My virtue is itself the virtue of heaven" (The *Analects, Shu-Erh*).

From the literature on virtue quoted above, we see how virtue is taken as the characteristic of man in the teachings of Confucius and the Idealists of latter periods. Within the context of the phrase "nature by the Mandate of heaven," this characteristic is good, that is, a corporeal nature suited for the *li* (principle) of human nature. This type of characteristic may be called talent or ability. These characteristics need cultivation and nurturing in order for them to flourish. If man cultivates these characteristics, his good talents flourish. Once the human mind has achievements, then he can fulfill his human nature. In this way, man's life can be said to have "reached the ultimate goodness." This idea concurs with the idea of Mencius. Mencius affirms that the human mind is endowed with the rudiments of the four virtues of humanity, righteousness, propriety and wisdom. Man is supposed to nurture his mind for him to cultivate these virtues. The human mind is good. In the first chapter of the *Ta-hsüeh*, the human mind is described as brilliant virtue. Chou Tun-i wrote that "when operations are harmonized, we have virtue." The disposition is what is meant by the passage "when these feelings are aroused and each and all attain due measure and degree, it is called harmony" in the *Chung-yung*. The phrase "due measure and degree" itself refers to goodness. Human nature is good. This nature is concretized in the mind, which takes it as foundation. This is the way how the rudiments of the four virtues of humanity, righteousness, propriety and wisdom are endowed in the human mind. The cultivation of these rudiments is itself the nurturing of virtue. Although Confucius said, "Heaven produced the virtue that is in me," he also said, "The lack of cultivation of virtues causes anxiety in me."

To cultivate virtues, one must "aspire to ease the mind," Mencius taught. This means that the mind, fixed on external things, must be retrieved. One must maintain the good rudiments of the mind as suggested by Confucius' advise on "the gentleman contemplating on virtue" and "being founded on virtue." In fact, maintaining the virtues of one's mind is not sufficient but also requires further cultivation. Mencius said: "In nurturing the mind, there is nothing better than reducing desires" (*Chin-hsin* Part I). Chu Hsi wrote that "cultivation refers to the proper nurturing of virtue," after which one can fulfill his nature. Fulfilling one's nature refers to the development of one's human nature in its totality. And since human nature penetrates with corporeal nature, the fulfillment of corporeal nature is made possible after fulfilling one's human nature. This way, one can participate in praising the generation of Heaven and Earth and thus attain the realm of supreme good where Heaven unites with man.

The cultivation of virtues benefit the mind. In terms of substance, the characteristics of human nature are made to flourish. In terms of life, the cultivation of virtues encourages the formation of the habit to do good deeds. These habits dispose man to get used to observing ethical laws in all his actions. This disposition was described by Confucius as "at seventy I could follow my heart's desire without transgressing moral principle" (*Analects*, Ch. II *Wei-cheng*, Chan 22), "a superior man never abandons humanity even for the lapse of a single meal" (*Analects*, Ch. IV *Li-jen*, Chan 26), and again, "for three months there would be nothing in his mind contrary to humanity. The others could attain to this for a day or a month at the most" (*Analects*, Ch. VI *Yung-ye*, Chan 29). In his commentary on this chapter, Chu Hsi wrote: "Three months is such a long time. Humanity is the virtue of the mind. A person with nothing in his mind contrary to humanity has no private desires but rather has virtues." Mencius once taught that for one to cultivate virtues, he must control his private desires. If private desires are constantly and habitually put under control, the rudiments of the four virtues of humanity, righteousness, propriety and wisdom can mature. They are transformed into spiritual strength that allows man's mental life to flourish.

A person without the virtue of goodness has his mental life blocked by private desires. Thus, the rudiments of the four virtues of humanity, righteousness, propriety cannot be made to flourish in him.

It is perhaps similar to Mencius' comparison with "bald Mount Ox,"[1] that is, a person without virtues germinating and growing in him "cannot be considered a human being."

Confucians affirm that the virtue of goodness (*Shan-te*) comprises all the characteristics of human nature. Being the rudiment of goodness in man's heart and the power behind man's metal life, it must therefore be cultivated. With cultivation, the rudiment of goodness can develop for the benefit of man's mind. With this, man's mental life can be made to flourish.

Western ethics defines "virtue" as a good habit. St. Thomas explained virtue as a habit cultivated by man in this performance of good deeds. It makes it easier for man to be good. This habit of virtue is classified under man's habits related to feelings (St. Thomas).

Habit is a characteristic formed after birth. It is formed in man through his action that lead to a manner of behavior. The manner of the habit does not determine a good virtue for it is only related to the difficulty or ease of the actions. It is but an empty shell. A person who does evil can also cultivate evil habits. For instance, a thief improves his skill as time goes by. Therefore, for a virtue to be a good habit, it must not only be a habitual good. In addition, the subject possessing that habit must itself be good. The subject of a habit is man's actions. Actions may be good or evil. When an action is in conformity with ethical laws, it is good. If not, it is evil. When a person does a good action many times over a long period of time, he cultivates a manner of action. This manner is itself a habit. Fused with habit, good actions lead to virtues. The goodness of a virtue is derived from good actions. Similarly, the classification of virtue is also derived from good actions. For instance, if a person often shows love for the poor, he then possesses the virtue of charity.

---

(1) [Translator's Note] Niu-shan (Mount Ox) is found in Shantung Province. During the time of Mencius, Mount Ox was denuded because of rampant tree-cutting and pasture grazing (*Mencius, Kao-tzu*, Part I).

Actions come about owing to a type of power. The power to perform virtues belongs to the emotions, that is, what the Chinese call "pleasure, anger, sorrow and joy." Actually, love and hate, greed and dislike all occupy higher positions in the hierarchy of emotions. If these emotions "attain due measure and degree," then they are good. If this good becomes a habit, then it is called a virtue. This is why in Western philosophy, the term virtue connotes strength. Therefore, we can say that virtue is the "strength of life that is always in conformity with ethical standards in its actions." This definition has a close semblance with the Chinese definition of virtue. However, in Western philosophy, ethics is not explained ontologically. Instead, it is explained by way of the relationships between behavior and ethical laws. Because ethical relationships are relationships involving good and evil, ethical good and evil do not pertain to the substance but rather to ethical relationships. On the contrary, Chinese philosophy explains good and evil nature by an ontological discussion of ethical good and evil. For this reason, however, it cannot explain the source of evil thoroughly. Nevertheless, although ethical good and evil are explained through ethical relationships, the basis of the latter are ethical laws, themselves derived from man's ontological life. Goodness is necessarily beneficial to mental life and evil detrimental to it. Goodness is the pathway through which mental life is made to flourish while evil is the channel through which mental life is destroyed.

Virtue is a power of life as emotion is. However, the classification of virtues is not done based on the emotions because every type of virtue may include all emotions. For instance, the virtue of humanity may include love, hatred, anger, patience, greed and disgust provided these emotions, in their operations, are in conformity with the ethical laws on humanity (jen). Therefore, when virtue is called a habit, it is a habit when the emotions act. In contrast, the substance of a virtue is not a habit of emotion, but rather the power that makes mental life flourish much in the sense of what Mencius called the "rudiments of the four virtues of humanity, righteousness, propriety and wisdom."

In the Roman Catholic faith, there are the three virtues of faith, hope and charity, collectively called the "three infused virtues." These three virtues, infused by God upon baptism, must not be viewed solely as a habit, but rather as a supernatural strength or as supernatural rudiments of the virtues of faith, hope and charity. After baptism, a person depends upon the help and protection of God, the objective of his performance of the three virtues of faith, hope and charity in his endeavor develop his own supernatural life. Supernatural life results from these three virtues without which supernatural life would not exist at all. In terms of man's nature, Mencius said that by nature, mental life is derived from the four virtues of humanity, righteousness, propriety and wisdom. Without these four virtues, a person would not have mental life. He would therefore not be a human being, according to Mencius.

In my discussion entitled "Mencius' Doctrine on Virtue," I wrote:

> Yet, both Mencius and the *Chung-yung* used the concept of virtue in their explanations on how goodness is developed or in order to show the goodness in man's heart. They do not explain virtue in terms of doing good and forming good habits. The Confucian way of moral cultivation is done through the cultivation of mental life and is not limited to the so-called ' attaining of due measure and degree.' (Lokuang 129).

In Volume II of his book *Tao-te yao-yi* [Definition of Morality] where he discusses man's moral objective in life, Fr. Chou K'e-ch'in writes:

> In general, human life possesses ways that belong to human nature and virtues that belong to the human mind. (Virtue is the possession of Tao in one's mind.) This is the basis of man's morality or man's way of life. It is also the basis of man's sanctity or goodness. The ultimate morality or the (inner) objective of man's way of life lies in fulfilling man's virtuous heart and in fulfilling or perfecting man's moral nature. That is, it

consists in fulfilling human life in its totality or in becoming holy using all the rudiments that lead to all goodness. (69)

In my book *Ju-chia che-hsüeh* [Confucian Philosophy], I therefore wrote:

> Western philosophy draws a line between ethics and metaphysical ontology. Ethics merely deals with some laws on behavior and habitual good virtues. In contrast, such differentiation does not exist in Chinese philosophy where everything is learned through life. Being is life. Good virtues are the flourishing of mental life. (Lokuang 107)

In my explanation of the moral doctrine of the philosophy of life, I use the Confucian explanation of morality as basis.

III. Humanity (*Jen*) and Life

Confucian morality often discusses the four virtues of humanity, righteousness, propriety and wisdom to match the *I Ching's* concepts of origination, penetration, advantage, correct and firm (*yuan t'ung li chen*). Although Han Dynasty Confucianists talked about the Five Agents by matching them with the Five Virtues of humanity, righteousness, propriety, wisdom and trustworthiness (also called the Five Constants), the last--trustworthiness--was not considered as a type of virtue but rather a condition existing in all the other virtues. Among the four virtues of humanity, righteousness, propriety and wisdom, the most important is humanity, referred to as the "the hinge of virtues" (*te-shu*) or "the linking virtue" (*te-wang*). It encompasses all types of virtues which it happens to represent.

Confucius explained the matter of humanity (*jen*) from the angle of ethical behavior. The *Ch'ien-kua wen-yen* [I Ching's Treatise on the Ch'ien] says:

> What is called (under *ch'ien*) ' the great and originating' is

(in man) the first and chief quality of goodness; what is called
' the penetrating' is the assemblage of excellences; what is
called ' the advantageous' is the harmony of all that is right;
and what is called ' the correct and firm' is the faculty of
action. The superior man [gentleman], embodying benevolence
(humanity, *jen*), is fit to preside over men; presenting the
assemblage of excellences, he is fit to show in himself the
union of all propriety; benefiting (all) creatures, he is fit to
exhibit the harmony of all that is right; correct and firm, he is
fit to manage (all) affairs. The fact that the superior man prac-
tises these four virtues justifies the application to him of the
words--'*ch'ien* represents what is great and originating, penetrating, advantageous, correct and firm.' (Legge 408)

The "Appended Remarks of the *I Ching* " matches "the great and
originating" with humanity (*jen*) and also with *ch'ien*. It says: "Vast is
the great and originating (power) indicated by *Ch'ien* ! All things owe
to it their beginning; -- it contains all the meaning belonging to
heaven" (Legge 213). *Ch'ien* is the originating power of life. Originating power is the beginning of life. The "Appended Remarks" says:
"The great characteristic of Heaven and earth is to produce. The most
precious thing for the sage is [the highest] position. To keep his position depends on humanity." (Appended Remarks, Part 2, Chan 268)
The *I Ching* proposes that the sage imitate heaven. The great characteristic of Heaven and Earth is to produce, while humanity (*jen*) is
attained when a sage imitates Heaven. Humanity (*jen*) and production
are matched together. This idea continued from the Han Confucianist
T'ung Chung-shu until the Sung Dynasty. Sung Dynasty Idealists then
formally affirmed that "humanity (*jen*) is production (*sheng*)."

Chou Tun-i said: "Production is humanity (*jen*)." (*Chou-tzu chüan-
shu, T'ung-shu, Shun-hua* [Complete Works of Chou Tun-i], Bk. VIII)
In the "Appended Remarks of the *I Ching*," Ch'eng Yi-ch'uan said:

Origination is the beginning of the myriad things. Flourishing
is the growth of the myriad things. Advantage is the satisfaction of the myriad things. Firmness is the consummation of all

myriad things. (*Chou-yi Ch'eng shih chuan* [Chou-i's Biography of Ch'eng], Ch. I)

Furthermore, he wrote: "The mind is like a grain. The nature of production is called *jen* (kernel)." (*Erh-Ch'eng Chi-yi*, Surviving Works, Bk. XVIII)

Chu Hsi adopted this idea of production being equal to humanity (*jen*). He said:

> The meaning of production is humanity (*jen*). (*Chu-tzu yü-lei* [Classified Conversations of Chu Hsi], Bk. VI)

He further wrote:

> Take for example such things as seeds of grain or the peach and apricot kernels. When sown they will grow. They are not dead things. For this reason that are called *jen* (the word *jen* meaning both kernel and humanity). This shows that *jen* implies the spirit of life. (*Chu-tzu yü-lei* [Classified Conversations of Chu Hsi], Bk. VI, Chan 633)

Again, he wrote:

> *Jen* means production. It resembles the presence of spring in all the four seasons. In summer, there is growth. In autumn, comes maturity and in winter, harvesting. Yet, although they all have a climate of their own, the productive vitality of spring prevails in all cf them. Therefore, *jen* connotes action and goodness. (*Chu-tzu yü-lei* [Classified Conversations of Chu Hsi], Bk. XX)

Chu Hsi did not equate humanity with love. Instead, he considered humanity to be the principle of love. He said: "Jen is the principle of love, the Tao of production." (*Ta Hu Kuang-chung, Chu-tzu ta-chüan,* Wen-chi ta-chuan [Complete Literary Works of Chu Hsi, Response to Hu Kuang-chung, Collected Writings], Bk. XLII, Chan 633)

Principle of love refers to the reason why man loves. All things love their own existence, which they seek to maintain and make flourish, and hope to be naturally kept free from any harm. Human existence is life. All men love their own life. At the same time, the existence of the myriad things is also life. Heaven and earth, treasuring the life of the myriad things, constantly have their intention in the production and generation of things. Hence, it is said that "the great characteristic of Heaven and earth is to produce." Chu Hsi; affirmed that man possesses the mind of Heaven and earth. Therefore, the human mind is endowed with humanity (*jen*):

> What is called *jen* (humanity) is the mind of Heaven and earth to produce things. It also is the mind received by men and things. Thus, Heaven and earth and the things they produced possess a common mind. To say that this mind penetrates all is not at all wrong." (*Chu-tzu yü-lei* [Classified Conversations], Bk. XCV)

Chu Hsi; further wrote:

> In the production of man and things, they receive the mind of Heaven and earth as their mind. Therefore, with reference to the character of the mind, although it embraces and penetrates all and leaves nothing to be desired, nevertheless, one word will cover all of it, namely, *jen* (humanity). (*Jen-shuo, Chu-tzu ta-chüan, Wen-chi* [A Treatise on Jen, Complete Literary Works of Chu Hsi, Collected Writings], Bk. LXVII, Chan 593)

The cosmos is constantly in action. By the fusion of *yin* and *yang* principles, things are engendered. As *yin* and *yang* principles within things continue their activities, things continue to have life. The whole cosmos is one life. The life of each thing and that of the cosmos are joined together. Chu Hsi affirms that Heaven and Earth have no activities other than the generation and metamorphosis of things. "I consider Heaven and Earth to have no other function but to have the mind of producing things. One originating *ch'i* operates and circulates without ceasing to produce myriad things in bounty." (*Chu-tzu yü-lei* [Classified Conversations], Bk. I)

Transformations in the universe are made visible to man in the four seasons. What the four seasons show are the growth and harvesting of cereal crops. This phenomenon is repeated each year as the universe continues in the production and transformation of myriad things. The "good virtue" of Heaven and Earth is precisely this "production and metamorphosis." They manifest the love of Heaven and Earth, which represents the love of God. In the process of production and metamorphosis, the love of God is made manifest. As the myriad things perpetually generate and renew them selves through the producing actions of Heaven and earth, the myriad things themselves are filled with vitality and go on making their own life flourish. This itself is the humanity (*jen*) of the myriad things. The lives of the myriad things in the universe are mutually linked and are supportive of one another. In the process of making their lives flourish, they adjust and harmonize with one another according to their own natural heaven-bestowed principle. Man, for instance, possesses rationality and freedom. Man is naturally inclined towards loving his own life and those of other things. In this rational and free life, man necessarily has to cultivate this inborn loving care for life. Thus, this human aspiration for the flourishing of life is called "mind of humanity"(*jen-hsin*) The cultivation of the mind of humanity is the virtue of love (*jen-ai*).

All the efforts and activities of man are aimed at the maintenance and development of life. Human life is the life of the mind. The maintenance and development of the life of the mind is a virtue. Humanity (*jen*), viewed from the angle of making life flourish, is called origination" or spring." Therefore, humanity (*jen*) encompasses all the virtues. It is the main link leading to all the virtues. In other words, all the virtues can be classified under humanity (*jen*).

The life of the mind in the Roman Catholic faith is man's spiritual life. Through baptism, man's spiritual life fuses with the supernatural life of God. The maintenance and flourishing of this life also relies upon the virtue of love (*jen-ai*).

The virtue of love (*jen-ai*) fortifies the bond between man's spiritual life and God's divine life. As this bond grows closer, man's whole spiritual life is elevated to a higher level. Love (*jen-ai*) is the power behind spiritual life. It makes spiritual life flourish. If this power radiates outward, man's life is elevated to join God and is extended to join the lives of fellow men and of things. This joining together is love. Roman Catholic moral laws have love of God as the first commandment. Loving one's fellowmen ranks second. These two commandments are made to overlap because the loving heart (mind) is one and the same. Love includes all other commandments and encompasses all the other virtues. Ethical life is the life of the substance. Since ethical laws are the laws governing the life of the mind, then ethics and morality are themselves the flourishing of the life of the mind.

Works Cited

Aquinas, St. Thomas. *Summa Theologica*. 1-2, 9.58.a.3.

Chan, Wing-tsit. *A Source Book in Chinese Philosophy*. Princeton: Princeton UP, 1963.

Chou, K'e-chin. *Tao-te yao-yi*. [Definition of Morality]. Vol. 2. Taipei: Taiwan Commercial Press.

Hsiung, Shih-li. *Hsin wei-shih lun* [The New Doctrine of Consciousness-Only]. 374.

Legge, James. trans. *The I Ching*. New York: Dover, 1963.

Lokuang, Stanislaus. *Ju-chia che-hsüeh te t'i-hsi hsü-pien* [The System of Confucianism (Sequel)]. Taipei: Hsüeh-sheng, 1989.

Translated by Carlos Tee

Chapter XVI

Transcendence of Life

The spiritual life of man tends toward the infinite and absolute Truth, Goodness and Beauty. Man's spiritual life is also fused with the divine life of Jesus Christ. In substance, the spiritual life of man, having partaken in the divine substance, transcends those of other creatures in the natural world. Furthermore, the spiritual activities of man also gradually transcend the universe and the myriad things each day that passes. Although living in the midst of the myriad things in this universe, man possesses a spiritual life that transcends the universe both in terms of its goals and its essence. In fact, his spiritual life is closely associated with the Creator--the absolute Truth, Goodness and Beauty.

In Chinese philosophy of life, Confucianism, Taoism and Buddhism all tend toward the search for transcendence of life. The Confucianists take as their goal, the unity between Heaven and man. The Taoists seek after a "fusion with the Tao," while the Buddhists aspire for the attainment of nirvana. All of them seek for a transcendence of the human life to attain union with the Absolute. In his 600-page work, *Life, Existence and the Spiritual State*, T'ang Chün-yi discusses the transcendence of life in both Chinese and Western philosophical traditions.

I. Transcendence of Life in Chinese Philosophy of Life

1. The Sage in Confucianism

In Confucianism, the mind is considered as the "subject" of man. Man's life is primarily spiritual (intellectual) in nature. When the human mind attains the state of vacuity, quiescence and clarity, it can be termed "spiritual" [*shen*]. For this reason, Confucian scholars have exerted much effort to develop their spiritual (intellectual) life.

Confucianists call the task of developing a person's spiritual life *hsiu-shen* (cultivation of oneself). The pathway followed to cultivate oneself is outlined in the classic *Ta-hsueh* (Great Learning). It says:

> The Way of learning to be great (or adult education) consists in manifesting the clear character, loving the people, and abiding (*chih*) in the highest good. . . The ancients who wished to manifest their clear character to the world would first bring order to their states. Those who wished to bring order to their states would first regulate their families. Those who wished to regulate their families would first cultivate their personal lives. Those who wished to cultivate their personal lives would first rectify their minds. Those who wished to rectify their minds would first make their wills sincere. Those who wished to make their will sincere would first extend their knowledge. The extension of knowledge consists in the investigation of things. (Chan 86-87)

In the *Ta-hsueh*, the manifestation of clear virtue serves as the foundation of one's spiritual life. Its goals consist in loving one's fellowmen and in abiding (*chih*) in the highest good. The manifestation of clear virtue is achieved by cultivation of oneself, caring for one's family and the administration of one's country. In turn, cultivation of oneself may be achieved by rectifying one's heart (mind), achieving sincerity, extending one's knowledge and investigating things. These methods are aimed at the cultivation of one's intellectual life. The goals of manifesting clear virtues are identical with those of cultivating one's intellectual life. The transcendence of spiritual life does not lie in its methods but in its goals. However, the Idealists of the Sung and Ming Dynasties did not place the goals of spiritual life on the transcendental plane. In his commentary on the *Ta-hsueh*, Chu Hsi writes:

> The Great Learning is the learning of the great man. The character *ming* means "clear." *Ming teh*, or illustrious virtue, is what man receives from heaven. It is pure and is what gives man the

reason (principle) to handle things well. Illustrious virtue is limited by matter and hidden by desires, making it sometimes unclear. However, it always exists. That goes to say that a learner enlightened by the Great Learning can restore its purity and make it revert to its original state. ' New' means throwing away the old. When someone manifests his illustrious virtues, he influences others to do the same, letting others throw away the old. To rest is to remain on a stand still at one point, the point of the highest good. The highest good is the factual truth of all things. When we say ' manifesting illustrious virtues and loving people', all must rest at the point of highest good and remain there, because it must reach the principle of heaven without any trace of selfish human desire. All these three make up the outline of the Great Learning.

In explaining the outline of the Great Learning, Chu Hsi never departed from ethical issues such as controlling one's passion to manifest the Heavenly principles existing in the human heart and the need to apply rationality on interpersonal matters and things.

Chapter III of the *Ta-hsueh* says:

As an emperor, one must aspire for benevolence. As an official, one must show respect. As a son, one must be filial. As parent, one must be kindhearted. In dealing with others, one must be trustworthy and sincere.

In his commentary on this passage, Chu Hsi writes:

To quote this is to say that it is the goal of the sage to reach the highest good. These five agents are the most elementary of virtues. If the teacher can find the real meaning and extend it to others by analogy, then he can abide in all things without doubt.

Chu Hsi's explained the "highest good" as "the factual truth of all things," thereby including the "highest good" within the scope of human affairs and not transcendent to it. Since the Great Learning is the learning of the great man, then "highest good" must not refer to the "truth of all things" but rather the "highest good" that makes a great man what he is. In the *I Ching*, "great man" is explained as someone who "unites his virtues with Heaven and Earth (*Commentary on the text of the Ch'ien*)." Here, it can thus be clearly seen that the spiritual life of the "great man" is one that is transcendent to the world and things. Chu Hsi failed to see the "abiding of all in the highest good." Instead, he only noticed the abiding in the highest good through the practice of various good actions.

The *Chung-yung* deals with the ways of the sage and the gentleman (*chūn-tzu*). It says:

> Great is the Way of the sage! Overflowing, it produces and nourishes all things and rises up to the height of heaven...Therefore the superior man honors the moral nature and follows the path of inquiry and study. He achieves breadth and greatness and pursues the refined and subtle to the limit. He seeks to reach the greatest height and brilliance and follows the path of the Mean. (*Chung-yung*, Ch. 27)

Confucian tradition only placed strong emphasis on the way of the gentleman. Confucianists have often discussed the primary importance of honoring moral nature and following the path of inquiry and study. The former is represented by Lu Hsiang-shan and Wang Ch'uan-shan and the latter by Chu Hsi. Regardless of whether they are right or wrong, this trend was a deviation from the Confucian goals on spiritual life. The passage above clearly says that: "Great is the way of the sage! Overflowing, it produces and nourishes all things and rises up to the height of heaven." This is such a pre-eminent realm! The goal of Confucian personal cultivation consists of becoming a sage despite the difficulties involved. In the same chapter, the *Chung-yung says*: ". . . a talented and virtuous man must first appear before all these can be made a reality. Hence, it is said: "Without a highly virtuous person, those great and exalted principles cannot find fruition." Here, "great and exalted principles" refer to the ways of the sage while "highly virtuous" alludes to the virtue of "generating and transforming the myriad things." Without the latter, it would be impossible to concretely manifest the virtues of the sage. The "highest virtues" mentioned in the *Chung-yung* are the same virtues referred to in the *I Ching* when it says: "The sage unites his virtues with Heaven and Earth."

In the *I Ching*, the virtues of Heaven and Earth are described as follows:

> It is the great virtue of heaven and earth to generate life. It is the great treasure of the holy sage to stand in the right place. How does one safeguard this place? Through benevolence (*jen.*) (Appended Remarks, Part II, Ch. 1)

All the goals of the Confucian spiritual life can be summarized in one line: "uniting with the virtues of Heaven and Earth," or what is ordinarily called "unity of Heaven and man." In the phrase "unity of Heaven and man," the word "Heaven" represents Heaven and Earth, both of which represent celestial Heaven. Heaven and Earth, which work towards the perpetual renewal of life, unite to form the myriad things in the universe. Heaven and Earth possess the creative power to perpetually renew life. All the myriad things are also endowed with the principles of perpetual renewal. The creative power to perpetually renew life circulates around the myriad things, causing their generation and transformation. The universe is a living univese. It is torrent of life that flows endlessly.

Man shares with Heaven and Earth a mind that is benevolent. Man has personal desires, except the sage who is born without them. He is clear and pure, and deeply aware of Heavenly principles. The sage can penetrate the mind of Heaven and Earth. He unites the creative power to generate life which is inherent to his own mind with that of Heaven and Earth. Hence, it is said that the sage praises the generating and transforming actions of Heaven and Earth, and "assists in their generation of the myriad things (*Chung-yung*, Ch. 22)."

The *I Ching says*:

> The great man accords in his character with heaven and earth;
> in his light, with the sun and moon; in his consistency, with the
> four seasons; in the good and evil fortune that he creates, with
> gods and spirits. When he acts in advance of heaven, heaven
> does not contradict him. When he follows heaven, he adapts
> himself to the time of heaven. If heaven itself does not resist
> him, how much less do men, gods and spirits! (Baynes 382-383)

In the *I Ching*, Heaven and Earth are symbolized by the *ch'ien* and
k'un trigrams. In turn, *ch'ien* and *k'un* are characteristics of *yang* and
yin respectively. Both these two are basic trigrams in the *I Ching*. On
the Ch'ien, the I Ching's Commentary on the Decision says: "Great
indeed is the sublimity of the Creative [*Ch'ien*], to which all beings
owe their beginning and which permeates all heaven" (Baynes 370).
On the *K'un*, it says: "Perfect indeed is the sublimity of the Receptive
[*k'un*]. All beings owe their birth to it, because it receives the heavenly with devotion" (Baynes, 386). Both *Ch'ien* and *K'un* are the
origins of the generation of the myriad things.

The *I Ching* further says:

> The way of the Creative [*Ch'ien*] works through change and
> transformation, so that each thing receives its true nature and
> destiny and comes into permanent accord with the Great
> Harmony: this is what furthers and what perseveres. He towers
> high above the multitude of beings, and all lands are united in
> peace. (The *Ch'ien*, Commentary on the Decision, Baynes 371-
> 372)

> The Receptive [*k'un*] in its riches carries all things. Its nature
> is in harmony with the boundless. It embraces everything in its
> breadth and illumines everything in its greatness. Through it,
> all individual being attain success. (The *k'un* Commentary on
> the Decision, Baynes 386-387)

The great virtue of Heaven and Earth consists in the perpetual renewal of life through the endless circulation of their creative power of generation. The highest virtue of the sage lies in uniting with the creative power of Heaven and Earth to perpetually renew life and the myriad things.

> Therefore absolute sincerity is ceaseless. Being ceaseless, it is lasting. Being lasting, it is evident. Being evident, it is infinite. Being infinite, it is extensive and deep. Being extensive and deep, it is high and brilliant. It is because it is extensive and deep that it contains all things. It is because it is high and brilliant that it overshadows all things. It is because it is infinite and lasting that it can complete all things. In being extensive and deep, it is a counterpart of Earth. In being high and brilliant, it is a counterpart of Heaven. In being infinite and lasting, it is unlimited. Such being its nature, it becomes prominent without any display, produces changes without motion, and accomplished its ends without action. The Way of Heaven and Earth may be completely described in one sentence: They are without any doubleness and so they produce things in an unfathomable way. (Chan 109)

Prof. Thomé Fang writes:

> "The great excellence of heaven and earth is to bring forth life not only once for all as it is in the ordinary static mode of creation but also continually in a dynamic process of iteration. In the *Book of Change*, the expression ' sheng-sheng' means literally in Chinese to beget and to beget or to create and to create. So all along I have taken the Whiteheadian idiom ' creative creativity' for its Chinese equivalent. (Spirit, 111)

The spiritual life of the great man or the sage is thus closely associated with the perpetual renewing action of Heaven and Earth. His creative power to generate life participates in the creative power of Heaven and Earth, through which they jointly generate and transform the myriad things. The sun and the moon, the four seasons and the spirits are all tools of Heaven and Earth to exercise their creative power.

Hence, the great man or the sage can associate himself with the sun and the moon, the four seasons and the spirits. In such a case, his spiritual life expands to include Heaven and Earth, and embraces the myriad things. This manifestation of life is exactly what Mencius called "flood-like *ch'i*" (*hao-jan chih ch'i*). He writes:

> This is a *ch'i* which is, in the highest degree, vast and unyielding. Nourish it with integrity and place no obstacle in its path and it will fill the space between Heaven and Earth. It is a *ch'i* which unites righteousness and the Way. Deprive it of these and it will collapse. (Mencius, Lau 57)

For Mencius, the mind (spirit) is described in the following words: "The myriad things are in me in every possible way" (*Chin-hsin*, Part II). For this reason, ". . . he is human to all people and feels love for all creatures" (*Chin-hsin*, Part II, Chan 81).

Such a manifestation of life also matches Confucius' description of his own spiritual life. He says:

> At fifty I knew the Mandate of Heaven (*T'ien-ming*). At sixty I was at ease with whatever I heard. At seventy I could follow my heart's desire without transgressing moral principles. (Chan 22)

In these few lines, Confucius modestly described his experience in developing his spiritual life. Yet, his achievements--knowing the Mandate of heaven, being at ease with what he heard and following his heart's desire without transgressing moral principles--are no ordinary feats. Only when the spirit tends toward extreme goodness can one attain such a level of ascetic height.

The Chung-yung extols the greatness of Confucius' spiritual life. It says:

> Chung-ni (*Confucius*) transmitted the ancient traditions of Yao and Shun, and he modeled after and made brilliant the systems of King Wen and King Wu. He conformed with the natural

order governing the revolution of the seasons in heaven above, and followed the principles governing land and water below. He may be compared to earth in its supporting and containing all things, and to heaven in its overshadowing and embracing all things. He may be compared to the four seasons in their succession, and to the sun and moon in their alternate shining. All things are produced and developed without injuring one another. The things are produced and developed without injuring one another. The courses of the seasons, the sun, and moon are pursued without conflict. The lesser forces go silently and deeply in their mighty transformations. It is this that makes heaven and earth so great. (Chan 111-112)

This chapter of the *Chung-yung* coincides with the Commentary on the Text of the *Ch'ien* trigram in the *I Ching*. The latter says: "The Great Man (Sage) unites his virtues with those of Heaven and Earth. He shares his brightness with the sun and the moon. He matches the order of the four seasons." The great man or sage in Confucianism lives a spiritual (intellectual) life by uniting with the great virtue of Heaven and Earth to perpetually renew, such that "all things are produced and developed without injuring one another." This spiritual life transcends the universe and the myriad things in it, and participates in the generating virtues of Heaven and Earth. This virtue to generate is actually the creative process of the Celestial Heaven in which the sage participates. This union between Heaven and man is not manifested in the substance of man or that of the Creator. Instead, it is seen in the work of creation. They unite in this generating process. This is a transcendental state wherein the sage's spiritual life is not subjected to any form of restriction or aimed at any material thing as goal. Rather, it has as its goal the generative process of Heaven. The development of the spiritual life of the sage is as lofty as the heavens and deep as the earth. As the *Chung-yung* describes it, it is ". . .great as the heavenly expanse and deep as a bottomless chasm" (Ch. XXXI)

Prof. Thomé Fang takes Confucianism's transcendence of life as transcendental and immanent, and thus different from the Western preternatural transcendence (Fang 28-30). The difference between

Western transcendence of life and those of Taoism and Buddhism will be discussed in the later sections. Confucian transcendence of life is a type of spiritual activity, or rather, a type of transcendence of the spiritual life. Such a transcendence does not lie in the substance of life, but instead in the activities of life. Life is the "being" of an object. It is that object's most realistic "ego." Thus, the activities of life are the activities of the ego itself. Since Confucian transcendence is a transcendence of the spiritual life, then it is a transcendence of the ego's activities. Transcendence is still founded on the "ego." Confucius always taught about "following one's desire without transgressing moral principles." The *Chung-yung* deals with how Confucius practiced the way of Yao, Shun, Wen and Wu so that "all things are produced and developed without injuring one another." The *I Ching* deals with how the great man "unites his virtues with Heaven and Earth." All these represent an uplifting of the ego's persona as it tries to transcend mundane desires and to praise and participate in the generating and transforming actions of Heaven and Earth.

However, this type of transcendence does not lead to a transcendence of human nature but rather to the development of the ego. Prof. Thomé Fang takes the Confucian spirit as that of the Time-man (Fang 44-48). And since it is a "man of the times," then it exists in time, and thus, also within the cosmos. Confucianism does not transcend the universe. It proposes union with the universe by praising and participating in the creative action of the universe, in such a way "that the myriad things are in me in every possible way" (Mencius, *Chin-hsin*, Part II). It can thus be said that Confucian transcendence is ethical in nature. It matches the way of benevolence (*jen*) with perpetual renewal of life (*sheng-sheng*).

2. The Perfect Man [*Chih-jen*] in Taoism

The process of development of the Taoist spiritual life is divided into various levels in a manner comparable to how the Confucianists have scholars, gentlemen and sages. In Taoism, there are the so-called farm man [*tien-yuan jen*], the vacuous and quiescent natural man [*hsu-ching tzu-jan jen*] and the perfect man [*chih-jen*].

The basis of Taoist philosophy lies in the ontological *Tao*. *Tao* is an infinite substance. It is "born before heaven and earth." Describing Tao, Chuang-tzu writes: "It is its own source, its own root. Before Heaven and Earth existed it was there, firm from ancient times. It gave spirituality to the spirits and to God; it gave birth to Heaven and Earth" (Watson 81). It is the origin of the myriad things.

Tao itself is hazy and changeable. The *Tao Te Ching says*:

> As a thing the way (*Tao*) is shadowy, indistinct. Indistinct and shadowy, yet within it is an image. Shadowy and indistinct, yet within it is a substance. Dim and dark, yet within it is an essence. This essence is quite genuine and within it is something that can be tested. (Ch. XXI, Lau 31-33)

Tao is hazy and changeable and possesses the power to change itself--ten (virtue). Because of this virtue, *Tao* changes, and it changes without ceasing. Lao-tzu further writes:

> The Way begets one; one begets two; two begets three; three begets the myriad creatures. The myriad creatures carry on their backs the *yin* and embrace in their arms the *yang* and are the blending of the generative forces of the two. (Lau 63)

Tao generated the myriad things. It is also present in them. The substance of the myriad things is *Tao*. The myriad things are the external forms of *Tao*. On *Tao*, Chuang-tzu writes:

> Master Tung-kuo asked Chuang Tzu, "This thing called the Way--where does it exist?" Chuang Tzu said, There's no place it doesnt exist." " Come," said master Tung-kuo, "you must be more specific!" "It is in the ant." "As low a thing as that?" "It is in the panic grass." "But that's lower still!" "It is in the tiles and shards." "How can it be so low?" "It is in the piss and shit!" Master Tung-kuo made no reply. Chuang Tzu said, "Sir, you questions simply don't get at the substance of the matter. When Inspector Huo asked the superintendent of the market how to test the fatness of a pig by pressing it with the foot, he was told

that the lower down on the pig you press, the nearer you come to the truth. But you must not expect to find the Way in any particular place--there is no thing that escapes its presence! Such is the Perfect Way, and so too are the truly great words. ' Complete,' ' universal,' ' all-inclusive'--these three are different words with the same meaning. All point to a single reality. (Knowledge Wandered North, Watson 240-241)

In terms of substance therefore, all the myriad things are equal. This made Chuang-tzu propose the "Discussion on Making All Things Equal" [*Ch'i wu lun*]. He writes:

Heaven and Earth were born at the same time as I was, and the ten thousand things are one with me. We have already become one, so how can I say anything? But I have just said that we are one, so how can I not be saying something? (Watson 43)

Changes in the Tao absolutely concur with the natural world. Tao possesses no passion. In the *Tao Te Ching*, Lao-tzu described it as "forever free of desire, it can be called small" (Lau 51). And since it has no passion, then it does not act. Lao-tzu writes:

The way never acts yet nothing is left undone. Should lords and princes be able to hold fast to it, the myriad creatures will be transformed of their own accord. After they are transformed, should desire raise its head, I shall press it down with the weight of the nameless uncarved block. The nameless uncarved block is but freedom from desire, and if I cease to desire and remain still, the empire will be at peace of its own accord. (*Tao*, Lau 55)

The humanism of Lao-tzu is founded on his own philosophical ontology. Man's substance is spiritual, or Tao. The human body is but a form. This form is worthless. What matters is the spirit. When the needs of the form are reduced to the bare minimum, spiritual growth is least restricted. In order to reduce the needs of the form, Lao-tzu proposed "a return to truth [*chen*] and simplicity" and following things' natural course. The *Tao Te Ching* says: "Exhibit the unadorned and embrace the uncarved block. Have little thought of itself and as few desires as possible" (Lau 27-29).

Based on this sense of values, therefore, the first level of Taoist spiritual life corresponds to the so-called *t'ien-yuan jen*. The *t'ien-yuan jen* favors a life in the farm where he is close to nature. He rejects fame and fortune, as well as official positions. He aspires not for a life of luxury and prosperity. The *t'ien-yuan jen* is a recluse who is wise and playing it safe. He finds joy in tilling the soil. In ancient China, there were the so-called *t'ien-yuan shih-jen* (field-and-garden poets).

On of them is the T'ang Dynasty poet T'ao Ch'ien who writes:

I built my hut in a place where people live,

And yet there's no clatter of carriage or horse.

You ask me how that could be?

With a mind remote, the region too grows distant.

I pick chrysanthemums by the eastern hedge,

See the southern mountain, calm and still.

The mountain air is beautiful at close of day,

Birds on the wing come home together.

In all this there's some principle of truth,

But try to define it and you forget the words. (*Drinking Wine*, Poetry, Watson 135)

Another celebrated T'ang Dynasty poet, Wang Wei wrote the following lines:

Middle age--I grow somewhat fond of the Way,

My evening home at the foot of the southern hills.

When moods come I follow them alone,

To no purpose learning fine things for myself,

Going till I come to where the river ends,

Sitting and watching when clouds rise up.

> By chance I meet an old man of the woods;
>
> We talk and laugh--we have no "going home" time. (*At My Country Home in Chung-nan*, Poetry, Watson 202)

In another poem he writes:

> In evening years given to quietude,
>
> The world's worries no concern of mine,
>
> For my own needs making no other plan
>
> Than to unlearn, return to long-loved woods:
>
> I loosen my robe before the breeze from pines,
>
> My lute celebrates moonlight on mountain pass.
>
> You ask what laws rule "failure" or "success"--
>
> Songs of fishermen float to the still shore. (*To the Assistant Prefect Chang*, Hucker 246)

Having rejected social affairs as mundane and officialdom as filthy, these people avoided daily social contacts and lived in the wilderness where they enjoyed things of the natural world everyday of their lives. They aspired not for the satisfaction of the senses but sought for spiritual contentment. The *t'ien-yuann jen* was transcendent to the world, from which he constantly hid away. His happiness lies in basking in natural scenery and enjoying the peace and quiet of his spiritual consciousness.

The second spritual level in Taoism is the so-called *hsu-ching tzu-jan jen*. It is the level of human life favored by Chuang-tzu.

The *hsu-ching tzu-janjen* first empties himself and then forgets about his existence. On this, Chuang-tzu writes:

> I smashed up my limbs and body, drive out perception and intellect, cast off form, do away with understanding, and make myself identical with the Great Thoroughfare. This is what I mean by sitting down and forgetting everything. (Great and Venerable Teacher, Watson 90)

He forgets about his physical form and abstains from bodily enjoyments. Without desire and actions, he thus attains spiritual vacuity.

Chuang-tzu writes: "Emptiness is the fasting of the mind" (Watson 58).

Such a "fasting" mind is freed from material desires, and is thus constantly self-sufficient. Hence, Lao-tzu writes: "Know contentment and you will suffer no disgrace. Know when to stop and you will meet with no danger. You can then endure" (Lau 67). When the heart attains vacuity, it enjoys peace and serenity.

In his work, Chuang-tzu writes:

> Master Kuang Ch'eng sat up with a start. "Excellent, this question of yours! Come, I will tell you about the Perfect Way. The essence of the Perfect Way is deep and darkly shrouded; the extreme of the Perfect Way is mysterious and hushed in silence. Let there be no seeing, no hearing; enfold the spirit in quietude and the body will right itself. Be still, be pure, do not labor your body, do not churn up your essence, and then you can live a long life. (Let It Be, Leave It Alone, Baynes 119)

In the chapter entitled "Way of Heaven," he further writes:

> The sage is still not because he takes stillness to be good and therefore is still. The ten thousand things are insufficient to distract his mind--that is the reason he is still. Water that is still gives back a clear image of beard and eyebrows; reposing in the water level, it offers a measure to the great carpenter. And if water in stillness possesses such clarity, how much more must pure spirit. The sage's mind in stillness is the mirror of Heaven and earth, the glass of the ten thousand things. Emptiness, stillness, limpidity, silence, inaction--these are the level of Heaven and earth, the substance of the Way and its Virtue. . . . Resting, they may be empty; empty, they may be full; and fullness is completion. (Watson 142)

Stillness results when the heart attains spiritual vacuity. Stillness, being a spiritual activity, is in harmony with nature, and thus, interlinked with Heaven and Earth. It is "similar to the Great Way." A vacuous, quiescent and natural man transcends the myriad things. His heart is not attached to anything at all. It instead freely circulates between Heaven and Earth. Such a man can be identified with what Prof. Thomè Fang called the "Space-man" (Fang 34).

In Taoism, the highest state of spiritual life is that of the *Chih-jen* (perfect man). Using parables, Chuang-tzu had described the perfect man or the spiritual man whom he envisioned to pervade Heaven and Earth and to transcend the four directions.

The perfect man forsakes form and appearance and forgets himself to unite himself with Tao. This way, he finds his own substance--the Tao--and forsakes a formal individuality. Tao generates the myriad things and takes shape through the ether (*ch'i*), which is unity and being. The perfect man unites his *ch'i* with the *ch'i* of Heaven and Earth. He allows the *ch'i* of Heaven and Earth to unite with the Tao, and thus, forget his own self. This way, he unites with the real ego--Tao itself. The perfect man knows not through his mind but through *ch'i*. This knowledge through *ch'i* is known as *shang-chih* (supreme knowledge). The virtue of the perfect man is called *shang-teh* (supreme virtue). Chuang-tzu writes:

> He who does not depart from the Ancestor is called the Heavenly Man; he who does not depart from the Pure is called the Holy Man; he who does not depart from the True is called the Perfect Man. (In the World, Watson 362)

> The Way does not falter before the huge, is not forgetful of the tiny; therefore the ten thousand things are complete in it. Vast and ample, there is nothing it does not receive. Deep and profound, how can it be fathomed? Punishment and favor, benevolence and righteousness--these are trivia to the spirit, and yet who but the Perfect Man can put them in their rightful place? (The Way of Heaven, Watson 151)

So I will take leave of you, to enter the gate of the inex-
haustible and wander in the limitless fields, to a form of triad
with the light of the sun and the moon, to partake in the
constancy of Heaven and Earth. (Let It be, Leave It Alone,
Watson 120)

The True Man of ancient times did not rebel against want, did
not grow proud in plenty, and did not plan his affairs. A man
like this could commit an error and not regret it, could meet
with success and not make a show. A man like this could climb
the high places and not be frightened, could enter the water and
not get wet, could enter the fire and not get burned. His knowledge was able to climb all the way up to the Way like this. The
True Man of ancient times slept without dreaming and woke
without care; he ate without savoring and his breath came from
deep inside. . .The True Man of ancient times knew nothing of
loving life, knew nothing of hating death. He emerged without
delight; he went back without a fuss. He came briskly, he went
briskly, and that was all. He didn't forget where he began; he
didn't try to find out where he would end. . . So I began explaining and kept at him for three days, and after that he was able to
put the world outside himself. When he had put the world
outside himself, I kept at him for seven days more, and after
that he was to put things outside himself. When he had put
things outside himself, I kept at him for nine days more, and
after that he was able to put life outside himself. After he had
put life outside himself, he was able to achieve the brightness
of dawn, and when he had achieved the brightness of dawn, he
could see his own aloneness, he could do away with past and
present, he was able to enter where there is no life and no
death. (The Great and Venerable Teacher, Watson 77-78, 82-
83)

The attainment of the state of being a perfect man or real man
depends on the observance of truth. Lao-tzu once said that although
the substance of Tao is hazy and unsettled, yet "in it is found essence,
an essence that is true." Here, "truth" is explained in the same way as

"truth" in the substance of the Tao. Truth represents the substance of Tao. Such a substance is truth, being and ether (*ch'i*). As mentioned earlier, the perfect man or the real man unites his ether with that of Tao. In the Chapter entitled "Mastering Life," Chuang-tzu writes:

> Master Lieh Tzu said to the Barrier Keeper Yin, "The Perfect Man can walk under water without choking, can tread on fire without being burned, and can travel above the ten thousand things without being frightened. May I ask how he manages this? The Barrier Keeper Yin replied," This is because he guards the pure breath--it has nothing to do with wisdom, skill, determination, or courage. (Watson 198)

In the chapter entitled "Great and Venerable Teacher," he also writes: "Even now they have joined with the Creator as men to wander in the single breath (ether) of heaven and earth" (Watson 87). By uniting his *ch'i* with Tao, the perfect man attains great wisdom. He is conscious that his own substance is Tao, which transcends the cosmos and is totally infinite and limitless. The perfect man is thus transcendent to everything in the cosmos. This transcendence of the perfect man arises from the transcendence of his substance. The common man usually possesses small wisdom. His substance is his own mind, through which he lives. In contrast, the perfect man transcends his own mind. He takes Tao as his life. Taoist transcendence differs from that of Confucianism in that the latter's transcendence of life is a mere "union of one's virtues with those of Heaven and Earth." It is not an ontological transcendence, as in the case of Taoism. The substance of the perfect man is no longer that of a human being, a relative substance that is finite and to which time and space apply. The substance of the perfect man is the substance of the infinite Tao.

Similarly, there are also differences between Taoist transcendence and the Roman Catholic view of transcendence. We shall deal with these differences later. However, the spiritual transcendence of life in Taoism, Buddhism and Roman Catholicism share certain similarities. This transcendence is both mysterious, contradictory and yet absolutely overlapping. Spiritual life is the very zenith of human life, where all things are beyond description and explanation. Chuang-tzu used the parable of the roc which flies to the edge of the firmament to illustrate this idea. Its wings resemble the clouds of the sky, and yet, it is still not sufficient for expression.

3. Buddhahood

Buddhism has always stressed spiritual life. It teaches the so-called Four Significant Truths to help man rid himself of sufferings and reach Nirvana, the world of ultimate bliss where constancy, joy, ego and purity reign. Yet, in spite of this, Confucianists have often derided Buddhist teachings for extracting humanity from man, who is then relegated to mere "dead trees and cold ashes." Confucianism and Buddhism totally differ in their views on life, as well as in their metaphysical foundation. Hence, their concepts and ideals on the development of spiritual life are also poles apart.

In Buddhism, the present life is perceived as suffering and as a state wherein man constantly finds himself beset by pain, disease, old age and death. Sakyamuni Buddha sought for the dependent origination of life's sufferings in his desire to find release from them. He pointed out that the cause of life's suffering lies in lack of enlightenment or ignorance. He taught that the myriad dharmas in the cosmos do not really exist, as against man's usual belief. Because of man's belief in the reality of the dharmas, he experiences selfish craving, which in turn gives way to all other types of desires and aspirations and leads to all sins. Sins lead to chastisement in a person's coming life, and thus his life enters an endless process of reincarnation. For him, the path towards release from suffering consists in eradicating man' ignorance. By thus becoming intelligent, man becomes sensitive. Hence, two words--reality and emptiness--became central ideas in Buddhist teachings.

Theravada Buddhism, or the Lesser Vehicle, confirms that the myriad dharmas are a reality. It takes the universe and all things as being made up of the four greats--earth, water, fire and wind. Lying in their midst are the myriad phenomena on earth. Theravada Buddhism denies the existence of the "ego." Some schools accept the reality of the three worlds while others only accept the concepts of the present world and the next to come. Still some only accept the reality of the present world.

The Abhidharma-kosa-sastra proposes the reality of the three worlds and the lasting existence of the dharmas. From the latter was derived the concept of *t'i-yung* (reality and function), in which the dharmas are said to be absolutely not generated nor annihilated. Instead, it propounds that only their functions experience generation and annihilation and such other changes.

Neither does the Theravada sect of Indian Buddhism accept the reality of the myriad dharmas. The Abhidharma-kosa-sastra led to the "Treatise on Karma-Origination." The reality of all dharmas arises from dependent origination. Although they are reality, they actually are not. The Abhidharma-kosa-sastra touches on the chain of twelve dependent origination to explain the reincarnation of the ego. Reincarnation involves the three worlds: previous, present and future. The present life was formed from karma in the previous life. Similarly, the present life determines the future. This karma is a result of one's actions, evaluated using the yardstick of moral good and evil. Evil karma has leakage while good karma has not. A leaking karma will mean chastisement in the life to come in the form of lack of enlightenment and ignorance. In turn, lack of enlightenment leads to actions, actions to consciousness and consciousness to name and form. Name and form lead to the six sense organs. The six sense organs generate contact, contact generates sensation, sensation generates craving. In turn, craving leads to attachment, attachment generates existence and existence generates birth. By birth, there arises death. This is the so-called chain of twelve dependent origination. They continue in rotation to form a cycle of life samsara.

However, if the myriad dharmas are not existing, then only dependent origination would exist. How did they come into being? Vasubandhu and his brother Asanga started the Mahayana school, or the Greater Vehicle. This school and Theravada Buddhism can be bridged together by the Doctrine of Consciousness-Only, which proposes that the myriad dharmas are mere consciousness. They only exist because of consciousness. Asanga authored the Mahayana-samparigraba-sastra which laid the foundation for the Doctrine of Consciousness-Only. Vasubandhu's Vijnaptimatra-sastra later formed the fundamental scripture of the Yogacara sect. The Doctrine of Consciousness-Only proposes the Eight Consciousness, the first six being sight, smell, hearing, taste, body and will. The remaining two are Manah (mind) and the Alaya-vijnana. The Alaya-vijnana is also called the "treasury." The Alaya-vijnana bears seeds, both naturally and by merit. Seeds by merit are those formed by karma in the previous life. Because of sense organ actions of the present life, these seeds are corrupted to cause the formation of "condition," an object of the senses. When seeds of the previous life are corrupted to show the condition" of the previous life, the sense organs become aware of this condition, and thus they are triggered to sense. Consciousness is mental in nature. The mind leads to a sensitive consciousness. Through the Manah, the mind concludes that this consciousness is existing, thus leading to the "grasping of oneself and things" [*wo-chih and wu-chih*]. Grasping of oneself happens when the mind affirms and insists that the self is a reality. Similarly, grasping of things happens when the mind confirms that the myriad dharmas are a reality and sticks to this view. The reality of the myriad dharmas results from the human mind's grasping of oneself and things. In turn, these two graspings come from the consciousness of the self. Based on this logic, the myriad dharmas are mere emptiness and all realities are mere consciousness. The Consciousness-Only doctrine of origination is based on the doctrine of karma origination. Explaining karma origination involves not only the concept of cyclic life samsara, but also the creation of conditions and consciousness that generates the myriad dharmas.

Mahayana Buddhism went a step further. If consciousness emanates from the mind and if the myriad dharmas are mere consciousness, then it would be proper to say that the myriad dharmas are merely in the mind. Thus, Mahayana Buddhism paid more attention to the mind.

Mahayana scriptural texts that deal with the mind form part of the

Prajnaparamita-sutra. An important work that explains the Prajna-paramita-sutra is the hundred-volume Maha-Prajnaparamita-sastra, translated into Chinese by Kumarajiva. Prajnaparamita is wisdom. With its brightness, the actual world received illumination. On this, Prof. Thome Fang writes:

> . . . dialectically transfigured and exalted into exuberant light of Dharmas, being continually purified of sullied elements and enriched with noble ideals. And this liberating spirit, just because of its possession of the pervasive wisdom, closely aware of all phenomena observable in their purity of essence, is able to come upon anything without attachment and to enjoy its own perfect freedom in the contemplation of the Ultimate Reality utterly devoid of all defective liminations. (Chinese Philosophy, 196)

The Mahayanic explanation of the Prajnaparamita-sutra often starts with the concept of the "mind." The Lankavatara sutra's preface says: "As mentioned above, the mind is the link to the capacity of the mind of all Buddhas, the key to the reason of all canons." It proposes that all things are generated through dependent origination. Dependent origination is not a reality but rather arrived at in the mind, which is often presumptuous. Thus, all things are not real; neither is dependent origination. Therefore, generation and annihilation can neither be a real phenomenon.

Since the mind is presumptuous, how is it possible to find a real mind? The Mahayana sect believes in the "Treatise on the Origination of All Things from the Tathagatagarbha." The Tathagatagarbha is fundamentally a pure mental condition into which man's presumptuous mind must enter. Man must break through his presumptuous mind to attain the realm of the Tathagatagharba. This realm is no other than Buddhahood, the state of wisdom and right vision. It means detachment from forms of the outside world. It does not mean breaking away from forms to attain emptiness. Rather, it calls for actual vision so as to attain *chen-ju*. The Treatise on the Awakening of Faith [Mahayana-Sraddhotpada-sastra] explains the origination of the *chen-ju* by saying that the mind is itself *chen-ju*. The *chen-ju* is an absolute reality. However, it involves two tenets: the mind as bhutatathata [*chen-ju*] and the two gates of the mind--creation and destruction. The substance of the *chen-ju* is beyond description because it is absolutely beyond human intelligence. The *chen-ju* shows a manifestation of no-self externally. This is the so-called "two gates of the mind." The presumptuous mind, upon seeing the myriad things and transformations in the universe, mistakenly thinks they are real. However, when wisdom is attained, these "realities" are found to be but emptiness, and emptiness is "reality." Everything is then absolutely equal.

It is this wisdom that makes human life transcendent that the Mahayanic Prajnaparamita deals with. It also focuses on the Pranya-mula-sastra-tika of the Madhayanuka (Middle School). The Pranya-mula-sastra-tika deals with the Eight Negations--no ceasing nor arising, no constancy nor impermanence, no unity nor difference, and no coming nor going. The basis of the Eight Negations is the denial of dependent origination. This "Middle Doctrine" is not to be confused with that of Confucianism bearing the same name. However, some among the Idealists of the Sung and Ming Dynasties took "medial principle" as part of the human substance, a practice that is essentially an imitation of the Buddhist Middle Doctrine. The Buddhist Middle Doctrine takes substance as *chen-ju* itself. Since the *chen-ju is* medial, then all the myriad dharmas also have "medial principle" as their substance. Therefore, they are neither reality nor emptiness. Reality and emptiness are not opposing and are not mutually realizing. They are two sides of the same substance. According to the Two Tenets associated with the Treatise on the Awakening of Faith, there is no need to deal with the issue of reality or emptiness. Instead, it proposes the use of "examination" [*kuan*].

The first topic discussed in the Middle School is the "Examination of Self-nature," in which reality and emptiness, and causality are taken as neither real nor unreal. Thus, all dharmas are considered neither real nor unreal. After all, they are all virtually empty. The actual form of virtual emptiness is the Tathagata, the opposite of what is relative. Yet, the Tathagata is not deliberately confirmed as absolute reality. In the "Examination of the Tathagata," the Tathagata is described as both real and non-real. Heretical ideas contend that the Tathagata is a non-reality. Biased views take the Tathagata as a reality. In truth, the Tathagata is both real and non-real. Virtual emptiness is taken as the supreme mystical principle. It is a mystical emptiness that stresses neither reality nor emptiness. Neither does it deal with non-reality nor emptiness. Instead, it only deals with denial. In the "Examination of the Nirvana," these idea of the "Examination of the Tathagata" becomes even more obvious.

Chapter XXV of the "Examination of the Nirvana" says:

> If all this is empty, then there is neither arising nor ceasing. Therefore, through the abandonment and ceasing of what does one expect Nirvana? If all this is non-empty, then there is neither arising nor ceasing. Therefore, through the abandonment and ceasing of what does one expect Nirvana?

By the time the Mahayanic Perfected school [*Yuan-chiao*] evolved, this examination method characterized by denial had already shifted its course to an affirmative view. The Perfected school is made up of three sects: Huayen, T'ient'ai and Ch'an [or Zen]. They all confirm the absolute reality of the *chen-ju*. The myriad dharmas of the universe are the no-self manifestation of the *chen-ju*. The Ch'an sect teaches direct vision as a means to look into the *chen-ju* that lies deep within one's mind. It considers the *chen-ju* as the real self, real mind and actual form. The follower of the Ch'an teachings tries to empty himself of all knowledge and anxieties in his efforts to directly see the *chen-ju* in his mind. The *chen-ju* is absolute and infinite. It is beyond description and cannot be transmitted. Man has words that correspond to his concepts. In the case of the *chen-ju*, it is absolutely impossible to transmit or describe it using words. The Ch'an sect emphasizes experiencing. It gives little attention to verbal expression.

Both the T'ient'ai and Huayen sects propose using methods of examination to see through the real form of the *chen-ju* and the myriad dharmas in the universe. The myriad dharmas and the *chen-ju* are interlinked and mutually accessible. The *chen-ju* is one. Everything is the myriad dharmas. One is everything and everything is one. One penetrates all and all penetrates the one. The T'ient'ai sect teaches the Maha Chih-kuan, which proposes rest of the body for clearness of vision and which also propounds that one dharma assimilates all dharmas. It propounds that all the three Tripitakas are mutually harmonized and all things are mutually assimilating and harmonized, such that "one concept covers three thousand worlds." The Huayen sect pays special attention to the "Three Meditations on the Relationship of the Noumenal and Phenomenal," "Treatise on the Absolute Void," "Treatise on the Unimpeded Interaction of Noumenon and Phenomenon," and the "Ten Philosophic Ideas."

I says:

> One must follow the ascetic way, making efforts to enter the world of dharmas, so as to make his mind one with the *chen-ju*, and witness the overlapping of the myriad dharms with the *chen-ju* of one mind, and the harmonization of all dharms. This world of harmony is the world of the *hua-yen* or of *chen-ju* itself.

The transcendence of spiritual life in the Mahyanic Perfected school is similar to the Taoist spiritual transcendence. Both of them are transcendence of the substance. When man has abandoned his presumptuous mind and has seen through his own unreal self, he gets a direct vision of the substance--the *chen-ju*. Adherents of the Mahayanic Perfected school unite their substance with the *chen-ju* and directly see their substance, with all their absoluteness, stability and transparency. They experience their own real self, which is permanence, joy and purity. This is the state of Nirvana. The enlightened followed of the Ch'an sect who has attained Nirvana directly sees the absolute *chen-ju*, through which he sees the myriad dharmas. The myriad dharmas are in harmony with one another and with the *chen-ju*. Everything is absolutely equal.

The Monk Hui-neng (638-713 A.D.) once said:

The Supreme Maha Parinirvana is perfect, permanent, calm and illuminating. Common people and the ignorant erroneously call it death, while heretics arbitrarily equate it with annihilation. Adherents of the Sravaka Vehicle or the Pratyeka Vehicle take it as non-action. These are all intellectual speculations that led to the sixty-two fallacious views. Since they are only fictitious names invented for the occasion, they are not in anyway related to the Absolute Truth. Nirvana is fully understandable only to those with great minds, who behave neither with indifference nor attachment towards it. They know that the five Skandhas, and the "self" that results from the union of Skandhas, along with all external things and forms, and the various sounds and voices are equally unreal as dreams or illusions. They do not distinguish between a holy man and an ordinary man, nor do they have any arbitrary idea on Nirvana. They are beyond "affirmation" and "negation" and they break the barrier of the past, the present and the future. They use their sense organs when needed but the idea of "using" does not arise. They may particularize on all things but the idea of particularization does not arise. The real and eternal bliss of "perfect rest" and "cessation of changes" of Nirvana remains the same and does not change even during the catastrophic fire at the end of a Kalpa, when the seas are burnt dry or during the wheezing of the destructive wind when mountains fall one on top of another.

It urges man to have his feet flat on this mundane world but his mind entering Nirvana. He sees things of this world but his heart remains free from worldly attachment. Fu Ta-shih, a contemporary of the Boddhidharma, once wrote a poem. It says:

With bare hands I hold a hoe,

As I travel on the buffalo's back.

Across the bridge I walk,

Feeling the bridge flowing away,

As the waters remained on a standstill.

Thus, all contradictions cease to exist. Everything is equal. In the *"Wu-teng Hui-yuan Collection,"* a passage says:

> Wen-yen [Founder of the Cloud-Gate Monastery in Kwangtung in the early 10th c.] once held his staff up and said: ' I see the staff as staff and the post as post. What's wrong with that?' What is important is that the mind refrains from making a confirmation nor a denial. It does not matter if one says yes or says no, as long as there is no worry whatsoever in one's mind.

Transcendence of life in the Mahayanic Perfected school can be directly traced to the absolute reality of the *chen-ju*. It takes the absolute substance as substance, self-ego and real mind. The myriad dharmas are emptiness and yet are manifested as the form of the absolute substance. It is both reality and non-reality. The mind is empty and the spirit has no attachments. When life has cultivated the absolute life and is never attached to mundane things, it is an enjoyment of the eternal bliss and purity of the state of Nirvana.

The Mahayanic Perfected school and Taoism share the concept of substantial transcendence in their idea of transcendence of life. The concepts of "concordance with Tao," "unity with the *chen-ju*," and the Confucianist transcendence of virtues bear certain similarities with transcendence of life in Roman Catholicism. However, both Buddhism and Taoism take the myriad things as substance or *chen-ju* or Tao itself. Ignorance has made people erroneously believe that the myriad things each have a substance. This false belief imposes on Buddhism and Taoism the task of correcting misconceptions. When one overcomes this error, he attains great wisdom. As a consequence, real life presents itself and one enjoys eternal bliss. This transcendental process leads from the outside to inside. Seeing through one's own real self does not mean elevating one's substance to the level of the absolute substance. Therefore, it is neither preternatural transcendence nor supernatural transcendence. Rather, it is the internal discovery of one's nature. Ontologically speaking, Mahayana Buddhism confirms that the myriad dharmas have no substance but are only all types of manifestations. Although Taoism explains that Tao exists in all things and propounds the Discussion on Making All Things Equal [*Ch'i-wu lun*], it does not clearly deny the reality (substance) of the myriad things. When Taoism deals with emptiness, what it teaches is the emptying of one's mind. It does not propound that the myriad things are empty. In fact, Lao-tzu taught that the myriad things are beings, created from ether. Chuang-tzu explained that man resulted from the fusion of ether. When ether disperses, man dies, whereupon ether returns to join the great ether of Heaven and Earth. Thus, Taoist transcendence lies in the condensation and dispersion of the transcendent ether. Direct fusion with ether leads to Tao. In contrast, Buddhist transcendence is the transcendence over the manifestations of the myriad dharmas and the direct return to the substance or *chen-ju*. Spiritual life is union with the life of Tao or life of the *chen-ju*, whereupon man exists forever to become the perfect man [*chih-jen*] or to attain Buddhahood.

II. Spiritual Transcendence of Life in Roman Catholicism

1. Metaphysical Principles

When contemporary Chinese scholars talk about spiritual transcendence of life, they often mention Western spiritual transcendence of life. Western spiritual life is often equated with Catholic spiritual life. These scholars often hold wrong ideas about Roman Catholic spiritual transcendence of life. Of them, the most common lies in condemning Western spiritual transcendence of life for its "neglect of the interior character of personal spiritual life." They argue that when a person believes in a supernatural God, his personal spiritual life is made to transcend the universe and is united with God, a union that is external in nature. Then from this external union, one returns to the things of the universe. Thus, it is a rise from the earth to heaven, and then a return to the earth from heaven. Prof. Thomé Fang called this transcendence "absolute" or "preternatural". In comparison, Prof. Fang took Chinese spiritual transcendence of life as either transcendental or internal. The development of spiritual life in the West is often a matter of duality between opposing forces of good and evil. Western spiritual transcendence often puts the body against the spirit and teaches that man's original sin has brought damage and imperfection to human nature. On this, Prof. Thomé writes:

> Such a metaphysics as this has been very rarely appropriated, if appropriated at all, by the Chinese thinkers. The Chinese have taken this stand not so much for the reason that preternatural metaphysics lays great stress upon the supreme ideals of value, which we do all the more, as for the reason that it has the tendency, explicitly, to impair the concordance and continuity of Nature with Supernature and, implicitly, to hurt the integrity of the human individual which is a healthy soul merged in a sound body so as to form a unified personality or wholesome character. (Spirit, 19)

Prof. Fang showed much optimism on the issue of integral persona. In contrast, the issues of good and evil nature which have often fared in the debates of Confucianists for many generations show that they did not believe in a sound, integral persona as universal to mankind. Chu Hsi's discussion of material force and matter, and evil or good nature enters the realm of metaphysical ontology. He never took a person's substance as always sound and good. On good virtues, Confucianism has always proposed their attainment by ascetic means. They are not something naturally possessed by everyone.

Roman Catholic teachings on human spiritual life are backed by strong metaphysical basis. A human being is an aggregate of body and soul. All the independent activities of man are done by a subject that is a union of body and spirit. Man has a good nature. His body is also good. However, the human heart often craves for corporeal enjoyment. Even when he pursues spiritual aims, such as honor, position and knowledge, he is still often stimulated by earthly considerations such as the attainment of a high social status. The ancient Chinese, whether Confucianists, Buddhists, or Taoists, considered this tendency as a direct consequence of human passion. Why does human passion tend towards evil? Only Chu Hsi said that it is because of the clarity and turbidity of the *ch'i* that *li* (material principle) is not manifest. But what made the *ch'i* turbid? What makes one's *chi* this clear and another person's *ch'i* that turbid? Chu Hsi's only answer to this question is that *li* (material principle) limits *ch'i* and vice-versa. This hardly answers the question. In Roman Catholicism, the tendency of human passion towards evil is a result of the poison of original sin. Man's original ancestors failed a test given by God by disobeying his warning. This tendency to disobey was transmitted to their descendants, through which the poison of original sin continues to wreak havoc. Man's tendency towards sensual enjoyment leads to evil, through which he goes against rules. In the *Chung-yung*, it says that when passion is "central and regulated" [*chung-chieh*], it leads to harmony. Failure to make passion "central and regulated" will mean a lack of harmony, which is essentially evil. Roman Catholic teachings never say that human nature is damaged by original sin, and is therefore evil.

Man originated from God, the Creator, who made man in his own image and likeness. Thus, the value of man far exceeds that level described in Confucianism as "having received the fair *ch'i* of Heaven and Earth and became the spirit of the myriad things." Man's soul is spiritual, created in God's likeness. Human body has its own corporeal beauty. Roman Catholicism has never rejected the Greeks' appreciation for the beauty of the human body. At the Sistine Chapel of the Apostolic Palace, Michaelangelo's nude paintings adorn the ceiling. The reredo of the front altar features a depiction of the Last Judgment, acclaimed as the best work of Michelangelo and which shows nude human forms. Because of the human heart's inclination towards sensuality, he often fails to suppress himself. This explains why Roman Catholicism frowns upon the aesthetic enjoyment of nudity.

It is a universal fact that man's tendency towards the pleasure of the senses is not often regulated, which leads him to commit sins. Although man has the ability to use his mind over his passion, he often finds himself weak in spirit. It is partially a consequence of the failure of man's first ancestors who had disobeyed God's commandment. They were separated from God and their descendants got lost in pagan practices. In his desire to lead man back to the right path and so that man may have control over his passions, God sent his only son to be incarnated as man — Jesus Christ. By entering the life system of the universe, He then has become a part of human history.

Jesus Christ gave up his life as a ransom for man's sins. He instituted the sacraments, using baptism to wash away the sins of man and unite the spiritual life of man with his own life. Through this sacrament, the baptized person becomes God's son or daughter. Such an elevation is an elevation of the substance. Thus, human life is transformed into the divine life of God. It is not an elevation that is merely an action but is rather an elevation of the substance of life. Hence, it is called supernatural life and not merely "preternatural."

God the Creator is an absolute spiritual reality. He is *ipsum esse subsistens*. He transcends everything in this universe. The universe and the myriad things were created by God, not generated; neither were they derived from God's substance. Creation is an action. It is a capability. The substantial relationship between the myriad things and God is one that has to do with capability and action, or what may be called "creative" relationship. God and the myriad things do not share the same substance. The myriad things are relative. God is absolute. The myriad things were created, started to exist and became beings. The being of the myriad things is not self-subsisting; it is a result of God's creative action *ex nihilo*. For the being of the myriad things to continue existing, creative power must continuously sustain them. The Creator's creative action transcends time and space. If viewed from the angle of a finite universe, creative action and sustaining action follow a certain chronological order. However, the concept of before and after does not apply to the actions of God. He creates and sustains at the same time. This explains why Roman Catholicism teaches the presence of God in the myriad things. It means that God's creative action always exists in the myriad things, an existence of power. This is similar to the idea proposed in the *I Ching* when it says: "Generation is the great virtue of Heaven and Earth."

The natural world in its entirety, including man, does not have the same nature as God. Their substances differ from God's Creative action which is inside the myriad things and sustains their existence without changing their nature.

Jesus Christ suffered, died and resurrected. The resurrected Christ is a pure spiritual substance. His body has lost its physical attributes. When a person receives baptism, his spiritual life is elevated and united with the life of Christ. The life of the resurrected Christ is divine spiritual life in the fullest sense. The substance of his life is both divinity and a divinized humanity. In contrast, the substance of man's spiritual life is the soul. When he is united with the divine life of God, his soul unites with the substance of Christ. Man's soul is then divinized. He becomes a son of God. Fathers and sons are said to look alike. Thus, man appears in the likeness of God not only because he was made in the image of God; his union with Christ enables him to share God's nature and substance. Such a transcendence belongs to the substantial plane. It is transcendence to the nature of the natural world; not that man's substance has been elevated to heaven, but rather God entering the soul, making it united with him. God thus resides in the heart of man.

When man's soul and the life of Christ are united into one, man does not, as a consequence, leave the universe. He continues remaining as himself. It differs from the Taoist teaching on "Tao" which takes it as the substance of the myriad things, including man's. Neither is it similar with the Buddhist *chen-ju*, the substance of the myriad dharmas or man's true self. In Buddhism, when man's real self is united with Tao or the *chen-ju*, he ceases from being himself. What remains is the Tao or the *chen-ju*. Although man's soul is divinized by its union with God, it remains a human soul. This soul remains united with the body as one. Instead, what happens is that man's activities become divine activies. His whole life becomes divine because of a divinized substance.

A divinized life can be manifested in this life through the human mind. He possesses a divinized consciousness and a desire to live a life of union with God. In the present life, man's perception and intelligence cannot lead him to directly see God. He can only rely on faith. Hence, divinized life in the present world is a life of faith. Although a life of faith is not a life of the intellect, which cannot fully understand mysteries, it is neither a fantasy nor some form of blind superstition. The intellect understands that a life of faith is not contradictory with intellectual life, the former being transcendent to the latter.

However, in this world, transcendence of the spiritual life can also transcend faith, which leads to a life of "direct vision" of God. The soul's direct vision of God does not occur through the eyes nor through the intellect. It is achieved through spiritual vision in a way that is utterly mysterious and unfathomable, and through which spiritual life reaches its apex. It is an experience beyond words and description. In spiritual vision, God is an absolute reality: Truth, Goodness and Beauty. He is not emptiness or an impersonal, empty being. God is a personal God, a God who is benevolent, loving, omniscient, intelligent and merciful. The good that comes out of spiritual vision is beyond the expectation and aspirations of man. It satisfies all that man desires and longs for. It is the realm of bliss. However, although this realm exists in one's heart, it is beyond the human mind, and thus, it does not last forever. It is a fleeting experience. It is desired but cannot be sought for. It comes when you do not sought for it. It comes and does not stay long, in a way that is mysterious, unfathomable and beyond words. When man dies, his soul is detached from the body, whereupon the soul exists alone. It does not leave God because of sin. Afterwards, both spiritual beings are brought face to face with each other. At this moment, the soul sees God directly and enters the divine spiritual life for all eternity.

2. The Emptying of Oneself

A. Viewing One's Sins

Mystico-spiritual life can be aspired for but is not necessarily achievable by all. But heaven rewards the persevering, as the saying goes. A person who prepares himself with a sincere disposition can receive divine life from God.

In such a preparatory work, the most basic requirements involve living a life of faith and morality. If one wishes to have a divine spiritual life and to directly see God's substance, he must, driven by a constant faith in the mercy and love of God, spare no effort to direct his spiritual life towards God. One's sense of values must place God above everything else as the goal of his life. One must be driven by a strong belief that his own substance has become transcendent and united in one body with the living substance of God. As St. Paul says:

> . . . and I now live not with my own life but with the life of Christ who lives in me. The life I now live in this body I live in faith: faith in the Son of God who loved me and who sacrificed himself for my sake. (Galatians 2:19)

This life of faith is a life that is vibrant, with the power of faith supporting a person's entire life. Faith also guides a person to pray in contemplation of God.

Thus, if a person wants to obtain a mystico-spiritual life and enjoy the beauty and goodness of God, he must live a righteous life. He cannot say that he commits no sins or say that he has attained the peak of moral life. St. John once said:

> My dear people, we are already the children of God but what we are to be in the future has not yet been revealed. All we know is, that when it is revealed, we shall be like him because we shall see him as he really is. (1 John 3:2)

However, St. John also said:

> If we say we have no sin in us, we are deceiving ourselves and refusing to admit the truth; but if we acknowledge our sins, then God who is faithful and just will forgive our sins and purify us from everything that is wrong. To say that we have not sinned is to call God a liar and to show that his word is not in us. (1 John 1:8)

A person knows his own weaknesses as others know their own. Not one of us is perfect and unblemished. We commit many faults and omissions everyday, both large and small. As Confucius once said: "By viewing the sin one has committed, it is possible to discern the presence or absence of benevolence in one's heart" (Analects, *Li-jen*). Elsewhere, he writes: "Forget it! I still have to meet a man who detects his own fault and truly feels sorry for it" (Analects, *Kung-yeh chang*).

Knowing man's weakness, Jesus Christ instituted the sacrament of penance. It is inevitable for man to commit sins after receiving baptism. If a person is sorry for his sins and reproaches himself, Jesus Christ will grant him forgiveness.

What I mean by a righteous life is not the total absence of defects. Rather, it means being aware of one's sins, and because of such awareness, changing one's behavior. It means a constant effort to improve and to walk towards his ideals. If a person were satisfied with his present life and does not keep himself going forward, then he would be on his way to degeneration. Without the will to improve and without any ideal, he cannot develop his spiritual life. A person who constantly does every effort to improve always aspires for the infinite future, the absolute Truth, Goodness and Beauty. He prepares his spiritual life for the eventual acceptance of a mystico-spiritual life.

A person who constantly tries to improve in his spiritual and moral life is said to be setting the foundation for spiritual elevation. God is the absolute Truth, Goodness and Beauty. When a person, as a relative truth, goodness and beauty, meets and fuses with the absolute Truth, Goodness and Beauty, the former's relative character ceases to exist. It is not a substantial disappearance but instead, one in the realm of consciousness. A lamp or a candle under bright sunlight does not appear as a source of light. Thus, for a person to achieve his aspiration for a divinized spiritual life and a life of union with God, he must necessarily empty himself.

B. Emptying of One's Consciousness

A person may be full of his own self-consciousness. He may be aware of his own status and position. He has his own plans. He always shows his opinions and preferences. Consciousness of himself makes him aware that he is his own master, that he is the master of his own position. If someone goes against what he likes, says or does, he shows his displeasure on his face. Some say that such a behavior is manly or is second nature to a man of deeds. Yet, since a person is so sure of himself and does things his own way, how could he make his own spiritual life divinized and united with God's life? Although a person's soul is one with the substance of God's life, his life activities are still mastered by himself, not by Jesus Christ. Thus, a person must go through the stage of emptying his own consciousness.

This stage is divided into two phases. The first is active and the second is passive.

a. Active Emptying of One's Consciousness

This manner of emptying one's own consciousness requires self-control. One's mental activities are directed towards the holy will of God. He does everything that God wants him to do. Loving God becomes the goal of his actions. This is in imitation of Jesus' thirty-three years in this world, which he spent totally for the fulfillment of God's will. Jesus Christ said:

> My food is to do the will of the one who sent me, and to complete his work. (John 4:34)

> My teaching is not my own, but his who sent me. (John 7:16)

> . . . and that I do nothing of myself: what the Father has taught me is what I preach; he who sent me is with me, and has not let me to myself, for I always do what please him. (John 8:28-29)

> For what I have spoken does not come from myself; no, what I was to say, what I had to speak, was commanded by the Father who sent me, and I know that his commandments mean eternal life. And therefore what the Father has told me is what I speak. (John 12:49-50)

> The words I say to you I do not speak as from myself: it is the Father, living in me, who is doing this work. (John 14:10)

And the word that you have heard is not mine, but the Father's who sent me. (John 14:24)

Father . . . Now at last they know that all you have given me comes indeed from you; for I have given them the teaching you gave to me, and they have truly accepted this, that I came from you, and have believed that it was you who sent me. (John 17:8)

What Jesus has said and done in his lifetime were all made in obedience to the will of God, the Father. He did not assert himself but instead did everything for the Father. Before his arrest and crucifixion, he prayed to his Father:

Abba (Father)! Everything is possible for you. Take this cup away from me. But let it be as you, not I, would have it. (Mark 14:36)

The substance of God's life is made-up of his divinity and humanity. His humanity is perfect. He possesses intellect and will. He experienced fear at the moment of death. Yet he fulfilled the will of the Father.

All of us cannot reach the level of Jesus' life, which is a complete obedience to the will of the Father. Nevertheless, we must still exert the effort to reach such a level. The direction of our spiritual life must always be towards God. Confucius said: "At fifty I knew the Mandate of Heaven" (Analects, *Wei-cheng*, Chan 22). For a Christian, it is not merely knowing the Mandate of Heaven, it also means fearing it. The Analects says: "The gentleman has three things to fear: the Mandate of Heaven, great men and the words of sages" (*Chi-shih*). Fear commands acceptance and obedience. The Mandate of Heaven mentioned by Confucius is the will of heaven and the fate it has dictated for all. He did not mean directing one's actions to the will of God or, much less, directing one's heart to God because of adoration. The Old Testament says:

Like the deer that yearns for running streams,

So my soul is yearning for you, my God.

My soul is thirsting for God, the God of my life;

When can I enter and see the face of God?

How I would lead the rejoicing crowd into the house of God,

Amid cries of gladness and thanksgiving, the throng wild with joy. (Psalm 41)

To you have I lifted up my eyes, you who dwell in the heavens:

My eyes, like the eyes of the slaves on the hand of their lord.

Like the eyes of a servant on the hand of her mistress,

So our eyes are on the Lord our God till he show us his mercy.

(Psalm 122)

Since ancient times, slaves have always listened to the commands of their masters, never daring to assert themselves. For a person to empty his own consciousness, he must obey the will of God in everything. God's will is surely the best for everything one does, including one's performance in spiritual life. It is so for the reason that God sees thoroughly everything. He sees through our hearts. He is omnipotent and infinite. When a person follows God's will, he then benefits from God's perfect intelligence, and shares in the wisdom of God and in his omnipotence. His heart then finds repose in God.

But how can we see the will of God in everything we do? In prayer, in contemplation and in recollection, the silent voice of God sends inspiration to a person's heart and mind. He hears not the voice of God. He does not see a flash of lightning or other extraordinary signs. Yet, in the silence and peace of his heart, the person who yearns for God hears his voice without the sound of words.

b. Passive Emptying of One's Consciousness

Passive emptying of one's consciousness is of a higher level than the active way. Although in active emptying, a person tries to orient himself to the will of God, that person still has full control of himself.

Self-consciousness still resides in him. In contrast, passive emptying calls for the acceptance of God so as to empty oneself. It means being emptied to the extent of losing oneself and of knowing nothing about one's actions. St. John of the Cross called this state the "dark night." He writes:

> We may say that there are three reasons for which this journey made by the soul to union with God is called night. The first has to do with the point from which the soul goes forth, for it has gradually to deprive itself of desire for all the worldly things which is possessed, by denying them to itself, the which denial and deprivation are, as it were, night to all senses of man. The second reason has to do with the mean, or the road along which the soul must travel to this union--that is, faith, which is likewise as dark as night to the understanding. The third has to do with the point to which it travels,--namely God, Who, equally, is dark night to the soul in this life. (19-20)

In this passage, "dark night" has its usual meaning. However, the real "dark night" is the process of passive emptying of one's consciousness. The first stage of this passage focuses on one's desire for mundane things. Everything that happens everyday are against his wishes. People he meets do not share the same dispositions with him. He does not get what he wants. He had wanted to be healthy but he got sick. He had wanted to have peace for a moment but someone came to discuss something. When these things become common occurrences, he must remain unaffected and calm. This unaffected disposition is even more difficult to achieve than Mencius' version. For Mencius, an unaffected disposition means the development of one's ability to shoulder burdens, which shows one's personality. In contrast, the unaffected disposition required of a Christian is the emptying of his own consciousness, in forgetting himself. It is not identical with Chuangtzu's "smashing of one's form and body." It is forgetting one's existence. He must make himself smaller and smaller until he stops seeing himself. It resembles the emptying of oneself that Zen Buddhism teaches. In the latter case, however, it is more of a lack of mental consideration that leaves the mind empty. In contrast, the emptying of oneself required of a Christian is more of being unaffected when faced with contradictions. It is not lack of feeling or numbness. His feeling remains sensitive. Although all things go against his wishes, he remains calm and unaffected as though he has no feeling at all. Such a disposition requires personal cultivation. St. John of the Cross further writes:

> The first is whether, when a soul finds no pleasure or consolation in the things of God, it also fails to find it in any thing created; for, as God sets the soul in this dark night to the end that He may quench and purge its sensual desire, He allows it not to find attraction or sweetness in anything whatsoever. (373)

> But, as I say, when these aridities proceed from the way of the purgation of sensual desire, although at first the spirit feels no sweetness, for the reasons that we have just given, it feels that it is deriving strength and energy to act from the substance which this inward food gives it, the which food is the beginning of a contemplation that is dark and arid to the senses; which contemplation is secret and hidden from the very person that experiences it; and ordinarily, together with the aridity and emptiness which it causes in the senses, it gives the soul an inclination and desire to be alone and in quietness, without being able to think of any particular thing. . . (375)

This stage is the so-called "dark night" wherein the soul remains in an abyss of aridity. It has lost all interest in things of the world and heaven above. It can be considered a total deprivation of interest. In this state, the soul feels frightened. It starts to become afraid of being abandoned by God, and launches itself into a panicky search for a way out. Yet, it falls into mistakes one after another, through which the value of the dark night is lost. Although this dark night of the soul emptied from mundane attachments is dreadful, it is still much more bearable than the hardships of emptying oneself of spiritual desires. St. John of the Cross writes:

It is well for those who find themselves in this condition to take comfort, to persevere in patience and to be in no wise afflicted. Let them trust in God, Who abandons not those that seek Him with a simple and right heart, and will not fail to give them what is needful for the road, until He bring them into the clear and pure light of love. . . The way in which they are to conduct themselves in this night of sense is to devote themselves not at all to reasoning and meditation, since it is not the time for this, but to allow the soul to remain in peace and quietness, although it may seem clear to them that they are doing nothing and are wasting their time, and although it may seem to them that it is because of their weakness that they have no desire in that state to think of anything. The truth is that they will be doing quite sufficient if they have patience and persevere in prayer without making any effort. What they must do is merely to leave the soul free and disencumbered and at rest from all knowledge and thought, troubling not themselves, in that state, about what they shall think or meditate, but contenting themselves with no more than a peaceful and loving attentiveness toward God. . . (379-380)

In the face of spiritual aridity and fear brought about by the empty-ing of one's consciousness, a person should stay calm and try to strengthen his faith. God will not allow him to turn desperate. He will support a person's constant struggle to seek for a mystico-spiritual life, an entry further into the dark night so as to empty a person of his desire for spiritual matters.

Faith is required in the search for a mystico-spiritual life. Although faith is obscure for the intellect, things of faith being unex-plained by reason, the soul always feels the presence of an inner light in faith. This light guides him in all activities of his spiritual life. But God snuffs out the light of faith to destroy a soul's self-confidence. Thus, faith becomes a total darkness for the soul. He becomes blinded. A thick layer of black fog shuts away the existence of one's life in the future. St. Therese of the Child Jesus once had this experience. Writ-ing on her painful experience, she said:

He allowed pitch-black darkness to sweep over my soul and let the thought of heaven, so sweet to me from my infancy, destroy all my peace and torture me. This trial was not something lasting a few days or weeks. I suffered it for months and I am still waiting for it to end. I wish I could express what I feel, but it is impossible. One must have traveled through the same sunless tunnel to understand how dark it is. But I will do my best to explain it. (Story 117)

Despite her extreme pain, St. Therese remained calm. She said:

And so, in spite of this trial which robs me of all sense of pleasure, I can still say: "Thou hast given me, O Lord, a delight in Thy doings." For is there any greater joy than to suffer for love of You? The more intense and hidden the suffering is, the more pleasing it is to You. And if--which is impossible--You knew nothing of it, I should still be happy to suffer in the hope that, by my tears, I could prevent or perhaps atone for a single sin against the Faith. (118)

In the face of this dark night, one should uproot all the satisfaction residing in his inner self. He should not have any iota of his self-confidence remaining. He must be aware of his own uselessness and sinful nature. Furthermore, he must have a different perception of the soul's joy and satisfaction. To develop spiritual life, joy and satisfaction of the soul are not necessary. In fact, they are obstacles. Seeking for the joy and satisfaction of the soul must be supported by a sweet feeling. Giving up the joy and satisfaction of the soul, and facing the dark night of the soul are needed to stand up and walk, and to face the many challenges.

In his work, *Journey of the Mind to God*, St. Bonaventure said that the first step consists in passionately loving the cross, sacrificing everything. He writes:

Yet the road to peace and harmony is to passionately love the cross. This passionate love lifted St. Paul to heaven and made

him unified with Christ that he called out in a loud voice:
"have been crucified with Christ, and I live now not with my
own life but with the life of Christ who lives in me" (Gal. 2:19)
. The same passionate love also entered the heart of St. Francis.
Two years before his death, the stigmata of the five wounds of
Jesus appeared on his body. (Breton 426)

Everyone has his own way or method in developing spiritual life
according to one's preferences. In the dark night of emptying one's
spiritual desires, this preference must likewise be destroyed. A
person's ways and methods usually do not work because they confuse
him on which to adopt. Once a person's self is totally annihilated, he
loses all preferences for things. In fact, he stops making choices and
leaves everything in the hands of God. However, this attitude is absolutely not pessimism, despair or laziness; neither is it a "dead tree or
cold ash." Rather, it is life reaching its peak whereupon the soul's love
overlaps with the love of God, whereupon God's will becomes one's
will. Zen Buddhism often proposes the emptying of oneself from all
worries and the emptying of the self to directly see the *chen-ju* of
one's substance. The emptiness proposed by Zen Buddhism is cold and
barren. In contrast, seeking the emptying of oneself by God is motivated by love. Two persons who truly and passionately love each other
try to empty themselves to accept each other. In the dark night, a
person seeks for the love of God to empty oneself of all, to offer his
whole self to the love of God and to accept God in his fullness.

Unable to see God face to face in the dark night, a person suffers
the second level of pain in the emptying of his spiritual desire to
contemplate God. The first level of suffering comes from faith. The
second level is derived from God. St. John of the Cross writes:

But the question arises: Why is the Divine light (which, as we
say, illumines and purges the soul from its ignorances) here
called by the soul a dark night? To this the answer is that for
two reasons this Divine Wisdom is not only night and darkness
for the soul, but is likewise affliction and torment. The first is
because of the height of Divine Wisdom, which transcends the

talent of the soul, and in this way is darkness to it; the second, because of its vileness and impurity, in which respect it is painful and afflictive to it, and is also dark. (406)

God is absolute Truth, Beauty and Goodness. He is infinitely beyond the grasp of human intellect. Furthermore, he infinitely transcends man's purity. The soul who seeks for a mystico-spiritual life abandons all the things of the earth in search of God. Yet he realizes that God's absolute transcendence can never be measured up in any way. He feels powerless and filthy in front of the absolute Truth, Beauty and Goodness. His soul gropes for light in the dark, feeling sorrowful and anxious. Such pain resembles that of a person who has been away from home for a long time and who returns after experiencing hardships. Standing before his family's house, he sees its door closed. Inside him he feels unworthy of seeing his parents, his heart tormented by an extreme pain. Such a pain makes the soul feel its nothingness. Jesus Christ said:

> I bless you, Father, Lord of heaven and of earth, for hiding these things from the learned and the clever and revealing them to mere children. Yes, Father, for that is what pleased you to do. (Luke 10:21)

Dashing man's pride in himself and not allowing man to feel he is intelligent and virtuous enough to reach the majesty of God, God instead grants mystico-spiritual life to a person with child-like humility. In this spiritual dark night, although the soul feels an excruciating pain, his heart and soul remain extremely calm. He has no aspirations other than reaching God. St. John of the Cross further writes:

> It now remains to be said that, although this happy night brings darkness to the spirit, it does so only to give it light in everything; and that, although it humbles it and makes it miserable, it does so only to exalt it and to raise it up; and, although it impoverishes it and empties it of all natural affection and attachment, it does so only that it may enable it to stretch forward, divinely, and thus to have fruition and experience of

all things, both above and below, yet to preserve its unrestricted liberty of spirit in them all. (422)

Thus the soul is emptied of everything. It is emptied of its consciousness. That person no longer makes plans using his intellect. Without any preference, he no longer follows his tendencies. His soul then becomes blank and unblemished. It resembles a clean blackboard, without the slightest writing on it, waiting for the teacher to scribble something on it. This teacher is God. Using the light and beauty of his substance, he penetrates the soul in its entirety, a soul that waits with total eagerness for God.

C. The Fulfillment of Charity

a. Fulfillment With God

After experiencing the dark night, the soul is purified. He is now empty. The Absolute Reality--God--directly shows himself to the soul. This showing is a close union. It resembles sunlight shining through glass. Sunlight penetrates the glass totally, reaching all of its parts and with which it becomes united.

When the soul--a relative being--meets the origin of its own being, it joyfully enters the absolute being. The mystery of mysteries-- the absolute Truth, Beauty and Goodness--is presented before the soul, insignificant and small. Faced with the infinite Truth, Goodness and Beauty, the soul is entirely satisfied, its heart filled with immense joy. As Confucius once said:

"To know it (learning the Way) is not as good as to love it, and to love it is not as good as to take delight in it" (Chan 30).

Standing before the absolute Truth, Goodness and Beauty, the soul feels nothing else but goodness and joy. God is right there, needing no contemplation, analysis or scrutiny. The intellect loses its function of reasoning out. It can only enjoy what stands before it.

As God presents himself, his substance is spiritual and resplendent. He illumines the soul not through the use of imagination or through concepts. The soul directly sees God. This experience is absolutely not done through the senses. The body, although living, has become like a corpse. Such an experience is not a dream. Imagination and the senses stop working. It is the soul directly facing God. Relating his own experience, St. Paul writes:

> I know a man in Christ who, fourteen years ago, was caught up--whether still in the body or out of the body, I do not know; God knows--right into the third heaven. I do know, however, that this same person--whether in the body or out of the body, I do not know; God knows--was caught up into the paradise and heard things which must not and cannot be put into human language. (2 Corinthians 12:2)

Spiritual vision, contemplative vision, facing God, and the appreciation of the absolute Goodness and Beauty cannot be put into concepts and are beyond description. Much less, words cannot be used to adequately describe them. Human concepts, languages and literature are all relative, localized and often obscure. They can never be used to adequately express the absolute Truth, Goodness and Beauty. Even memory fails. It can only allow recalling that a spiritual vision occurred. What exactly happened is beyond recall.

Spiritual or contemplative vision happens when spiritual life has transcended the summit of spiritual life, a level when the soul becomes aware that it is directly facing God. Contemplative vision, through which one silently appreciates the Absolute Truth, Goodness and Beauty, is like looking at a very beautiful painting, a natural scenery or a work of art. One can only open his eyes, stupefied by what he beholds. The mind concentrates, unoccupied by the slightest thing. The heart feels satisfaction and joy. Contemplative vision is the appreciation of God's substance in which one's substance is immersed in God and in which one is filled with joy and bliss. His soul basks in complete satisfaction.

The absolute Truth, Beauty and Goodness is infinite. Although the soul comes face to face with God, as a finite spiritual being, it cannot comprehend God in his entirety. When the soul has entered eternal life, contemplative vision continues forever. But what it beholds is always a new Truth, Goodness and Beauty. This is called beatific vision.

Those who were fortunate enough to have experienced spiritual vision in this life were only granted a transitory experience. Back in ordinary life, their spiritual life remains in a supernatural state. They have a faint recollection of the contents of spiritual vision or the joy of contemplative vision. Yet, the love felt during the vision remains sustained, and in fact, keeps on growing.

Spiritual or contemplative vision leads the soul to appreciate God's substance. Out of this appreciation, adoration results. A soul's love of God is a love directed at the origin of life. It is the love for the source of all graces. God's love is love for a life he himself has created. It is a love for his chosen ones, a love for the pure and the unblemished.

Love is the bestowing of life. God the Creator gave his own substance to souls. Thus, the Creator's substance is the foundation and source of life. It is also the spring of all beauty and goodness. When a soul offers himself up to God, it places its life into the life of the Creator. Both of them are the bestowing of life, and thus, join in the fulfillment of love.

In Western cultural ideas, the most intimate love on earth is love between a man and a woman. A man and a woman who love each other marry one another, thus becoming one body and one life. Hence, the Catholic Church uses the symbolism of the love between a man and a woman to describe the completion of love between the soul and its Creator. The Church calls the union of the soul with Jesus Christ "spiritual marriage." Spiritual marriage is not marriage in the usual sense of the word. It is only used to allude to the love between a couple and to symbolize the fulfillment of love. In the Old Testament, the Song of Songs (*Cantici Canticorum*) echoes love songs, which the Catholic Church often takes as symbolizing the union between heaven and man. It says:

Set me like a seal on your heart, like a seal on your arm. For love is strong as Death, jealousy relentless as Sheol. The flash of it is a flash of fire, a flame of the Lord himself. Love no flood can quench, no torrents drown. Were a man to offer all the wealth of his house to buy love, contempt is all he would purchase. (Sg 8:6-7)

This symbolism is an outright sacrilege if viewed from the Chinese cultural perspective. In Greek mythology, gods and goddesses fall in love and often engage in incestuous relationships. In contrast, the Song of Songs is symbolic of a pure and true love. St. Therese of the Child Jesus writes:

Now I wish for only one thing--to love Jesus even unto folly! Love alone attracts me. I no longer wish for either suffering or death and yet both are precious to me. For a long time I've hailed them as messengers of joy. I've already known suffering and I've thought I was approaching the eternal shore. From my earliest days I have believed that the Little Flower would be plucked in the springtime of her life. But today my only guide is self-abandonment. I have no other compass. I no longer know how to ask passionately for anything except that the will of God shall be perfectly accomplished in my soul. I can repeat these words of our Father, St. John of the Cross: "I drank deep within the hidden cellar of my Beloved and, when I came forth again, I remembered nothing of the flock I used to look after. My soul is content to serve Him with all its strength. I've finished all other work except that of love. In that is all my delight." (109)

The Taoist Tao and Buddhism's *chen-ju* are absolute realities. However, they are hazy, impersonal realities. They are not spirit and cannot love. God is a personal deity, supreme and absolute Beauty and Goodness. He feels a strong love and a wisdom that is compassionate to man. God is all perfect, good and sublime. Similarly, his love is also perfect, good and sublime. When a soul's life is united with the life of God, it accepts the infinite love of God in which it becomes totally immersed. Such a love cannot be aptly symbolized by love between a man and a woman. Instead, it can be called "the love of life." God is the fountain of all life, which he gives out of love. When a soul receives the life which God has bestowed, its life is drawn into the fountain. Thus, the life of the soul and God give love to each other. Both loves are as deep as life itself.

Spiritual or contemplative vision elevates the soul to see the substance of God. It allows a relative life to revert to its own absolute roots, whereupon shared truth, goodness and beauty are poured into the absolute fountain of Truth, Goodness and Beauty. This fills the soul with an appreciative joy. Its life is totally transformed into love, which fuses with divine love. Thus, his life is divinized into love. After receiving baptism, a person's substance becomes elevated to a state of union with Jesus Christ's substance. He or she becomes a son or daughter of God. Spiritual or contemplative vision presents to the soul the divine life of Jesus Christ. It leads to a direct view of the substance of God. In the love of the bestowing of lives, they fuse and are completed.

Spiritual or contemplative vision is a form of supernatural transcendence. It represents a rise above one's nature wherein a relative life fuses with the Absolute Life. In the face of the absolute Truth, Goodness and Beauty, the soul feels an immense joy that is beyond words. Spiritual vision happens rarely and only for a fleeting duration. When one enters eternal life, beatific vision becomes a lasting enjoyment.

Once spiritual or contemplative vision has disappeared, the fusion of the "love of life" continues existing. With it, the soul lives a life of the "fulfillment of love" in its earthly journey.

b. Fulfillment With Things

In his *Journey of the Mind to God*, St. Bonaventure describes the soul's path in its rise from the natural world to God. It tells about how the human soul, created in the likeness of God, is raised up to God--an elevation of man's material substantial existence to God. The state of "fulfillment of love" keeps the soul constantly in a "vision of love's fulfillment," united with God in charity. In the case of Taoism, transcendence affords man to attain great wisdom through knowledge of the *ch'i* (*chi chih*), after which he sees the equality of all material things. Buddhism's transcendence adds a "vision of love's fulfillment" wherein things and dharmas fuse together, such than one exists in all and all exist in one. In contrast, Roman Catholic transcendence brings to the soul the "vision of love's fulfillment," in which man sees the love of God in everything and sees everything in the love of God.

c. Fulfillment of the Universe

A vision of love's fulfillment makes one appreciate the goodness of each thing in the natural world. He loves these good things, taking them as signs of the goodness of God. Poets praise the beauty of nature. They inject their own feelings into the myriad things. Thus, flowers, mountains and rivers are made to show joy and sorrow, reflecting poets' sentiments. Pious believers of God laud the goodness of God as they see the beauty of flowers, the majesty of a moonlit sea and the awe-inspiring spectacle of a waterfall. A vision of love's fulfillment does not lead to the personification of things in nature; neither does it lead one from the beauty of things to God, the source of beauty. Rather, it means viewing things in nature with the love of God. The goodness of things in nature is a manifestation of God's love. The more beautiful things of nature are, the greater is the love of God that one feels. Such that facing the natural world is like facing the Creator himself. In enjoying the goodness of each thing, the soul joyfully experiences the love of God. The natural world actively praises the wonder of God's love. Thus, things of nature also becomes divinized. They also become the children of God. As St. Paul writes:

> For creation was made subject to vanity--not by its own will but by reason of him who made it subject--in hope, because creation itself also will be delivered from its slavery to corruption into the freedom of the glory of the sons of God. . . waiting for the adoption as sons. . .(Romans 8:20-21, 23)

The universe and all myriad things, created by God, join to form a single life. They are placed in the hands of man. When the human race had fallen into sin, it drifted away from God. Similarly, things of the natural world also drifted away from God. By the birth and death of Jesus Christ, man became united with him. As a consequence, man once again became a son of God. Similarly, things of the natural world also became children of God again, for which they praise the goodness of the Creator. The vision of the fulfillment of love has helped realize the natural world's aspiration for becoming children of God. The love of God receives praise from the myriad things. St. Francis of Assisi often took things of the natural world as his brothers and sisters. It is said that natural things also treat him that way, such that wolves and leopards used to follow him like domesticated pets. Wild birds used to perch on his hands as they listened to his songs. In his *Canticle of Brother Sun*, he writes:

> Most high, all-powerful, all good, Lord!
> All praise is yours, all glory, all honor
> And all blessing.
> To you, alone, Most High, do they belong.
> No mortal lips are worthy
> To pronounce your name.
> All praise be yours, my Lord, through all that you have made,
> And first my lord Brother Sun,
> Who brings the day; and light you give us through him.
> How beautiful he is, how radiant in all his splendor!
> Of you, Most High, he bears the likeness.
> All praise be yours, my Lord, through Sister Moon and Stars;
> In the heavens you have made them, bright
> And precious and fair.
> All praise be yours, my Lord, through Brothers Wind and Air,
> And fair and stormy, all the weather's moods,

By which you cherish all that you have made.

All praise be yours, my Lord, through Sister Water,

So useful, lowly, precious and pure.

All praise be yours, my Lord, through Brother Fire,

Through whom you brighten up the night.

How beautiful is he, how gay! Full of power and strength.

All praise be yours, my Lord, through Sister Earth, our mother,

Who feeds us in her sovereignty and produces

Various fruits with colored flowers and herbs.

All praise be yours, my Lord, through those who grant pardon

For love of you; through those who endure

Sickness and trial.

Happy those who endure in peace,

By you, Most High, they will be crowned.

All praise be yours, my Lord, through Sister Death,

From whose embrace no mortal can escape.

Woe to those who die in mortal sin!

Happy those She finds doing your will!

The second death can do no harm to them.

Praise and bless my Lord, and give him thanks,

And serve him with great humility. (Fahy 130-131)

The vision of love's fulfillment is neither legend nor fairy tale. It is the rhythm of spiritual life. It means using fulfilling love to link together and divinize the universe and all things in it. Imbued with the divine love of God, all myriad things are beautiful.

Works Cited

Baynes, Cary F. *The I Ching*. Princeton: Princeton UP, 1967.

Breton, Valentin. St. *Bonaventura--Textes et studes*. Paris: Aubier.

Chan, Wing-tsit. *A Source Book in Chinese Philosophy*. Princeton: Princeton UP, 1963.

Fahy, Benen, trans. *The Writings of St. Francis*. Chicago: Franciscan Herald Press, 1963.

Fang, Thomé. *Chinese Philosophy: Its Spirit and Its Development*. Taipei: Linking, 1968.

Hucker, Charles O. *China's Imperial Past: An Introduction to Chinese History and Culture*. Stanford: Stanford UP, 1975.

Lau, D.C. *Tao Te Ching*. Hong Kong: Chinese UP, 1982.

---. *Mencius*. Vol. 1. Hong Kong: Chinese UP, 1984.

St. John of the Cross. *The Complete Works of Saint John of the Cross*. Trans. Silverio De Santa Teresa. Vol. 1. Westminster: Newman Bookshop, 1946.

St. Therese of Lisieux. *The Autobiography of St. Therese of Lisieux: The Story of A Soul*. Trans. John Beevers. New York: Doubleday, 1957.

Watson, Burton. *The Complete Works of Chuang Tzu*. New York: Columbia UP, 1968.

---. *The Columbia Book of Chinese Poetry: From Early Times to the Thirteenth Century*. New York: Columbia UP, 1968.

Translated by Carlos Tee